MADRONA

The
REALSIMPLE
GUIDE
TO
REAL LIFE

Adulthood made easy.

Edited by Noelle Howey

Illustrations by Serge Bloch

Oxmoor
House.

REALSIMPLE

Adulthood.

"It was the best of times, it was the worst of times." Quick—who wrote that? If you answered, "Charles Dickens," then congratulations—you paid attention in that English seminar. And you are undoubtedly smart. But...do you know how to ask for a raise? Organize your kitchen? Treat adult acne? (Yes, unfortunately, it's real. And even if you did receive an A in molecular biology, you still might get it.)

That line from *A Tale of Two Cities* pretty much summarizes the whole post-school experience, if you ask me. Your 20s are a time of incredible highs and lows. Or, per Mr. Dickens: *"It was the season of Light, it was the season of Darkness, it was the spring of hope, it was the winter of despair, we had everything before us, we had nothing before us."*

OK, you get the picture. But you're not living in London or Paris during the French Revolution. You're living in the 21st century, with a shiny, new adult life. Which sometimes is really spectacular and sometimes positively sucks.

I speak from experience here. Oh, I was happy to graduate from college and put the constant pressure of schoolwork behind me. But when I graduated, I looked at my diploma and thought, *What am I supposed to do with this?* I mean, exactly

which real-world situations does college prepare you for? Learning that there was an important difference between, say, Tom Wolfe and Thomas Wolfe was great, but it did nothing to help me understand my legal rights when I moved into my first big-girl, roommate-free apartment and there were opera singers—specifically, opera singers who practiced at home— living on the other side of the wall. As it turns out, I didn't need to tolerate their incessant, very loud singing!

But I didn't know that, because I didn't have this book when I signed the lease on that apartment. What you hold in your hands is (hopefully) the only reference you will ever need to navigate the practical side of adulthood—or the beginnings of adulthood, at least. Résumés, roommates, easy recipes, budgeting, beauty tricks, small-space solutions, breakup advice, 401(k)s, thank-you notes, stain-removal tips, how to buy a bra, how to clean an air conditioner: This book covers it all.

So enjoy. But one last thing: I suggest you don't try reading this book in one sitting. After all, you're not going to be tested on it. And isn't that *fantastic?*

Kristin van Ogtrop

CONTENTS

CHAPTER 1

FINDING A PLACE TO LIVE

You're a grown-up, but you still need a crib.
And finding an apartment or a house
can be a nail-biting prospect. But you're ready—
because you have a caring and responsible
roommate; a list of ideal locations and
the amenities that matter to you most; and
a comprehensive understanding of renter's
insurance. Wait, you don't? Well, at least
you have this book.

On the following pages, you'll get all the info
you need to land your dream pad.
(Warning: "Dream" may rapidly downsize
once you learn the true cost of apartments
with walk-in closets.)

Ready to find a roost that rules?
Let's get moving.

Should I live here?

Just because it has a working shower—which, by the way, did you check?— and isn't located above your parents' garage doesn't mean it's the place for you. Before you sign on the dotted line, ask yourself these 10 make-or-break questions.

1 | Is it in my budget?

You need to determine how much you can afford in rent while meeting your other obligations, including socking away savings. A rule of thumb: You shouldn't pay more than 30 percent of your gross salary (meaning before taxes) in rent. So if you are making $30,000, don't sign on for more than $750 a month. You also need to factor in utilities if they aren't included and other expenses, like parking. Do not assume that once you move you will develop a cheaper lifestyle—the housing equivalent of buying jeans two sizes too small because you are *definitely* going to start exercising. "Lots of people say something like 'Oh, it has a nice kitchen. I'll cook more and spend less money eating out,'" notes Janel Laban, the executive editor of the website Apartment Therapy. "But life usually gets more expensive, not less." In short: Have a firm maximum price, and don't look anywhere that exceeds it.

2 | Is it close to my workplace?

Your commute can determine whether you have a great day or a Terrible, Horrible, No Good, Very Bad Day. Even a rain-head shower won't make up for the fact that it takes three bus transfers to get to your desk every morning. Before you commit to any location, test out the commute, by car or public transportation, at the time of day that you'll typically be traveling. It's also helpful to keep in mind where you go besides work. Do you have a second or part-time job someplace? Will you die if you can't make the weekly trivia night at a certain bar? Do all of your friends live— and hang out—in a particular neighborhood? Map out all your favorite locales, then find a sweet spot that's convenient to as many of those places as possible.

3 | Will I feel safe walking home from the bus stop at night?

Or will your mom be buying pepper spray for your key chain after her first visit? You may be tempted to just do a gut check, but a little research can pay off. Look up the local police blotter online, or simply call the department and ask about the crime rate in your prospective neighborhood. Think about it this way, says Laban: You spend hours online planning a vacation and looking up reviews of hotels, so why give this decision less time and effort?

4 | Does the dry cleaner close at 6 P.M.?

This can be a problem if you have to wear suits to work and you never get home before 7:30. You should consider your neighborhood an extension of your home, says Laban. "If there are no cafés or restaurants and you aren't someone who likes to cook at home, that's going to seriously impact your life," she says. You may want to sacrifice square footage to afford a neighborhood that improves your quality of life.

5 | Does the apartment have (some of) the amenities I want?

Make a list of what you would love to have. (For help deciding among key amenities, see page 16.) "At first, just dream. Write it all down," says Laban. "Then cross out what's completely unrealistic." (Sayonara, roof deck.) Whatever is left, put in order, and know what your top three or so

priorities are. Once you start looking, you may realize that your budget is going to allow for only one. If you want a dishwasher, you may not have a view or high ceilings. But this list can also help you immensely in the search. If you have time to see only four apartments on a weekend, this must-have list can narrow down your options.

6 | Does the place fit my lifestyle?

Think about what happens regularly inside the apartment. Do you have a sister who crashes on your floor twice a month? Then maybe it's worth taking the apartment that is a four-story walk-up but has an air-mattress-size alcove off the living room. Do you make your own clothes? There had better be a spot for a sewing machine. Are you training for a triathlon? You need bike storage (or a roomy foyer). In the same vein, don't be shy about skipping popular amenities that you know you won't use. A rental agent can go on and on about stainless-steel appliances and a gas stove, but if you "cook" entirely in the microwave, a pro kitchen isn't worth paying for.

7 | What can I change?

For most rentals, it won't be much. Paint, possibly. So ask the landlord or rental agent—whoever shows you the apartment. If you love to decorate, make sure you know the rules on nailing things into the wall, hanging curtain rods, or adding wallpaper to a bathroom.

8 | What can't I change? And will those things drive me bonkers?

There are certain biggies you probably won't be able to change: flooring, closet space, natural light (or lack thereof), and electrical outlets. "The ugly tile in your kitchen is always going to be the ugly tile in your kitchen. If you don't like it now, you won't like it in six months," says Laban. If an apartment has dirty, stained carpet, for example, don't assume you'll just live with it. Move on. Or if everything else about the icky-carpet place is perfect, consider asking the landlord to replace it. When it comes to storage and natural light, the more you get, the better. Storage and organization solutions abound, of course, but you'll have to be really clever and creative to make up for no actual closet space. Are you up to the task? As for electrical outlets, Laban advises: "It may seem like a small thing, but we all live very wired lives. If there's a perfect corner for an office but nowhere to plug in a laptop, that can drive you nuts."

9 | Is there a school within earshot?

Anywhere kids congregate will be noisy in the morning and afternoon. Count on it. Other noisy spots: firehouses, hospital emergency rooms, nightclubs, bars. Take those things into account when you're scouting the block—especially if you're a light sleeper.

10 | Do my friends think this place is a good idea or a bad one?

Ask those who know and love you best to weigh in. Maybe you've never lived without laundry facilities but you have an uncanny ability to spill something on yourself every time you eat. Your best friend might be able to tell you that the great apartment with the swoon-worthy balcony but no washer and dryer isn't right for you. No friends available to see the place with you? That's what social media is for. Snap pics of the apartment (no pretty Instagram filters allowed!) and ask for verdicts online. "It's like taking a step back emotionally and seeing a place through someone else's eyes," says Laban. "Maybe you'll find that the entryway is a little smaller and darker than you remember."

APARTMENT WTF No.1

The neighbor has the unfortunate habit of leaving her smelly trash in the hallway. Vermin have noticed.

YOUR FIRST STEP: Speak to the neighbor, if you feel comfortable doing so. If not, call the super or landlord. Be polite and say, "Hi, I'd like to report a building rules violation, and I'm hoping you could get back to me about it as soon as possible."

IF THAT DOESN'T WORK: Create a paper trail. Write a letter and deliver it in a way that you're sure the landlord received it. (Try sending it certified mail.) That way, if you need to report your landlord to a housing authority, you'll have documented the complaint. In the letter, remind the landlord that your lease states that he is responsible for the upkeep of the building and will handle issues in a timely manner (or whatever language your lease uses).

YOUR LAST RESORT: You'll need to write your landlord another letter and send it (again) certified mail. This time, say that if he doesn't move the trash, you will deduct the cost of your time from your next rent payment for moving the trash yourself. But be careful: Withholding rent can backfire. A landlord could sue you. Before you take the risk, consult a lawyer first. Check with your city council or a housing advocacy group to find an appropriate attorney.

APARTMENT WTF No. 2

The guy above you is bouncing a basketball or playing drums at 3 A.M. You are about to take that drum stick and...yeah, let's get to the solution.

YOUR FIRST STEP: The following day, calmly talk to Lebron upstairs. The way to approach it nicely is to assume he has no idea he's being loud. (He truly might not know.) Say, "You probably don't know, but I can hear you in the middle of the night. Would you mind keeping the noise down?" Follow up with, "I hope you'll let me know if I do anything to disturb you." (So you don't seem like you're on your high horse about being a perfect neighbor.)

IF THAT DOESN'T WORK: Write a note and send it via certified mail. Explain that you are still having a problem with the noise and are going to brainstorm with the super or landlord about what to do. This communicates that (a) you are willing to problem-solve but that (b) you're not going to suffer in silence.

YOUR LAST RESORT: Actually talk to your landlord or super. Explain that you've tried to resolve the noise situation on your own to no avail. Ask if he can introduce quiet hours in the building. If nothing works, your last option, unfortunately, may be checking with an attorney or contacting a local tenant's-rights organization to find out what recourse you can take.

Beg, borrow—and deal

How could I find a decent apartment when I had a rock-bottom credit score and no job? Well, I got, ahem, *creative. By **Molly Antopol***

THE SUMMER MY BOYFRIEND AND I SEARCHED for our first apartment together, we were at opposite ends of the country: I was in San Francisco, issuing directives by phone, and he was on the ground in New York, carrying them out.

I'd just finished graduate school, which meant that I had to relinquish my blissfully cheap university apartment. School was over, adulthood loomed, and my boyfriend wanted me to move into his place, a rent-controlled apartment on the Upper West Side. It was cheap, yes, but he'd lived there for almost seven years and didn't have a single thing hanging on the primered white walls. It was a dark, moldy one-bedroom split into two by a fake wall he and his brother had engineered with a ruler and a bread knife. There was a mysterious brown spot on his sofa, shaped like Sweden.

I was nervous about moving in together and had fantasized about a bright, beautiful place with original built-ins and pressed-tin ceilings, where we'd combine our books and cook meals together in a sunny yellow kitchen with herbs growing on the fire escape. But how to get such a place when our credit score qualified us not for the apartment of our dreams but for a series of rejections from American Express, Visa, and Mastercard?

While I slept on a friend's sofa in San Francisco, my boyfriend, a journalist, searched for apartments. Every evening, he'd take the train from Manhattan into Brooklyn and wander into open houses. Every day, he sounded a little more dejected. He looked at more than 30 apartments, where he kept bumping into the same couple. They resembled us, he told me, pale and dark-haired, only they both had jobs and decent credit: a better version of ourselves.

Then one day a new listing appeared on Craigslist: a one-bedroom taking up a floor of a brownstone. It had everything we wanted: hardwood floors, a clawfoot tub, a little nook we could turn into an office. It was way out of our price range but seemed so perfect that we decided to reach. I suggested my boyfriend wear a suit to the open house—he had to borrow one from his brother—and charm the pants off of the landlords.

Every day, he sounded a little more dejected. He looked at more than 30 apartments, where he kept bumping into the same couple.

It worked. These landlords were artists and liked the idea of renting to young, aspiring writers. That night, across the country from one another, we celebrated with beers over the phone.

Then the landlord called back. They'd run a credit check, my boyfriend later told me. I could hear him twitching over the phone as he let me know it was over.

But it wasn't over. I had a plan. I booked a red-eye flight back to New York on my credit card, praying I'd have a job soon enough to pay the bill. The following morning, my boyfriend and I showed up on the landlord's doorstep and begged. She looked like a sweet woman, curly-haired and freckled, standing in the entryway with a toddler pulling at the hem of her denim cutoffs.

"I'm sorry," she said. "You both seem great, but I just can't in good faith rent you the place. You can't afford it!"

"Actually, I have a trust fund," I lied. The previous night, while I'd been flying cross-country, my boyfriend had asked our friends and families to lend us money for a single day—a total of $3,000. I'd deposited it into my bank account that morning and would return it to everyone once the landlord verified my balance. "I'm a little embarrassed even mentioning it," I said. "But a bunch of

money gets deposited into my account every month."

Something about the way she looked me up and down made me want to run home and iron all of my clothes. I knew I was lying, I suspected she knew I was lying, but there we were, an anxious, eager couple on her doorstep, and finally she sighed and said, "You promise you can make the rent?"

"I promise," I said.

And I did. I didn't know that morning that making the rent would mean working four jobs at once—freelance writing, a gig at a pharmaceutical company, and teaching at two dueling language schools. Or that after two years in Brooklyn, my boyfriend (now my husband) and I would head out west, realizing that our Herculean effort to land that perfect apartment ultimately wasn't worth it, when we were working so much that we were rarely there. But I didn't know any of that then. All I knew was that I was in love with him and with that mythical apartment and so I swore to the landlord that we could make our rent, over and over, before she could change her mind.

MOLLY ANTOPOL IS THE AUTHOR OF THE SHORT-STORY COLLECTION *THE UNAMERICANS*.

APARTMENT-AMENITY SMACKDOWN

Get some background on your options—on key issues ranging from flooring to A/C—so you can make the best possible decision.

CENTRAL AIR   VS.   WINDOW UNITS

CENTRAL AIR

THE GOOD
- Heavenly relief from the heat and cold that is consistent and quiet.

THE BAD
- Depending on what utilities are included in your rent, it can be more expensive, unless you remember to adjust the thermostat or turn it off when you leave.

WINDOW UNITS

THE GOOD
- You cool only the rooms that you need. Hooray, environment!
- You might just open the windows. Fresh air is good for you!

THE BAD
- Unless it's the Mercedes-Benz of window units, it's probably noisy.
- Many models leave little gaps around the edge that let in outside air *(brrr)* and dust *(blech)*.

GAS STOVE   VS.   ELECTRIC STOVE

GAS STOVE

THE GOOD
- You're in full control. It's hard to adjust an electric stove other than low, medium, high, but gas can be raised or lowered by tiny degrees, making it easy to keep a pot at a barely-there simmer.
- It looks cool.

THE BAD
- It's an open flame. Watch your ponytail and pot holders.
- Heavy cast-iron grates can be hard to maneuver to clean.

ELECTRIC STOVE

THE GOOD
- Gets hotter faster. Because every inch of the electric eye comes into contact with the bottom of the pan, it's more efficient. With gas, some of the heat wafts out into the kitchen.

THE BAD
- Can be difficult to maintain low heat.
- If you have old-fashioned coils instead of a flat surface, they can be tough to clean—especially if the oatmeal boils over.

HARDWOOD FLOORS   VS.   CARPETING

THE GOOD

- *Oooh,* pretty!
- Easy to clean.
- You can customize your decor and color palette with rugs, instead of having to decorate around peach carpet.
- Red wine wipes up instead of staining for all eternity.

THE BAD

- If you have pets, their claws can scratch the wood, which means no more security deposit.
- High heels are loud when you stomp around.
- To make it feel cozy, you'll need to buy a few rugs.

THE GOOD

- Friends can comfortably lounge on the floor.
- Warmer on your feet in February.
- You won't see dust bunnies swirling around. (They're just better hidden.)

THE BAD

- You're stuck with it. Carpet isn't an easy fix, so if it's stained or heinously ugly, it can be a deal-breaker.
- You have to vacuum.
- Two words: cat pee.

TOP FLOOR   VS.   BOTTOM FLOOR

THE GOOD

- You generally get more light the higher up you are (and the shorter the surrounding buildings are).
- No neighbors walking overhead at the crack of dawn.
- Possible unsanctioned access to the roof. (Prop the door open.)

THE BAD

- If there isn't an elevator, note that groceries can get really heavy at right about the third floor.
- Sometimes higher floors can have lower water pressure, since water is often piped up from the basement.

THE GOOD

- Heavy walker? Like to do Zumba before work? No problem.
- If you live in a first-floor apartment with a garden, you probably have the best—or only—access to it.

THE BAD

- Lower-level apartments can be dark.
- Oddballs and nosies on the street can see into your living room.
- Drunk people on the sidewalk at 2 A.M. sound like they're in your bedroom.
- You may be more likely to have roaches or mice sneak in off the street (or through the garbage pickup, which is also at street level).

How to read the fine-print, rental edition

Your apartment- or house-rental lease is no page-turner—more Heidegger than Highsmith—but it is nonetheless required reading. Know what to look for before you sign your life away. (Kidding!)

Make sure the landlord can't boot you on a whim.

In most cases, he isn't going to pull the rug out from under you. But check for any clauses that allow the landlord to terminate the lease early—and note how little notice he's obliged to give you.

Know what you will or won't pay for a hot bath.

Are utilities included? Which ones—electric, gas, hot water, trash collection? Make sure you understand which monthly expenses you are responsible for in addition to your rent and what the landlord covers. If you are renting a house, find out if the landlord expects you to perform any maintenance duties, such as mowing the lawn or cleaning the gutters. Bear in mind that "the landlord should be responsible for all repairs," says Catharine A. Grad, a tenant lawyer in New York City.

Suss out wording that might leave you open to big rent hikes.

The lease notes what you will pay every month, of course, but it may also say whether the landlord can raise the rent and by how much. If you live in a city like New York, you may live in a rent-stabilized apartment, in which case the rent can increase only by a certain, regulated amount.

Others are market rate, which (sadly) means the landlord can charge whatever he wants when the lease is up. You should also make sure that there aren't any riders (meaning additions) to the lease that change the rules. "Some landlords might add a provision that there's a penalty, or the rent goes up substantially for the month, if you pay late," says Grad.

Check that the landlord is cool with Sir Barks-a-Lot.

Really, you shouldn't be all the way to the point of signing a lease before you ask whether your Maltese or parakeet will be allowed on the premises. But this is your last chance to ensure that there are no misunderstandings about your pet. Will you be required to pay a higher security deposit? Do you have to refinish the floors or clean the carpets before you move out? Ask. You should have the terms written into the lease.

Determine the landlord's definition of "wear and tear."

Most leases allow for reasonable wear and tear on an apartment. That generally means dirt, grime, and minor scuffing on things is OK and not grounds for the landlord to keep your security deposit. But he may have a different idea. Find out what the rules are, and be sure to get them in writing. Would a nick in the bathroom sink void your deposit? What about painting the bedroom Tasmanian Teal? Some landlords may require you to return the walls to their original color to get your money back, and it helps to know that at the outset.

Find out if you can sublease or not.

"Almost all leases have a provision against subleasing," says Grad. So don't sign a two-year lease assuming that you can transfer it to your little brother in nine months, when you move for graduate school. And if it is permitted? Remember: You are still legally and financially responsible. So if your bro tries to roast s'mores on the fire escape and scorches the windowsill, it's ultimately your problem.

Choose a cosigner with care.

We know...it's insulting to need a Genuine Grown-Up (a.k.a. a person deemed to be a financially responsible adult) to cosign your lease. But if you want that sweet studio, you may not have a choice. And Mom, Dad, and your doting Uncle Pete say that they are up for it. Still, before your cosigner commits, make sure he or she knows what is involved. For example, if you live with roommates and you decide to move out after a year while your roommates keep the apartment, guess what? Depending on the terms of the agreement, Uncle Pete may still be responsible for those roommates, even though you no longer live there. "Whatever problems you create, you could be imposing on this helpful relative," says Grad. Which could cause problems at future Thanksgiving gatherings. Not to mention that getting financial backing from Mom may also mean, surprise, that she thinks she's entitled to decorate. So you and your loving cosigner need to be on the same page about your arrangement.

> ### IF YOU DO ONLY ONE THING...
>
> "Don't choose a bigger space over the right neighborhood—a big mistake! An easier commute and a safer area is always worth more than a roomier living room."
>
> **BARBARA CORCORAN** is a real estate mogul and "shark" investor on ABC's *Shark Tank*.

SHOULD YOU LIVE WITH THIS PERSON?

Just because you and Heather harmonized beautifully in your college a cappella days (go, Decibelles!) doesn't mean you'll blend as roommates. Before you invite her—or anyone else—to share your 2 BR, 1 BA, take a look at this 100 percent foolproof* flow chart.

*ONLY NOT AT ALL. GOOD LUCK!

YES

START HERE:

YES

COLLEGE ROOMMATE?

NO

DO YOU ALREADY KNOW HER?

NOT EVEN. Then **NO.** Start over.

NO

Mutual friends or siblings.

HOW DID YOU FIND EACH OTHER?

Craigslist, alumni network, flyer in the grocery store.

DO YOU TRUST THESE PEOPLE?

Sort of?

DO YOU HAVE THINGS IN COMMON?

Um, we both like cats?

TOTALLY. Then, **YES.**

DOES THE PERSON SEEM NEEDY?

NO

GREAT! BUT THAT'S NOT ENOUGH. DO YOU KEEP SIMILAR HOURS?

YES. We are both vegan astronomy buffs from large southern families. **YES.**

IS THE SOUND OF THE BLENDER AT 6 A.M. GOING TO DRIVE YOU NUTS?

YES, FOR SURE. NO.

NAH. We don't believe you. **NO.**

OMG, YES. NO!

NO. She has to make a green smoothie every morning at 6 A.M., and I sleep until 11.

YES

IS SHE TIDY?

HOW DID THAT GO?

HELL. Then **NO.** (Duh.)

EEK! NO.

AWESOME. We split all the chores and were compatible in every way! **YES.**

YES

HAVE YOU DATED?

NO

NAH, she seems normal. **YES.**

ANY REALLY ANNOYING HABITS?

YES

Are you just Instagram friends?

NO

So you're friends from work, spin class, or high school science-lab days?

YES, YES, YES!

Yes (sniffs constantly, hums all the time).

Yep. Are there any photos to suggest she plays the bongos?

NO!

Seems to. And she posts lots of photos of homemade doughnuts!

YES

Can you live with that? If yes, **YES.** If no, **NO.**

BATHES REGULARLY?

NO. Obviously.

OMG, YES. THEN: NO!

NOPE. PIPE SMOKER?

NO

YES

And agrees not to eat your Greek yogurt?

YES

And will comfort you during a breakup without being intrusive?

You bet.

YES. NO!

AND WEARS THE SAME SIZE SHOES AS YOU?

NO

DO YOU CARE?

NO. I AM SLOBBY, TOO. Besides, she said I could have the bigger bedroom. Then, **YES.**

YESSS. Score! *We'll* move in with her!

Renter's and homeowner's insurance: a primer

Yeah, we'd like to skip this part, too. We're falling asleep just thinking about it. Except one day someone might break into your apartment and steal that sweet flat screen and... Oh good! You're back! We'll be quick.

RENTER'S INSURANCE

Even if your couch is really a futon and the rest of your furniture was passed down from your nana's assisted-living quarters, you need renter's insurance. Here are three reasons why.

1 | You do not want to pay for those Ikea Billy bookcases again. Should a worst-case scenario, like a fire, befall you, you won't have to shell out cash to replace your stuff. (You do still have to assemble them—ugh.) If you have a renter's policy, the provider will help you promptly replace your belongings, from clothes to electronics, after you pay the deductible (generally $500 to $1,000, according to State Farm insurance). One caveat: If the damage is from a flood or an earthquake, you're on your own.

2 | Because Clumsy Clarissa will totally sue you. You have a party. Someone slips on the spilled sangria and breaks her clavicle. If she's a terrible friend and blames you, renter's insurance will cover your liability, says Robert Hunter, the insurance director of the Consumer Federation of America, an advocacy group.

3 | It's cheap. The average policy costs only $187 a year, according to the National Association of Insurance Commissioners. You can pay even less if you go with a cash-value plan—that is, it reimburses you for the current market value of your stuff (like returning a shirt that went on sale after you bought it and getting only the sale price back). If you have a valuable baseball-card collection, an original Van Gogh (the *Starry Night* poster does not count), or heirloom jewelry, you'll need an additional insurance rider. The cost may vary, but it can be a small price to pay for peace of mind.

HOMEOWNER'S INSURANCE

A homeowner's policy will pay for damage to or destruction of your structure (meaning the house itself) and your belongings (from your furniture to your bunny slippers), and it covers liability. (So if Clumsy Clarissa does a header down the stairs and sues you, you won't lose everything you own.) Unlike with renter's insurance, you generally can't opt out of getting a policy. If you have a mortgage, the lending institution will insist that you are covered. Before you buy, here are three things worth knowing:

1 You should be smart and choose a replacement-cost policy that will cover the total cost of rebuilding your house and replacing your belongings at current prices.

2 If you get your auto and homeowner's policies from the same insurer, you should reap significant savings. For more on choosing an auto policy, see page 144.

3 Policies aren't cheap—$978 annually on average nationwide, according to the most recent figures from the Insurance Information Institute, an industry group. But you can shave costs in a few ways.
• Maintain a rock-solid credit score. (Clueless about credit scores? Turn to pages 135 and 139.)
• Install safety devices. Many insurers offer discounts of about 5 percent to homeowners who add smoke alarms and dead bolts to their homes. That's easy enough—and, you know, *safe.*
• Boost your deductible. Increasing it from $500 to $1,000 should save you a bundle on insurance costs every year.

APARTMENT WTF No. 3

My landlord is raising my rent 300 percent. What, does he think I work for Google?

YOUR FIRST STEP: First check to see if your landlord has the right to raise the rent. He probably does, if your lease is up and there aren't any local laws (such as those in New York City) to protect you.

IF THAT DOESN'T WORK: Negotiate. Landlords generally like it when tenants stay put. They save money on cleaning, repainting, and showing the apartment.

YOUR LAST RESORT: Alas, you might have to move. If you have a very good deal and the market rate is substantially higher than what you pay, you're probably out of luck. It's still worthwhile to call and ask. Say, "I've been a great tenant and can't quite pay this amount. Can you work with me?" Caveat: You'll probably have more wiggle room with an individual person who is the landlord than with a huge management company.

Buying a home: what you need to know

Excited?! You should be. And a bit daunted, too. After all, this is one of the most complex and pricey things you'll ever do—and that includes your dual Russian-literature/military-history degree. Happily, these handy tips will guide you through every step.

Stage 1: How to make your best offer and negotiate the close

BID SMARTLY. There's no rule of thumb for what your initial offer should be or how many times you should go back and forth with the seller. Most inexperienced buyers simply make a bid that's a certain percentage—say, 10 or 15 percent—off the listing price, says Ilyce Glink, the author of *Buy, Close, Move In!* But that's not always a wise strategy. The smarter move: Ask your real estate agent for prices of comparable homes in the area that have recently sold. Use those figures to determine the max you're willing to pay, then submit a bid that's a tad lower. Next, start haggling.

MAKE CLEAR DEMANDS. Be up-front about extras—those polished-nickel bathroom sconces, the dramatic velvet living-room curtains—that you want included with the house.

USE THE CLOSING DATE AS A NEGOTIATING POINT. Be flexible if you can. "As long as you don't need to relocate by a specific date, you'll possibly get other concessions from the seller that won't cost you anything," says Glink.

ASK THE SELLER TO BUY YOU A HOME WARRANTY. A good one will run about $300 to $400. It can cover the cost of repairing or replacing appliances and major systems, such as plumbing, for a year after closing.

Stage 2: How to get a mortgage

ASK FOR REFERRALS. There's no one easy way to find a lender, so try hitting up friends and family for recommendations. (You want someone known for good customer service.) Or ask your real estate agent for loan-officer suggestions. And make inquiries at local credit unions, whether you're a current member or not. They often have rock-bottom rates if you qualify for membership, and it's typically easy to join.

CALCULATE YOUR DOWN PAYMENT. To avoid having to buy private mortgage insurance, you need to pay at least 20 percent of the purchase price before closing costs. (Ouch, we know.)

OBTAIN QUOTES FROM FOUR TO FIVE TYPES OF LENDERS. Consult with mortgage bankers (who work in-house with big institutions, like J. P. Morgan Chase and Wells Fargo) and with mortgage brokers (who shop around with all lenders) to get the best interest rate. Also, check with your local credit union, online mortgage companies, and local or regional banks. Ask each loan officer how much her institution charges for closing expenses, including the underwriting fee and the cost of faxing documents. Make sure you are dealing with someone who is accessible and willing to take the time to explain the loan-approval process. That kind of person is more likely to be straight with you about *all* the costs. And remember to ask the lender if putting more money down can land you a better rate.

DECIDE IF YOU WANT TO PAY POINTS TO LOWER YOUR RATE. Sometimes a bank will let you buy prepaid interest (points, in finance-speak) in exchange for a reduced interest rate. Points aren't cheap. Each one will cost you 1 percent of the loan amount. So if you're buying a home that costs $209,700 (the national average) with 20 percent down, then you'll have to pay about $1,678 per point. Don't have that much cash on hand? Ask about purchasing a half or even a quarter point. If you're going to stay in the house for at least nine years and you can afford to do so, it makes sense to shoulder the extra expense up-front, as it will cost you less in the long run.

Stage 3: How to have the house inspected

FIND A LEGITIMATE INSPECTOR. This is one situation in which you shouldn't take a recommendation from your real estate agent. She could encourage you to go with someone who overlooks problems in order to make the deal go through as smoothly as possible. Instead, contact a professional organization (ashi.org or nahi.org) to find an accredited, self-employed expert who has performed at least 1,000 inspections. In many states, there isn't a licensing program, but these associations usually require their members to meet certain standards and participate in continuing education.

REQUEST A DETAILED INSPECTION REPORT IN ADVANCE. Ask how much time the inspector typically needs to conduct an analysis (an average home should take one to three hours) and what the finished report will look like. You want it to be at least 10 pages in length, and it should include photographs of anything that's wrong.

CONSIDER ADDITIONAL ASSESSMENTS. Ask your real estate agent and primary inspector if they recommend scheduling additional inspections above and beyond the standard one. These might include analyses of the chimney, the sewer, and the oil tank and testing for mold and radon. What you need to do usually depends upon the age, the condition, and style of the house. For example, radon is problematic in some basements, but if your house has only a crawl space, you probably don't have to worry.

GO TO THE INSPECTION. This is your opportunity to ask questions about the infrastructure of the house. Be sure to learn about the operation and the location of the gas and water shut-off valves and the breaker box.

Stage 4: How to address the physical defects

GET WRITTEN ESTIMATES FROM ANY CONTRACTORS YOU'LL BE HIRING TO PERFORM HOUSE REPAIRS. Your real estate agent will submit to the seller the anticipated costs for any problems found during the inspection.

ASK FOR A PRICE CREDIT. You can control the quality if you have the repairs done yourself. Request that the cost of any fixes, whether large or small, be deducted from the sale price and have the work done after the purchase is final.

Stage 5: How to hire an appraiser and buy title insurance

HAVE THE PROPERTY APPRAISED. To determine its value, you need an appraiser. But generally you can't hire one; your lender does this. You can, however, help the assessment go smoothly. Ask the seller to be present so that any questions the appraiser has about the home can be answered. He also should have a copy of the sales contract to verify exactly what is (and isn't) being sold.

TELL YOUR MORTGAGE BROKER TO PROVIDE A LIST OF COMPARABLE PROPERTIES. Point out where the home being appraised has been improved (like renovated bathrooms) and how that differs from other recent sales.

Stage 6: How to navigate the closing process

CONSIDER HIRING AN ATTORNEY. In some states, it's not customary to hire a lawyer for residential purchases. "But even in those areas, you should get a lawyer if your situation is complicated or if you're buying a foreclosure or a short sale," says Glink.

LOCK IN YOUR INTEREST RATE. See opposite page for more details.

OBTAIN A DETAILED LIST OF CLOSING COSTS FROM YOUR LENDER. Besides the expenses tied to your loan, you may have additional fees, such as title services and transfer taxes. This information should be listed on your Good Faith Estimate form, which the lender provides when you lock in your rate.

WATCH FOR BOGUS FEES. Some lenders charge for preparing documents, messengering papers, or even printing e-mails. It's worth asking for these items to be removed from your bill, says Glink.

Stage 7: How to conduct the final walk-through

VERIFY THAT ALL INCLUDED APPLIANCES ARE IN WORKING ORDER. Turn on the oven, the dishwasher, the stove, and the washer and dryer. Don't forget to make sure the refrigerator works, too.

TURN ON EVERY FAUCET, AND FLUSH THE TOILETS.

PLUG SOMETHING INTO EACH OUTLET. You'll want an electrician to repair any broken ones right after you close on the house.

CHECK THE SMOKE DETECTORS. Light a match by each to verify that they're in working order.

TEST THE HEAT AND THE AIR-CONDITIONING. You don't want to find out that the furnace or the A/C doesn't work a few months down the road.

LOOK FOR WATER STAINS AND MOLD ON THE CEILINGS. They could be a sign of ongoing leaks.

EXAMINE FOR SIGNS OF VERMIN, including excrement (mice) and insect remnants.

NEGOTIATE A CLOSING CREDIT. If you find anything broken or missing, have your broker or lawyer request financial compensation.

SHOULD I LOCK IN MY MORTGAGE INTEREST RATE?

If you change your shoes 14 times before dinner, this level of commitment is going to be hard. But at some point you have to pull the trigger.

A bank can quote you an interest rate, but until you "lock it in," the rate can change, depending on the market. Up a fraction of a point one day, down a fraction of a point the next. Once you've put in a bid on a house and it's been accepted, you lock in your mortgage rate, which allows you to hold on to a quoted rate for a limited amount of time (typically 30 to 60 days). At that point, the clock is ticking. You need to close before the lock-in period expires. But before you can close, your lender will order an appraisal and an inspection, and the seller will prepare the house or make any agreed-upon updates. "There are multiple parties involved, so you should ask your lender how long it typically takes to close loans like yours," says Keith Gumbinger, a vice president of HSH.com, a mortgage-information site.

If your lender offers you a 30-day lock-in period but deals are taking longer than that to close, ask if you can have 45 or 60 days—and if there will be a fee involved. "Don't be risky and wait to lock in your rate because you think it will go down. Rates may go up," cautions Gumbinger.

APARTMENT WTF No. 4

I moved out of my place weeks ago, and I still haven't gotten my security deposit back.

YOUR FIRST STEP: Assume it's an oversight; the landlord may have forgotten to send the money. Call or e-mail him, politely mentioning that you took very good care of the apartment, and ask when you might receive the security deposit.

IF THAT DOESN'T WORK: If the landlord claims there's damage to the apartment, you pull out your photographs. Wait—you don't have photographs? OK, back up. When you move in, take pictures of any broken floorboards or chips on the vanity, just like you would note dents in a rental car before driving away with it. Then, when you move out, document the apartment again to show that nothing else is damaged. If a landlord refuses to give back a security deposit, he's going to have to say why. If the allegations aren't true, you are far better off if you have proof. Send a letter outlining what was expected in your lease with photographic evidence that you complied. No photos? Still send a letter and follow up if you don't hear back.

YOUR LAST RESORT: Head to small claims court. If you want the money back, you'll need proof that you're in the right. You don't need a lawyer in small claims court, but you should bring your photos or at least a reputable friend who can be a witness on your behalf.

The ultimate moving checklist

The day is coming when you will pack up your high school yearbooks and steal your dad's shrunken leather jacket from the 80s and move into your own place. It's going to be amazing...well, once you get past the taping-boxes part. This step-by-step timeline will help you get organized.

1 MONTH BEFORE

☐ **PURGE, PURGE, PURGE.** Been meaning to go through the 19 pairs of boyfriend jeans you own and give some to Goodwill? Now's the time.

☐ **CALL FOR MOVING QUOTES.** Start investigating moving-company options, including DIY. Before you assume a rental truck and your friends are the way to go, consider how much it's going to run you to buy supplies (like moving blankets and dollies, which moving companies generally provide) and gas. Check with your auto-insurance company to see if you're covered when driving a truck or if you'll need to buy extra insurance. Get quotes from several companies, and consider looking on Craigslist or asking around for people you could hire to help you load heavy furniture, even if you're the one driving the truck.

☐ **BE NERDY.** Make a moving binder. Use it to keep track of everything—all your estimates, your receipts, and an inventory of all the items you're moving.

3 WEEKS BEFORE

☐ **RAID THE RECYCLING.** Save your boxes. Ask your local liquor store or grocery store for castoffs. Hoard newspaper for wrapping dishes and other breakables. Order any extra boxes you may need, plus padding for breakables and permanent markers.

☐ **QUIT BUYING (AND START EATING) YOUR FROZEN PIZZA.** Use up things you don't want to bother transporting, whether it's the last few glugs of olive oil or half-empty bottles of cleaning supplies.

☐ **FIND A TAPE MEASURE.** Check the room dimensions at your new place, if possible, including the door widths and heights. You don't want to find out on moving day that your couch is too fat.

2 WEEKS BEFORE

☐ **CONFIRM YOUR MOVING ARRANGE-MENTS.** Select a company and get written confirmation of your moving date, costs, and other details. Or, if your plan is to rent a truck and have friends help, make sure that everyone's schedule is clear. And ask the rental company for help in determining how big of a truck to get. Leaving your favorite chair on the corner because it won't fit will make you sad.

☐ **PACK THE IRON.** Come on, it's not as if you're using it. Start boxing up the items you won't need before the move, like winter coats if you're moving in August. (For packing tips, see page 31.)

☐ **CREATE A SAFE BOX.** Separate out valuable items, like jewelry, that you don't want to get lost in the back of the truck. Put them in a box or a bag that you'll personally bring to the new place.

☐ **FILL OUT A CHANGE-OF-ADDRESS FORM.** Do it in person at the post office or online at usps.com. But in case there are stragglers, it's always wise to ask a neighbor to look out for mail after you've moved. Check in with her two weeks after the move.

☐ **GIVE IMPORTANT PEOPLE A HEADS-UP.** Alert the following of your move: banks, your employer's HR department, magazines you subscribe to, and credit-card, insurance, and utility companies.

☐ **ASK YOUR BOSS** if you can have your moving day off.

1 WEEK BEFORE

☐ **REFILL YOUR PRESCRIPTIONS.** It may take you a while to find the most convenient pharmacy or transfer medical records. So stock up on any prescriptions you'll need for the next few weeks.

☐ **TRY TO FINISH PACKING EARLY.** You want to spend your last few nights saying good-bye to your friends and your favorite manicurist, not cramming to get everything in boxes.

A FEW DAYS BEFORE

☐ **SET ASIDE SOME CLEAN UNDERWEAR.** Pack a bag with enough clothes to get you through a few days without embarrassment.

☐ **GET CASH AND/OR BEER.** If you're using a moving company (or just moving guys), you'll need to have some cash for tips at the end of the day. (Turn to the appendix, Should I Tip This Guy?, page 264, for specific tipping recs.) Shell out for pizza and beer for your friends.

THE DAY BEFORE

☐ **CONFIRM YOUR TRUCK—AGAIN.** Many rental companies can't guarantee your truck until the day before, so call to make sure they have the size you need at the location you requested. If not, they should be able to steer you to another location or give you a larger truck at no extra cost.

MOVING DAY

☐ **PACK SOME H_2O AND A SNACK.** Moving day is like a wedding day: You never remember to eat.

☐ **KEEP CALM,** thank your friends if they helped out, and make sure you don't leave anything on the sidewalk.

PACK IT IN (BETTER)

Hack your move with these eight smart tips.

1 | PUT STUFF YOU'LL NEED ASAP IN A CLEAR BIN.
That way, when you're in your new digs, surrounded by boxes, you can get to your toothbrush and cell-phone charger without playing archeologist.

2 | USE THE RIGHT SIZE BOXES.
Put weighty items—cast-iron pans, your copy of *Infinite Jest*—in small boxes. Stow light items, like sheets and pillows, in bigger ones. Large boxes packed with heavy items make movers (whether they're pros or pals) grumpy and their chiropractors happy.

3 | PUT HEAVIER ITEMS IN THE BOTTOM OF A BOX, LIGHTER ITEMS ON TOP.
And if you're loading the truck yourself, pack heavier boxes first, toward the front of the truck, for balance.

4 | DON'T LEAVE EMPTY SPACES IN THE BOXES.
Fill in gaps with clothing, towels, or packing paper. Why? You want to keep an even weight distribution whenever possible.

5 | AVOID MIXING ITEMS FROM DIFFERENT ROOMS IN THE SAME BOX.
This tip just saved you 15 minutes of walking back and forth, back and forth, between your bedroom and the bathroom. You're welcome.

6 | LABEL EACH BOX WITH THE ROOM IT'S DESTINED FOR AND A ONE- OR TWO-WORD DESCRIPTION OF ITS CONTENTS.
Number each box to make sure none went AWOL during the move.

7 | TAPE BOXES WELL.
Use a couple of pieces of tape to close the bottom and top seams, then use a nifty movers' technique——making a couple of wraps all the way around the box's top and bottom seams, where stress is concentrated.

8 | BUNDLE BREAKABLES.
As you pack your nicer dishes, put packing paper around each one, then wrap bundles of five or six together with more paper. Pack dishes on their sides, never flat. And use loads of bunched-up paper as padding above and below. Cups and bowls can be placed inside one another, with paper in between, and wrapped three or four in a bundle.

CHAPTER 2

GETTING A JOB (AND KEEPING IT)

Our first—and biggest—piece of advice: It's going to take time. To find something that pays you, to find something that pays you decently, to find something that pays you decently and that you love and that you can see yourself doing for years to come. So be patient—and have faith that even though 50 online personality quizzes have not yet helped you find yourself (You're a Shoshanna...so now what?), you will eventually find your Thing.

This chapter will nudge that process along. With tips on nailing the interview, negotiating a salary (you can do it!), finding a mentor, and managing stress once you're in the job, these pages will make you, in some ways, an overnight success.

How to apply yourself—and get the job you want

You got that department-store perfume-misting gig based on your BFF's recommendation. Bartending at the Biergarten happened because you practically lived there. So you may never have had to put yourself up for a job-job. No time like the present.

THE STRATEGY: Scour online job sites.

Yeah, they get a bad rap. And there are some good reasons why: Some employers post a job on online boards like Monster.com, only to hire one of the summer interns. Or by the time the job has posted, everyone in town has already thrown her hat into the ring. Maybe the position has a high turnover rate because the manager is a serious pill or the hours are the stuff of sweatshops. But... aren't you the slightest bit curious what might be out there? Think of these search engines as the Tinder of your work life: There you are, browsing for love, not necessarily expecting to find it. And—boom!—there it is. If you see something that looks promising, why not apply?

HOW TO WORK IT

• Go to job-search sites like Monster.com, CareerBuilder.com, and Indeed.com for any kind of position, as well as more specialized sites, like Dice.com (for techies) and MediaBistro.com (for new media, PR, journalism, and advertising).

• Incorporate into your résumé keywords that come up often in job postings, such as "customer relations" if you're in sales, and "creative" if you're in advertising. The HR departments of many big companies employ applicant-tracking systems to search for given terms on résumés. That way, they can immediately disqualify people who don't use the important terms and whittle down the pool by as much as 50 percent. According to studies, only

20 percent of hiring managers look at the majority of résumés, so those keywords are essential. (For more on acing the résumé, see page 37.)

• Post multiple versions of your résumé, with each version tailored to the position that you're applying for. Let's say you're applying for an editorial-assistant position at a website and a sales-assistant job at a book-publishing house. For the website position, you would focus your résumé on your writing skills, digital bona fides, and editorial experience (e.g., your illustrious year as the culture editor of the university newspaper). For the sales position, you would talk up your two years of retail experience at Barnes & Noble, where you sold more literary novels than anyone else at the store.

• To get your résumé to the top of the pile, visit the company's website to see if the position is cross-listed there, then send a message via LinkedIn to the HR manager (or whoever has posted the job). Also reach out to anyone you might know at the company or within the industry to get more information about the job and make introductions. Suddenly you'll go from being a semi-anonymous online applicant to a candidate people are vouching for.

THE STRATEGY: Take a temp job.

No, you're not slumming it. Temp jobs can (a) help you bide your time until the gig of your dreams materializes or (b) develop into the gig of your dreams. Depending on the parameters of the position, the opportunities available at the company, and the get-up-and-go you show at the office, you could turn that temporary coffee-fetching, Excel-spreadsheet-creating position into a career-track position.

HOW TO WORK IT

• Ideally, sign up with all the temp agencies in your area. (Do a couple each week.)

• Once you're in an office, act like you're a permanent employee: Get up from your desk and introduce yourself. You want to become a recognizable face in the hallway.

• Take on responsibilities that will get you involved with people and not get you stuck in a rut. Say you're working as an assistant in the sales department: Ask to be more involved in group projects, like helping to prepare for a big presentation. You will not only have the chance to showcase your skills and intelligence but you'll also have an opportunity to get to know them—and for them to know you. You are also demonstrating initiative and the willingness to be a team player.

• One caveat: Don't temp for too long. Candidates whose résumés have more temp jobs than permanent positions can lead potential employers to wonder why their work life isn't stable.

THE STRATEGY: Go speed-networking.

If you've ever speed-dated, you understand pretty much how this works. You meet someone, have a slightly awkward conversation (the whole time wondering if the arugula from lunch is stuck between your teeth), then try to frantically assess whether this random person (or, er, company) could be The One—or at least The One Until Something Better Comes Along. These carefully orchestrated musical-chair events are most frequently held for college alumni groups, professional organizations, chamber of commerce groups, and college or corporate orientations and allow you to spend one-on-one face time—usually between one and three minutes—with a host of industry professionals, most often from the fields of finance, communications, and law.

HOW TO WORK IT

• Prepare a 15- to 30-second bio beforehand. Be sure to mention your main professional aspiration and a recent project or accomplishment that you're proud of.

• Hand out business cards printed with your name, cell-phone number, and e-mail address and a generic title of the position you're looking for, like "marketing assistant" or "accountant."

• If a chat seems to go well, send a connection request via LinkedIn. Once you get an acceptance, thank the person for her time and insights, and ask if you can follow up with an e-mail or a phone call to stay in touch. Then, if she agrees, do stay in touch. Within two weeks, send a polite note requesting an informational interview or asking if she would mind keeping you in the loop about job openings.

• To find a speed-networking event in your area, check out speed-networking.meetup.com. Also contact local industry associations in your field of choice to see if they host such events.

THE STRATEGY: **Use alumni services.**

Just about every college and university likes to keep their students close and their alums closer for a number of reasons—to keep you connected to the school community and (more cynically) to help fund that spiffy new study lounge in the environmental-studies building. But look: Their love for you, and your dollars down the road, can be indispensable to you now. There's no greater gift than having a fellow alum give advice, advocate for you, or make introductions as you break into the job market.

HOW TO WORK IT

• Check out your alma mater's website to see what career services are available to alumni. If you don't live near the campus, chances are you can still work remotely through phone appointments with alums or attend webinars.

• Don't show up empty-handed. Have a résumé drafted and ready for critique by the career-services gurus on staff. Bring all your job-search materials—what you've tried, whom you've spoken to—so that the office can help you brainstorm your next steps.

• Network through your alumni association. Most have a database of alumni contact information that you can search by company or industry. Or attend an alumni event. That fortysomething suit at the tailgate party could be looking to hire. For all you know, there's a diehard alum right around the corner from you who's in desperate need of a right-hand woman.

SHOULD YOU TAKE AN UNPAID INTERNSHIP AFTER GRADUATION?

Opting for a gratis internship can be worth taking a financial hit. Rochelle Rubin, the director of creative recruiting for the Solomon Page Group, a staffing firm, explains why.

"An internship puts a brand on your résumé and gives you some recognition and some qualifications," says Rubin. "To get the stamp of approval from a company in your intended industry is meaningful to a future employer." Plus, if you've shown initiative, you may have dazzled your immediate supervisor or even a higher-up or two. And though a position at that company might not be available, you will walk away with something else that's indispensable: references.

"Let's say you have an internship at an ad agency and you're being mentored by someone and she's impressed by you," says Rubin. "She might pick up the phone and call a client or colleague and tell him about you."

Whether you work there for two or six months, you'll get a first-hand glimpse of the industry and of the company. You'll also gain an understanding of that business, which will make you a savvier prospect for employers. So it isn't all for nothing. There is a payday in the end. And, man, won't that first paycheck feel even sweeter?

Cover-letter and résumé do's and don'ts

All that white space can be daunting to fill— especially since you don't have loads of work experience. And what you do have (um, college-library book reshelver?) may not wow the corporate honchos. So be sure to follow these guidelines from top recruiters and HR muckety-mucks.

Cover letter

DON'T sweat it. Why? No one reads it. Really. "The only time I look at a cover letter," says Aileen Joa, a human-resources generalist from Fidelus Technologies, a technology company, "is when I'm not 100 percent sold on a résumé. But if your résumé doesn't say it, chances are I'm not reading it in your cover letter."

DON'T wax on about your goals and dreams. "I've noticed that applicants tend to ramble about what they want from their career paths, but I never want to read that," says Joa. "I want to know what you are able to give the company. Why should I hire you?"

DON'T be overly creative or precious. Try to resist the urge, for example, to write a cover letter for a magazine job that reads *(ahem)*, "I could make your life *Real Simple* if you hire me." Just be straightforward, and bear in mind that employers are skimming.

DO keep it short—about two paragraphs total. In that space, you should convey a few key points: why you want the job; what makes you best suited for the position and the company; and what you uniquely have to offer as a candidate.

Résumé

As far as the résumé goes, **DON'T** think of it as a monolithic document. It should be tailored to fit each position you apply for. Save each version of your résumé under the name of the company and position, so you don't carry the wrong résumé to the interview. (Yes, you need to bring a copy, even if you already sent one.)

DO make it *just one page*. There is nothing that you have done that cannot be summarized in a coherent, intelligent way on one page.

DO include the following information, says Caroline Ceniza-Levine, a coach with SixFigureStart, a New York City–based career-coaching firm: your name, mailing address, e-mail address, and cell-phone number; work experience; schooling; references; skills (such as proficiency in PowerPoint).

DON'T have an absurd e-mail address. If it's something like sexxxykitty@gmail.com, then get a new one for professional use. (You might consider getting a new one for personal use, too. No offense.)

DON'T have a stated objective ("I'm looking for a great job in a Fortune 500") that has no meaning. If you say you want to work in fashion and you send it to a fashion company, they can probably figure out your goal.

DO put your most relevant experience first—especially if this is your first or one of your first jobs. Chronology is less important. Employers want to see immediately that you have experience related to the job.

DON'T be afraid to list unpaid, volunteer, and ad hoc work. An internship is a job, experts say. So is being a volunteer or a research assistant. (Be sure to give yourself an appropriate title.) And anyone who can comment on your work is a reference. Remember the summer you stepped in as the booking manager for your friend's band? You got them five back-to-back gigs, four of which sold out. This proves you're a self-starter and a savvy marketer. Write that down, too.

DO use keywords you see in job postings. They lure recruiters and would-be bosses to look at your résumé when they're doing candidate searches. When those words are absent, the HR people will probably toss your résumé in the trash without reading it. "If I post a job saying I want someone who is 'detail-oriented' and 'creative,' echo my language," explains Joa. Maybe you were in the debate club and you organized all the details involved in planning the club meetings. Work a mention of 'detail-oriented' into that part of the résumé. "You're not cheating—you're giving me what I need," says Joa.

DO include references. You may think you don't have any. (After all, it might be weird to ask Mrs. Thompson next door to vouch for your stellar babysitting skills.) But that amazing ability to bang out a brilliant 25-page paper on the emergence of post-apocalyptic narratives in the post-9/11 world has got to count for something,

right? You think big and work on deadline, so list the prof who gave you that A+. Just make sure you ask before using her name.

DO inform (and, ideally, coach) your references before they get a call. Assuming that they agree to speak well of you, pass on some basic information. Tell them, for example, "You're going to get a call from Josie at This Big Company, Inc., and she's considering me for an associate accounting job." Remind your reference of your accomplishments. Say, "Could you mention that big project I did for you a year ago?" Says Ceniza-Levine, "People tend to be very grateful when you do that, because it's less work for them."

DO proofread. "I've seen people get homonyms messed up and other things that don't get caught in spellcheck. 'Pubic finance' is my favorite. Recruiters look at résumés all the time—we are super attuned and have an eagle eye for mistakes," says Ceniza-Levine. And your top priority: Make sure you have *all* the names right on *all* your correspondence—the people, the company name, every proper noun. It's worth the extra few minutes it will take to check.

How to look good online

The Internet knows what you did last summer—and all the seasons before that. You probably can't eliminate every last tag or tweet, but this advice will help you appear as upstanding online as you are in person.

Step 1: Play detective.

"Your first impression isn't made with a firm handshake," says Dan Schawbel, the author of *Me 2.0.* "It's with a Google search." If you have a common name, like "Anne Smith," do a few different searches—one under your name, and then work in a few specific identifying details, such as your alma mater, your hometown, organizations or teams you were involved in, other jobs you may have had, and other associations. The first page of search results is the most important. Studies show that 90 percent of people never venture beyond it. But assume that employers will peruse up to five pages, and make sure there isn't anything ominous or incriminating.

Step 2: If you find anything problematic, tidy up.

If everything is clean as a whistle, congratulations. Skip ahead to step 3. Otherwise read on.

Delete negative comments and inappropriate photos and videos you may have put on sites like Facebook, Instagram, Pinterest, Vine, and You-Tube. Request your archive from Twitter (go to support.twitter.com for instructions) and delete old tweets. If you blog using a platform like Wordpress or Tumblr, you can edit that material, too. If you feel the need to start fresh and create a more grown-up profile, then generally you can eliminate your accounts. Methods vary among sites, so check the Help function for instructions.

If someone has posted a comment, a photo, or a video about you, you'll need to ask that person to remove it, because you might not be able to. Keep in mind that while you can't delete another user's photo on Facebook, you can remove the tag of yourself so it no longer shows up on your profile page or in your network.

Having trouble getting rid of stuff? Or just don't want to deal with it yourself? There are a number of online-reputation management services—Reputation.com and BrandYourself, among others—that promise to clean up your digital profile. They're effective at burying inaccurate, inappropriate, or slanderous information. (Unfortunately none of these companies can delete news articles or court records.) But these services are expensive and probably worth investing in only if your online profile is riddled with red flags.

Step 3: Improve your (virtual) image.

Now that your skeletons are safely buried, take a few steps toward bolstering your online persona. If you haven't already, buy the rights to the URL of your name (hello, AnneSmith.com). That way, you can create your own personal website that shows you in the best light. On it, include samples of your work, a list of your major accomplishments, videos of presentations you have given, links to professional journals or associations, testimonials from your LinkedIn profile, and, of course, your contact information. Visit GoDaddy.com or BlueHost.com to see if your name or a variation of it is available. If yourname.com is taken, opt next for yourname.net or, worst case, yourname.org.

Then get active on Twitter, if you aren't already. Begin by following CEOs and other leaders in your industry. Once you familiarize yourself with the players, you can start weighing in, retweeting articles and blog posts you're reading, and making connections.

LinkedIn is another excellent way to build content for yourself—and attract prospective employers' positive attention. (See opposite page for more info.)

IF YOU DO ONLY ONE THING...

"Always say 'Next.' I learned this by reading a quote by Barry Diller after he lost a crucial fight for control of Paramount: 'They won, we lost, next.' At that moment, I realized that all those nights worrying that I'd done something stupefyingly stupid or had made a fatal mistake or that a flop might sink me were worthless wastes of well-needed sleep. There is no crisis that can't be undone, outlasted, or untangled. The solution to surviving in a career is to say 'Next.'"

LYNDA OBST has produced lots of your favorite films (like *Sleepless in Seattle* and *Interstellar*) and is the author of *Hello He Lied: And Other Truths From the Hollywood Trenches*.

LINKEDIN FOR BEGINNERS

LinkedIn is one of the only social networks that you had no use for until the moment you moved your mortarboard tassel from the right side to the left. And no wonder: It's visually blah, and there's not a LOLcat in sight. So do you need to join up?

In a word: yes. It's indispensable. If you work (or want to work) in health care, finance, marketing, event planning, law, technology, consulting, human resources, or sales or at a nonprofit, "the site is a great place to connect with people who can help you professionally," says Victoria Ipri, the CEO of Ipri International, a Philadelphia-based marketing firm. In fact, about one-fourth of companies research potential employees on the site, according to a recent study.

You want in on that. But interacting on LinkedIn is different than on Facebook, where you know which friend requests you want to accept and reject. Abide by these rules.

ACCEPT RANDOM (BUT USEFUL) CONNECTION REQUESTS. Should you connect with your best friend? She's a nurse and you're an accountant. (Answer: yes.) What about a stranger who's in your field? Again, yes. "You're connecting not just with a person but her network. Your friend may have a link to someone who could help you," says Viveka von Rosen, the author of *LinkedIn Marketing*. What about someone 100 percent random? Well…maybe. "When you receive a random invitation, look at the sender's profile and determine if it is a quality connection for your needs and circumstances before accepting or rejecting it," says Ipri.

Use caution if you include your home address or phone number in your profile.

BE CURIOUS. Consider further expanding your network by using the site's "People You May Know" tool to reach out to professionals with similar backgrounds and connections. If you're interested in working for a particular company, go to its page and click to follow it, then look at the list of people who work there. Next, find someone whose path you would like to emulate, then invite her to connect. To demonstrate that you would be a meaningful connection, write a note that conveys that you have done research on her employer and her personal accomplishments.

CHECK IT DAILY, BUT NOT COMPULSIVELY. Log on every day for a few minutes and once a week for about a half hour. That's the amount of time you'll need to write to a new connection or weigh in on a group discussion.

BE A BIT BRAGGY. Think of your LinkedIn profile as your résumé, plus everything else that you couldn't fit on it, like video clips of speeches that you delivered in college and links to school-newspaper articles you wrote, says von Rosen. The more thorough you are in describing yourself, the easier it is for an employer to assess your qualifications.

Nail the interview

You've schmoozed strangers, cold-called HR recruiters, and proofread your résumé a bajillion times. Now comes The Interview— otherwise known as time to close the deal. Here's how.

Before you walk in the door

BE A SNOOP. Make sure you know as much about the company as you can. Start by reading the company's website, where you'll find the names, titles, and bios of the big players on staff; the company's latest projects; and any other news they're willing to make public. Then take it a step further and Google them. This is where you might find the good stuff: who their competitors are; recent deals; who is coming in, who's leaving, who's been promoted; and other industry gossip. Also: Have you found out in advance whom you're meeting with? This is very important. "Research the people who will be interviewing you," says Alex Morgan, an account manager at the San Francisco tech firm 24 Seven. Most people light up when personal connections are drawn—suddenly you share something in common and you have a bond. Tell the woman interviewing you, "Oh, I saw on LinkedIn that you went to Goucher College. Me, too!" Or comment, "I know that you worked for so-and-so at such-and-such company. I've always admired his career."

VISUALIZE HOW YOU THINK THE JOB INTERVIEW WILL GO. Try to anticipate how the conversation might play out, then write down talking points for yourself—key things you want to convey in the course of the meeting. Read these points aloud before your interview—at home by yourself or in front of a trusted friend. This will help reinforce the points in your mind, which will make you feel more confident and self-assured when you stroll into that office.

PLAN TO ASK A FEW SURPRISING QUESTIONS ABOUT THE COMPANY. See "Do You Have Any Questions for *Me*?" (following page) for suggestions.

BONE UP ON THE COMPANY'S CHIEF COMPETITION (and don't get them confused with the place you're interviewing at). "I interviewed someone and he boasted about how much he loved one of our shows. The problem was that the show was on a competing network!" says Adria Alpert Romm, an HR executive for Discovery Communications. "It was clear to me that he knew nothing about us."

CHOOSE A NUMBER. In many interviews, salary isn't even mentioned. (That talk gets saved for the job offer.) Still, you should come to the interview with a salary in mind—or at least a range. If you don't know how much the position pays, go to salary.com, a search engine that provides the pay scale for most jobs based on geographic location. If you suspect you're asking for a salary on the high end, be sure to offer reasons why your skills and credentials—a second language, an advanced degree—might warrant more money.

On the day of the interview

DRESS AS THOUGH YOU WORKED THERE. Going too formal or too casual can create red flags for the employer. "One woman came in wearing flip-flops," says Beth Anisman, a recruiter and consultant with B&Co, a recruitment and consulting firm. "Another came in with a Birkin bag and Chanel shoes. It made me wonder if she even needed a job." (For specific guidelines on the best way to dress for every industry, go to page 90.)

DON'T WALK IN EMPTY-HANDED. Andrea Eisenberg, the managing director of Preferred Transition Resources, a career-guidance and placement firm, says that all too often, "applicants come to interviews without a pen, without a note pad, without a résumé." Bring all of these things—even if the employers have already received your résumé. You should always have a copy on hand and a pen and paper for taking notes.

OPEN THE CONVERSATION WITH A COMPLIMENT. Make a personal connection by praising the Hiroshige print behind the interviewer's desk or taking note of a cute photo of her twins on display. A warm moment will help you stand out in her memory.

BUT REMEMBER—THIS PERSON IS NOT YOUR FRIEND. No matter how casual the interviewer is, remain professional. That means you shouldn't over-share or gossip—and don't complain about former bosses or jobs. Another no-no: swearing. Anisman says that one candidate she interviewed was so relaxed that she "dropped the S-bomb. Another candidate burst into tears and told us something incredibly personal." Always err on the side of formality.

After the interview

E-MAIL A THANK-YOU TO EACH PERSON YOU MET WITH. It's the menschy thing to do. It's no small thing for a businessperson to take time out of her busy day to chat with you. A lovely, genuine note can tip a recruiter from "I'm not sure about her" to "Isn't she awesome?" Plus, not sending a thank-you note can turn off a prospective employer.

THEN SEND A FOLLOW-UP THANK-YOU BY MAIL. U.S. mail, that is. "My favorite thing is to see someone e-mail and say it was such a pleasure, so you get the immediacy of it, and then a day or two later that is followed up with a handwritten note. Then you know the person is on top of it," says Anisman. "If you met with a few people, don't write the same thing to every person you've met with in the company, because we're forwarding them to one another." She also suggests bringing up a detail or two that came up in conversation, "just to personalize it and demonstrate that you were engaged and show that this isn't a form letter. This will impress them even more."

THEN THANK THEM ONCE MORE—even if you don't get a job. Acknowledge via e-mail that you appreciate the opportunity to be considered. That kind of professionalism speaks volumes. And if you were a strong contender, you never know when a position might open up.

DO YOU HAVE ANY QUESTIONS FOR *ME?*

Never draw a blank in an interview again. Stick these four expert-recommended queries in your back pocket.

It's the moment that you've been dreading. Your prospective boss leans forward and asks the question about, you know, questions. Moments before, you were chatting away so easily. Now it's crickets in the conference room. These Q's will help you end your interview on a high note.

1 | WHAT IS THE MOST IMPORTANT QUALITY I NEED TO SUCCEED IN THIS POSITION? Your would-be boss's response can give you an inside look at how the company really works, says Allyson Willoughby, the senior vice president of human resources at Glassdoor.com, a career site. For example, if your interviewer says "accountability," you know that she will expect you to woman up and admit fault if you make an error. Plus, says Willoughby, "asking this question shows that you're thinking about the importance of your work style, not just the skill set you offer."

2 | CAN YOU DESCRIBE A RECENT STRESSFUL WORKDAY THAT YOU EXPERIENCED? Details about the not-so-great times can tell you as much, if not more, about the realities of day-to-day business as you would learn from abstract talk about the future. Your interviewer's reply can also show you how she handles conflict, says Shannon King, the chief operating officer of Levo League, a career forum. If you follow up by asking her what could have made that day less challenging, she'll understand that your aim is to make her life easier.

3 | WHAT WOULD YOU EXPECT A STAR PERFORMER TO ACCOMPLISH IN THE FIRST 30 DAYS? This question shows the boss that you will be driven and ambitious, and it gives you a preview of your future to-do list. "If you're interviewed by multiple people for the same position, you would be smart to ask this of all of them," says Priscilla Claman, the president of the Boston-based coaching firm Career Strategies Incorporated. "Then you can see if their answers differ."

4 | WHAT IS THE OFFICE CULTURE LIKE? Office culture matters—especially considering how much time you would be spending in it. Are the employees merry pranksters who goof on one another constantly or no-frills drones who do their work and keep to themselves? Does everyone go out drinking together on Friday night, or do people barely exchange pleasantries in the hallway? These may seem like frivolous questions, but it's good to know what kind of vibe to anticipate—and whether it will be a good fit for you.

Name your price
(and get it)

Sheryl Sandberg says to lean in. Which sounds great, but it's hard to do— especially when you (a) really need a job, (b) hate talking about money, and (c) don't want to annoy the recruiter. Oh, and (d) did we mention that you seriously need a job? Still, you can drive a harder bargain than you think.

The two-minute salary-and-benefits conversation you'll have after landing a job is your single best chance to get what you're worth, says Jim Hopkinson, the author of *Salary Tutor: Learn the Salary Negotiation Secrets No One Ever Taught You*. After all, "you may spend many more years working hard at this new job for an annual raise of 3 percent—if you're lucky."

The trick is getting the potential employer to say a number first. This puts you in an advantageous position. But what are you supposed to do if the question is put to you? Try to dodge the question gracefully, says Jessica Miller, a coauthor of *A Woman's Guide to Successful Negotiating,* who suggests countering with "I'm sure we can work out something that's fair. What do you have budgeted for the position?" Why this maneuver can work: Employers are "not looking for someone whose primary interest in the job is money," says Miller. "So make the discussion about fit and getting to a number that works for everyone."

What if you are pressed (again) for an answer? Rely on the salary research you did before the interview (see page 43 for more information), pick a number you can live with, then name a figure a few thousand dollars higher.

If you have some work experience—say, you've been in your job for a year or two and you're looking for a new gig—you're in a better bargaining position. You might say something like "My total compensation is in the mid–five figures, but every company has a different mix, so tell me how you see the compensation for this position being structured."

What if you're caught off guard and blurt out, "I make X amount"? Don't fret. "Mention discussions that you're having with other companies and what they're offering," says Miller. "You don't need another solid offer. You can tell them that you're in talks about another opportunity and the salary being discussed is in the range of Y dollars."

When you get an offer, resist the urge to yell, "I'll take it!" Graciously say, "Thank you so much. May I get back to you tomorrow?"

Are you my mentor?

Wanted: a cool, connected person who's been there and done that to share her wisdom and advice. Now, for finding that special someone...

Know what you want.

Are you looking for a supportive, weekly mentoring session with someone who will guide your career long-term? Specific advice for a project that you're grappling with right now? Or do you simply want a "coffee mentor," someone whose brain you can pick when the spirit moves you? Decide; then look for the person who fills that bill.

Cast a wide net.

Women tend to focus their mentor searches at their workplaces as opposed to within their wider networks, says Nicole Williams, a career expert for LinkedIn: "But you don't even need to choose someone in your own industry." When Williams was in her 20s and working in event marketing, one of her most powerful mentors was her next-door neighbor, a venture capitalist. Someone in virtually any walk of life could have significant career experience that mirrors yours or relates to the career that you want to have.

Bring goals to your first meeting.

Don't try to engage your prospective mentor with mint tea for two and a meandering chat. Instead, experts suggest that you come to the table with a clear agenda. Having specific, targeted questions is a sign that you respect that person's expertise and value her time. For example, instead of posing a vague question like "Hey, what advice do you have to share?" say, "I researched your background and would love to understand how you transitioned from one job to another."

Make yourself useful.

Offer your help with something she needs. "Say, 'I heard you're going to this conference. Can I come along? Can I take photos for you or live-tweet the event?'" says Rachel Sklar, a writer and a social entrepreneur. "Figure out what to ask that will both deepen the relationship and provide you with chances to shine."

Be realistic.

Mentors are there to expand your scope and to get you to think about how to frame your experience. They're not there to make decisions for you or serve as a therapist.

Don't assume that your mentor is always available.

Be careful about requesting her time, whether that's in person or by e-mail or phone. Early on, find out the ground rules about how often you can call on her and what you can expect from her.

Finally, pay it forward.

Once you've benefited from having a mentor, consider becoming one. According to a report by the nonprofit Catalyst, both male and female leaders who helped foster others' careers saw a stunning average of $25,075 in compensation growth for themselves over a two-year period of time. Why? Developing the careers of others increases your visibility and shows your boss that you're not just out for your own advancement. It's the right thing to do for someone else, and it pays dividends for you, too.

IF YOU DO ONLY ONE THING...

"The most important thing to look for in a job is an intangible: the culture of the company. But culture is tough to get your arms around, so you have to ask questions and do some digging. What do its employees say about the company? What stories do they tell about it? How has the company responded when it's made mistakes? Here's an important one: How do they talk about people who have left the company? How have they treated them? How do they talk about their customers? Then you can make the decision about whether the company's values align with yours."

SALLIE L. KRAWCHECK is one of the highest-ranking women on Wall Street. She is currently the chair of Ellevate Network, a global professional women's network.

Make your job work for you

There is this mythic creature called the Happy Worker Bee. Maybe you've even met this person— a total freak of nature who bounces into the office as if he's had a full pot of coffee before eight in the morning. But according to a Gallup poll, these Bees are a rare species, outnumbered by malcontents by nearly two to one. How can you get buzzed? Read on.

WHAT YOU WANT: A bigger paycheck

HOW TO GET IT: You've seen the Dow tick up. Don't you wish your income would, too? Of course, you do. "A raise not only demonstrates that your organization values you; it also motivates you to work harder," says Adrian Granzella Larssen, the editor-in-chief of the Daily Muse, a career-management website. Hopefully, you will get a cost-of-living bump at your annual review. But if you think you should get a bigger hike, you may want to ask for a merit raise. To get a sense of what is a reasonable bump, check what others at your level and in your field are making at PayScale.com and Glassdoor.com. Finally, make a list of your job duties, taking note of how they have changed since you started there. (At least a year should have passed; don't ask before then.) Now that you have a sense of what you ought to be making, schedule a meeting with your boss. Take a list of your accomplishments (goals met, clients landed, projects completed) to your supervisor. Explain that you feel your pay should be higher to match your level of responsibility. State the specific wage that you desire; don't round it off. (Say $56,250, not $55,000.) A Columbia Business School study reported that, when negotiating, you're more likely to get what you want with a precise amount. And if your boss says no? Find out what you can do to work toward it. If it's a matter of budget, ask instead for other perks, like more vacation time.

WHAT YOU WANT: **A promotion**

HOW TO GET IT: The best way to increase your chances for a work promotion is through self-promotion. No need to cringe—there are ways to bring your awesomeness to your boss's attention without looking like an egomaniac. It begins with something as simple as taking credit for your work. Corinne Moss-Racusin, an assistant professor of psychology at Skidmore College, in Saratoga Springs, New York, explains: "Many women are still raised to think that sharing their accomplishments is unbecoming. As a result, they often undermine themselves without realizing it." So when given a compliment, don't say, "I couldn't have done it without Erin," or "It was luck." Say, "Thanks!"

Then get proactive: Spearhead new projects (for example, a volunteer initiative); organize an event (such as hosting a panel on your area of expertise). When supervisors see you taking charge, you earn instant credibility, says Nancy Ancowitz, a business-communications coach and the author of *Self-Promotion for Introverts*.

WHAT YOU WANT: **More challenges**

HOW TO GET IT: If you're bored to death, there's no way to feel invigorated on the job. "So highlight the skills that you're hoping to utilize or hone," says Adam Grant, a professor of management at the University of Pennsylvania. "Then ask a mentor or boss for advice on how to expand your contribution." Say, for instance, "I've always been interested in event planning, so I would love to help organize the gala fund-raiser next month." Or, if you want to put your accounting chops to good use, draw up a memo on ways that the company can save money. If your boss doesn't see the value of challenging you (or simply doesn't have additional work to give you), find ways to streamline your current tasks—or even create new projects for yourself. Seriously, just make yourself look busy. Do something like scanning every document from before 2000 and create online files. She'll think that you're nuts. (And, in a way, you are.) But you'll look like a hero to your colleagues, and you'll get the message across that you're bored out of your gourd. (And while you're at it, you may want to consider sending out your résumé, if you haven't done that already.)

WHAT YOU WANT: **Less stress**

HOW TO GET IT: Is your workload giving you agita? Talk to your boss about how much is on your plate. She may not remember everything you are juggling. Once she sees your full workload, she may decide to give one of your responsibilities to someone else or extend a deadline for a large project you are working on, says career coach Caroline Ceniza-Levine. In addition, each Monday, check in briefly with her about your three biggest priorities for the week to make sure that the two of you are aligned in where your focus should be. If your office is tightly wound in general, it may be up to you to find a way to unwind. Try scheduling a regular after-hours outlet. You might like a bit of a bend-and-shvitz activity, like yoga, or duking it out in a boxing workout. Or consider taking an art or writing class. And there are always your besties to call on. They may well be enduring the same kind of challenges. Whatever it takes to get through, do it.

Love, sex, and an open-floor plan

Everyone warned you: Never date a coworker. But when you spend all of your time at work, how else are you supposed to find "love"? Which is maybe how you ended up making out with Avery from marketing after the holiday party. But now what do you do?

First, is this a relationship or a hookup? A brief fling doesn't require the boss's attention.

But if you and Avery want to pursue this thing, then you'll need to loop in work. Consult the employee handbook and see if there is a policy against dating a coworker. If there is such a policy, be up-front with your boss. Present her with possible solutions, like moving to another department, that will allow you both to stay at the company. No official policy? Then let your boss know that your new relationship will not create a negative situation in the office, says Nancy Monson, an executive coach in central California.

Once the cat is out of the bag and you've alerted your manager, you don't need to "create walls of formality that don't exist," says Tracey Levy, an employment lawyer. "There's no need to be surreptitiously meeting in the parking garage at an appointed time for your rendezvous. You can joke; you can converse. You just shouldn't hang all over each other, kiss in public, or share stories about your personal escapades."

The one thing that never flies is getting romantically involved with someone you report to. It happens, but it's prohibited for good reason, says Levy: "And usually that means somebody has to change roles or leave the company to create some distance, so they no longer have that direct-reporting relationship."

And if you and Avery hit the skids? The office can become a minefield. If you thought keeping your displays of affection in check was hard, how about those feelings of heartache? Know that the same rules apply: You have to work out your business outside of business hours and keep them far from the cubicle zone. That said, if your ex can't remain professional, speak up. "If somebody is misbehaving," says Levy, "then the person who is feeling victimized should let HR or a manager know about it so they can address it."

A field guide to nightmare coworkers

Sometimes the toughest part of a job is not the actual work but the personalities you have to deal with from day to day—it's like a human obstacle course. Here are six of the most common aggravating on-the-job personalities, with tips on managing them.

The Spotlight Stealer

HOW SHE DISRUPTS YOUR DAY: She strolls over to your desk and flatters you, always asking if she can pick your witty brain. The next thing you know, she's taking credit for your ideas without even flinching.

BEST WAY TO FINESSE: If a coworker poaches your idea in a meeting where you are present, immediately pipe up. Say, "I'm so glad Lisa picked up on what I mentioned. Lisa, thanks for recognizing my idea." If you hear about the theft only after your little gem has been presented and approved, sending an e-mail to your manager with a line like "I'm glad Lisa picked up my idea and was able to run with it. Let me know how I can help." After that, let it go—but zip your lips the next time the two of you have a private meeting or conversation.

The Clueless Overling

HOW HE DISRUPTS YOUR DAY: He is a master at appearing to be productive while meddling in everyone else's business. Which is apparently a full-time job. If he expended only half of his energy actually being productive, then you wouldn't have to spend twice as much energy doing triage while trying to get your own work done.

BEST WAY TO FINESSE: The only job you need to salvage in this situation is your own. Let his self-sabotaging behavior take its course. The boss's follies will eventually attract the attention of the (even) higher-ups, and with luck they'll make a change. But if things are unbearable and he seems to have a lifetime appointment to his job, you may have to seek out a boss in another department or even another workplace. "If this person is that clueless and you're on his or her coattails, your career could be in danger," says Marjorie Brody, a career coach.

The Ball-Dropper

HOW SHE DISRUPTS YOUR DAY: She starts projects, then expects them to magically finish themselves. Enter the magic elf: you. Lately you're making her look like an idea machine that follows through on everything.

BEST WAY TO FINESSE: Fire a warning shot. Explain to her that you were happy to help until now but that you can't do it anymore because your own work is suffering. If that doesn't fly, schedule a meeting with your supervisor to address your workload. If you continue to pick up the extra work, your stress level will become intolerable.

The Rumormonger

HOW HE DISRUPTS YOUR DAY: He's got the dirt on everyone. At first you found his stories enter-taining—until it dawned on you that anything you say or do becomes grist for the gossip mill, too. Now you trust him about as far as you can throw his desk.

BEST WAY TO FINESSE: Tell him nothing. Close the gossip down before he starts by making an excuse to leave the room (a deadline or a meeting, for example). You can't listen to the gossip and then complain. If you're cornered and he starts dishing about a coworker's behavior, reply with "I've never noticed that myself," then change the subject.

The Best-Friend Wannabe

HOW SHE DISRUPTS YOUR DAY: She asks if you have lunch plans at 9:15, then 9:30, then 10, 10:30, 10:45.... And how about a drink after work? Brunch on Sunday?

BEST WAY TO FINESSE: You should not be held hostage to somebody else's wishes or neuroses. Just because your coworker wants or needs constant companionship doesn't mean you have to provide it. Explain that you have obligations elsewhere, or say that you've made a rule to go straight home after work. If you open the door, you'll be in a worse situation than before. Say what you have to in order to avoid getting together. People catch on after a while.

The Chronic Complainer

HOW HE DISRUPTS YOUR DAY: The clock has struck the kvetching hour, and the office whiner hovers over your desk, just as he does every day, to moan about...well, what doesn't he moan about? His workload, his boss, his mother, his lack of a love life. Honestly, you should start charging him for your time, because not only are you giving him free therapy but he's also cutting into your workday. Not to mention the fact that he's seriously bumming you out.

BEST WAY TO FINESSE: Gently interrupt the person, saying, "Excuse me, but I've really got to meet this deadline. I can't talk right now." That way, you cut the conversation off without criticizing him. If you restrain yourself from jumping on the boo-hiss bandwagon and don't offer any feed-back, the complainer will probably leave you and search out someone more likely to join in.

5 WORK RULES YOU SHOULD BREAK

These on-the-job maxims are officially ready for retirement—here's why.

1 | DO WHAT YOU WERE HIRED TO DO.
"Your boss has to look at the bigger picture all the time. She'll admire you for doing the same. If you pay attention to your organization as a whole, you'll better appreciate what other people do, and you might come up with macro ways to help the company. It's a fine line between offering assistance and stepping on someone's toes. But if you have the best intentions at heart, you can say, 'I see an opportunity here that we're not taking advantage of.'"
ADAM BRYANT is the author of *The Corner Office.*

2 | LIVE AT THE OFFICE. "For many of us, our careers are not our life's passions. So it's essential to pursue outside interests—both for our happiness and to facilitate our creativity at work. Amazing discoveries and insights are often made when people are tinkering in the garage or riding a bike. Plus, hobbies help give us a sense of peace. And once we relax for a moment, the answer to a work problem will often reveal itself."
KAREN BURNS is the author of *The Amazing Adventures of Working Girl.*

3 | CLIMB THE CAREER LADDER. "There's pressure in our culture to earn more money and to have important titles. But not everyone wants more responsibility and power. And what we don't hear often enough is that it's OK not to want a promotion. So move laterally or choose self-employment if you think that will make you happy. It won't hold you back. On the contrary, having a nonlinear career path can make you more intriguing to bosses in the future, not less. They'll view you as having broader experience."
MICHELLE GOODMAN is the author of *The Anti 9-to-5 Guide.*

4 | AVOID TMI. "Say you and a colleague have different work styles or have clashed over a project, and as a result there is tension between the two of you. Tiptoeing around the issue may cause your productivity to suffer, so it's crucial that you confront your coworker. You can say, 'You seem to dispute every point I make, and I don't understand. Did I do something to upset you?' If you talk about it, the situation won't spiral out of control or become a pattern."
SEAN O'NEIL is a management consultant and a coauthor of *Bare Knuckle People Management.*

5 | NETWORK 24/7. "It's inefficient to walk into a cocktail party or industry event and start mingling. My suggestion? You can get in touch with important people who interest you, retweet messages of theirs, ask them questions, and strike up online relationships. From there, it can be easy to get them to meet you for lunch or coffee, where you'll connect in a real, personal way that will ultimately help your career."
PENELOPE TRUNK is the author of *Brazen Careerist.*

Take this job and shove it

I landed a primo position at the company of my dreams in June—and quit by August. How I learned when to stop trying so hard. By **Kirstin Chen**

IT WAS DAY NINE AT THE STARTUP. I hunched over my keyboard, clicking through the sort of website I ordinarily would never, ever think to pull up at work. I was not alone. A glance around my open workspace would reveal that, at that very moment, approximately 40 percent of my colleagues' computer screens featured hot schoolgirls or randy mothers. From the corner of my eye, I spied the boss, stalking the room like an assassin, pausing to glance at a screen or ask a question. She approached my desk. I ducked my head to demonstrate my industriousness and held my breath, exhaling only when she tapped the shoulder of the boy next to me. They both disappeared into her windowless office.

By the time we returned from lunch, his desk had been cleaned out.

Weeks earlier, when the recruiter called to offer me the job, I was told I would join the Startup's new pay-per-click advertising group. I accepted at once. The Startup was a highly coveted place to work in Silicon Valley, with Ping-Pong tables and roving massage therapists. Getting such a glamorous and impressive job felt like the logical culmination of my academic striving, like all those years of overachieving had paid off.

What I didn't know was that almost half of our potential clients were porn websites. Because the Startup had stringent ethical standards, it would do business only with sites that adhered to certain rules: no actors under the age of 18 and no nonconsensual sex. My job was to vet these sites. As the management reminded us fresh college grads in near daily pep talks, they were tracking our work at all times. Only the most productive would earn permanent positions.

For the rest of the day following my neighbor's sudden disappearance, I didn't dare take even a quick break to gorge on the free candy and juice. Instead, I stared at my screen until my eyelids twitched. At the end of the day, management gathered us and announced—*Survivor* tribal-council style—the names of those who had been let go, and then the rest of us tumbled out into the parking lot, near hysterical with relief to have made it past the first cut.

For the first time, I realized that not all authority figures were worth pleasing and not all duties were worth fulfilling.

I came back the next morning determined to tamp down my burgeoning dissatisfaction and work even harder. As the weeks passed, a number of my colleagues grew disillusioned, while I endeavored to be a stellar employee. They arrived at our casual workplace in suits, not bothering to hide that they were interviewing elsewhere. The girl across from me quit before lining up another job; she said she couldn't spend another minute looking at porn.

It was then that the indignities of my work grew too large for me to ignore. When I was growing up, I'd come to believe that academic success all but guaranteed life success. I'd been an exemplary student who had thrived on positive feedback, and in exactly the same fashion, I now craved management's praise. But for the first time I realized that not all authority figures were worth pleasing and not all duties were worth fulfilling.

Soon thereafter, I left to teach high school English, where I'd advise students against simply striving to meet teachers' expectations. "Think about what most intrigues you and go for that goal," I'd say. A few more years would pass before I'd accept my own advice and pursue my love of writing, but I was on my way.

KIRSTIN CHEN IS THE AUTHOR OF THE NOVEL
SOY SAUCE FOR BEGINNERS.

WHEN TO TAKE THE PROBLEM TO HR

Every once in a while, situations at work get so messed up that you alone can't fix them. Before doing anything drastic (or literally making a federal case out of it), consider calling in the professionals.

Think of human resources as the hall monitor of the workplace. They are mediators, gatekeepers of the rules and regulations, and run interference among all the employees. Don't be afraid to seek out help from them—they are empowered to improve your working situation. But they can do that only if they know about your problem. Here are four instances in which you might want to give HR a call.

1 | YOU BELIEVE YOU ARE EXPERIENCING DISCRIMINATION OR HARASSMENT. According to the U.S. Department of Labor, examples of illegal employment discrimination include "paying women less than men for the same work; repeatedly teasing employees who speak with an accent; promoting employees based on sex or race." Harassment can include "unwelcome sexual advances, requests for sexual favors, and other verbal or physical harassment of a sexual nature," per the U.S. Equal Employment Opportunity Commission (EEOC). The EEOC adds that "harassment does not have to be of a sexual nature, however, and can include offensive remarks about a person's sex. For example, it is illegal to harass a woman by making offensive comments about women in general." Your HR representative should be responsive and either address your concern directly or open an investigation.

If you feel she is not responsive, consider contacting an employment attorney, the EEOC, or your state or city's human-rights agency.

2 | YOUR LEGAL RIGHTS ARE BEING IGNORED (overtime pay is being withheld, for example), and you've been stonewalled by your immediate manager.

3 | YOU NEED ADVICE ON DEALING WITH A COWORKER who hasn't responded to your previous efforts. HR may have suggestions for dealing with the problem.

4 | YOU'RE UNSURE whether someone is acting legally or ethically, and you fear your boss may be involved or in the know.

Quitting with panache

The day has come. You're giving notice. You can't wait to break the news to your boss, who totally took you for granted. Or to the coworker who clears her throat every 10 seconds...all...day...long. Keep your gloating in check, though, and remember: You can be as impressive on your way out the door as you were on the way in.

Before you even think of tweeting the good news, updating your Facebook status, or whispering to colleagues, "I'm outta this hellhole," step back. You can't say anything until you've delivered the news to your boss. And whatever you do, don't crow about moving on—not in front of your work pals or your employer, advises Laura Williams, an advertising executive in Los Angeles. Excited though you may be, it's poor form.

This is not a text-message breakup conversation. You can't do it over e-mail, either. Excruciating though it may be to consider, guzzle that coffee like a cup of courage and brave the human contact this conversation demands. (Or if yours is a tele-commuting position, employ Skype or make a phone call.) It's not a bad idea to rehearse what you're going to say—especially if you and your boss have had a contentious relationship. Do everything you can to contain the vitriol. "Do not use this conversation as an occasion to air grievances," says career columnist Anne Fisher. "The smoke from burning bridges can come back to choke you later."

However, you should be honest about why you're leaving. Tell your boss that you've had an offer that better meets your needs. And, above all, be respectful. Remember—this person hired you over other applicants and showed you the ropes, enabling you to move on to the next level. After leaving one job, Williams says, she thanked her main boss in person, then left short thank-you notes on the chairs of her other bosses and office mentors. She adds, "The idea is to leave open as many doors as you can. Also, it's just polite." After all, you never know when you'll need to walk through one of those doors again.

CHAPTER 3

LOOKING GOOD

Time to cue your makeover montage. In the movies, a Cool Chick named Madison or Keira would take you to the mall and transform you from plain-Jane college grad to polished sophisticate—all while a "You go, girl!" anthem swells in the background. But this is a book. No mall epiphanies to offer. What we do have is expert know-how, easy tutorials, and (sorry, Madison) zero attitude.

You won't find any overly involved braid how-tos or insane eye-shadow colors here. Instead, we'll supply realistic ways to take care of your skin, foolproof makeup tips, and doable hairstyles. You supply the catchy beat.

What your skin is trying to tell you

#nofilter? No, thanks. If your complexion is constantly out of whack, you may not be giving it what it needs. Once you figure out your skin type, you can customize your daily routine and be selfie-ready in no time.

THE CLUES: You tend to be shiny along the T-zone but dry on the cheeks. You rarely experience redness and have relatively small pores. (Lucky you.) Although an occasional zit may surface, your hormones are usually to blame.

THE VERDICT: You have normal (a.k.a. combination) skin.

BEST REGIMEN: Opt for products that serve dual functions.

CLEANSER: At night, use a mild glycolic acid or a gentle nonsoap wash that won't strip away too much oil but will still tackle dirt and dead skin cells stuck in pores. Just splash your face with water in the morning.

DAY LOTION: Look for a lightweight variety that's labeled "oil-free" and has an SPF of 15 or higher. This will help balance your dry patches and greasy spots.

NIGHT TREATMENT: If you spot pimples (usually around your period), dot a cream with benzoyl peroxide or salicylic acid onto blemishes to help unclog pores before you add moisturizer.

TROUBLESHOOTER: Since the T-zone is prone to blackheads, help prevent them by applying an oil-absorbing clay mask to your forehead, nose, and chin once or twice a week.

THE CLUES: Let's see.... There are flakes, more flakes, and even more flakes. And after cleansing, your face may feel tight.

THE VERDICT: You have dry skin.

BEST REGIMEN: Choose cleansers and creams with powerful, fancy-sounding emollient ingredients, like ceramides (a potent moisturizer) and hyaluronic acid.

CLEANSER: Choose a creamy formula, and smooth it on with a wet washcloth to exfoliate gently at night.

DAY LOTION: Every morning, after rinsing your face with just water, apply a cream with a humectant (which keeps skin moist), like hyaluronic acid, plus sunscreen. If the flaking and peeling are noticeable and uneven, try a skin-plumping face oil (like argan or coconut) under the moisturizer. It will smooth out your skin in a flash.

NIGHT TREATMENT: While you sleep, nourish skin with a night cream that includes ceramides.

TROUBLESHOOTER: Even with a moisture-packed program, this skin type can still feel as parched as the Kalahari. Compensate with a hydrating mask once a week or whenever you could use some extra help. Go for the kind you slather on and remove with a washcloth. (The peel-offs can be drying.)

THE CLUES: How do we put this delicately? You're easily irritated. Almost any new cream or potion provokes a response, usually in the form of redness or stinging.

THE VERDICT: You have sensitive skin. (No offense.)

BEST REGIMEN: Read labels closely and pick products that are fragrance-free, offer soothing hydration, and contain as few ingredients as possible.

CLEANSER: Stick with a cleanser that contains calming botanicals, like feverfew and oatmeal, and steer clear of the instigators, like glycolic and alpha hydroxy acids (AHAs). Wash only at nighttime; rinse with water in the morning.

DAY LOTION: Choose a moisturizer with sun-blocking minerals, like titanium dioxide and zinc oxide, which are less harsh than chemical sunscreens.

NIGHT TREATMENT: Alleviate any itchies and blotchies with a cream that contains anti-inflammatory ingredients, like green tea and licorice-root extract.

TROUBLESHOOTER: A hydrating serum, layered underneath a day cream, will provide an extra shot of moisture on days when your skin is feeling particularly fussy.

THE CLUES: Blackheads, breakouts, and big, obvious pores are a daily battle. Basically, your face still thinks you're 13 years old.

THE VERDICT: This is probably not news, but you have oily skin.

BEST REGIMEN: Help keep your pores unclogged by regularly sloughing away dead skin cells with products that contain salicylic acid or AHAs.

CLEANSER: Wash morning and night. Consider using a battery-powered facial cleansing brush with a mild cleanser to curb breakouts.

DAY LOTION: It may seem like the last thing you need is to slather moisturizer on your already greasy T-zone, but it's important that you don't skip this step. If your skin gets dehydrated, your sebaceous glands, which produce oil, will kick in to overdrive and you'll be cruising to Slick City. The key is to opt for oil-free lotions and sunscreens, which won't exacerbate acne.

NIGHT TREATMENT: Use a retinol night cream to speed up exfoliation and prevent clogged pores.

TROUBLESHOOTER: Spot-treat blemishes with a drying potion that includes sulfur or a salicylic acid treatment to make pimples heal faster before you add moisturizer.

Zits for grown-ups

Cafeteria cliques may be a distant memory, but you're still battling with that other purveyor of high school angst: pimples. Gervaise Gerstner, a New York City dermatologist, explains how to fight these bad boys off.

What is acne anyway? Zits occur when pores become plugged with sebum (an oily substance produced by the sebaceous glands) and dead skin cells that haven't sloughed off properly. When bacteria that normally live on the skin's surface enter those clogged pores, they can multiply, release fatty acids that are irritating to the skin, and cause inflammation, explains Gerstner. In adults, acne most often pops up on the chin and the jawline but can also be found on the chest, the back, and the upper arms.

What are the top triggers?

YOUR PERIOD: Doctors believe that acne is often caused by the hormonal fluctuations of menstruation. Breaking out along the jawline is often a sign that your period is on the way. Pregnancy and going off birth-control pills are two other times hormone-driven acne can occur.

A LEVEL-10 FREAK-OUT: Stress will stimulate your body to produce more hormones, which may contribute to breakouts, says Gerstner.

MOM AND DAD: Bummer. Susceptibility to acne may be written in your DNA.

DRUGS: Skin reacts to certain medications, including lithium, Dilantin, and many oral or inhaled steroids that are prescribed for the treatment of asthma.

COSMETICS: Heavy creams can clog pores and cause acne cosmetica, which is exactly what it sounds like—pimples triggered by makeup.

HAIR PRODUCTS: Styling sprays, serums, and mousses applied too close to the face can cause what's called pomade acne.

SWEAT: Not wearing ventilated clothing or wicking fabrics while working out can make acne worse, especially on the chest. Keep a clean towel nearby when you exercise so you can dab off perspiration periodically. Showering immediately after hitting the treadmill will help, too.

YOUR PHONE: Dirt and bacteria congest pores and create acne. Cradling the phone against your chin or touching your face frequently, for instance, can cause you to break out, so clean your phone daily with an antibacterial wipe.

How can I zitproof my skin?

First wash your face no more than twice a day (but do wash right after exercising) with a mild cleanser and follow up with an oil-free moisturizer as described on page 61 for oily skin. "Use an acne wash only a few times a week to prevent skin from dehydrating, which could trigger more oil secretion and pimples, as well as leaving skin feeling tight," says Gerstner. "If necessary, apply a 2 percent salicylic acid spot treatment to the pimple."

Next, be sure to exfoliate three nights a week with a product containing alpha hydroxy acids (AHAs). Scrubs can be harsh. "I like to use glycolic acid pads to remove dead skin cells, improve texture, and loosen clogged pores," says Gerstner.

If your acne doesn't clear up with over-the-counter treatments, see a dermatologist. Two of Gerstner's favorite prescription remedies: a topical form of vitamin A, called Retinol, which can help clear up clogs in the T-zone area, and oral contraceptives, which are approved for acne treatment by the U.S. Food and Drug Administration (FDA), to regulate hormones. According to Gerstner, it will take about three months to see results with oral contraceptives, but unlike with an oral antibiotic, you'll get long-term effects.

How can I tame a pimple without leaving a scar?

Follow these three simple steps.

1 Soak a washcloth in hot water, then wring it out. Hold it on the top of the whitehead until the washcloth cools.

2 Using the cloth, press down gently around the blemish for about 30 seconds. This should be enough to draw out the whitehead without squeezing.

3 Apply a treatment that contains benzoyl peroxide or salicylic acid.

TIP: Handling a blemish before it's ready (before it's white at the top) may only push oil and debris in deeper, making the problem worse. To help bring the pimple to the surface, use an oil-free medicated concealer during the day; at night, apply a drying treatment with sulfur or clay.

IF YOU DO ONLY ONE THING...

"Get the right haircut. When I did the show *Sabrina the Teenage Witch,* I wanted to have really short hair—a bob. But it didn't work at all. I have a weak jaw, and it wasn't layered correctly, so it looked like more of a SpongeBob."

MELISSA JOAN HART
(a.k.a. Sabrina the Teenage Witch) is a film and television actress.

No eye cream for you

It's a $40 jar of goop that you don't need. But other anti-aging measures can be well worth your time and money.

1 | Wear sunscreen—every day.

Broken record, we know. But it's true: Sun exposure is the number one cause of premature aging. Ultraviolet light from the sun or a tanning bed breaks down collagen and elastin, the substances that keep skin free of laugh lines and jowls. This applies to women of all colors. On a daily basis, use a moisturizer with SPF 15; at the beach, kick it up to SPF 30.

2 | Get sunglasses with UV protection.

Beware of shady knockoffs. Read labels and look for sunnies that block 99 or 100 percent of UVA and UVB rays, recommends the American Optometric Association. Good sunglasses help prevent cataracts down the line and keep you from squinting.

3 | Avoid smoking and smoky rooms.

Another duh: Smoking is bad for you. But even nonsmokers should know that chronic exposure to secondhand smoke could bombard you with free radicals that make skin sallow, break down its collagen, and slow its ability to heal.

4 | Control your sweet tooth.

Turns out, when sugar breaks down and enters the bloodstream, it bonds with protein molecules, including those found in collagen and elastin (the fibers that support skin), through a process called glycation. Still with us? Well, this makes collagen and elastin inelastic, which in turn leads to sagging. If you've just got to satisfy a craving, savor a small square of dark chocolate, which is chock-full of antioxidants.

5 | Prep for airplane flights.

In a plane, you're as close to the sun as you're going to get, so it makes sense that you're more vulnerable to the solar rays penetrating the windows. Plus, the air up there is notoriously dry. Drink as much water as you can in flight; avoid alcohol and salty foods, which are dehydrating; and apply a rich moisturizer with SPF 15 or higher 30 minutes before boarding, as sunscreen needs time to be absorbed before it's effective. And if you're sitting next to a window, pull down the shade.

6 | Stabilize your weight.

Yo-yo dieting can take its toll on the skin's elasticity, leaving behind stretch marks. You'll see increased sagging from putting and keeping on as little as 10 to 15 extra pounds. Aim to keep your weight in the normal range, with a body mass index between 18.5 and 24.9.

7 | Get enough z's.

Shoot for seven to eight hours of sleep a night—the deep, even-a-dump-truck-can't-rouse-you kind. This is how the skin repairs daily damage. Start by shutting off all electronic devices a half hour before bed so the stimulation doesn't keep you up.

PORTION CONTROL: SKIN-CARE EDITION

How much of this stuff should you actually be using?

SUNSCREEN
A TEASPOON FOR YOUR FACE;
A SHOT GLASS–FUL
FOR YOUR WHOLE BODY

MOISTURIZER
A QUARTER-SIZE CIRCLE

FOAMING CLEANSER
A GOLF BALL–SIZE BLOB

EXFOLIATING SCRUB
A QUARTER-SIZE CIRCLE

**SALICYLIC ACID
SPOT TREATMENT**
A PEA-SIZE DAB

HYDRATING SERUM
A PEA-SIZE DAB

HYDRATING MASK
A NICKEL-SIZE CIRCLE

NIGHT CREAM
A QUARTER-SIZE CIRCLE

Put on a good face

You'd go broke overnight if you bought even a fraction of the beauty products out there. What's truly essential? Lori Taylor Davis, a global pro lead artist at Smashbox Cosmetics, is here to tell you.

Must-have makeup

☐ **EYE-SHADOW QUAD OR TRIO:** Skin-toned pinks and browns can take eyes of any color from day to night. A brown can also fill in your brows—but color in only the sparse spots. Don't go over the whole arch or they will look painted on.

☐ **EYELINER:** Black can veer dangerously Kardashian. But a brown pencil? Relatively goofproof and suits everyone.

☐ **MASCARA:** Davis says, "A swipe of mascara plays up your eyes and makes you look more awake."

☐ **CONCEALER:** It lightly veils problem areas while remaining invisible. For under-eye circles, choose a shade darker than you would normally use. Your face has peaks and valleys that cast shadows, so if you overly lighten the area, it won't look natural.

☐ **FOUNDATION:** You can go liquid or powder. But if you've ever noticed in photos that your head and neck are two totally different colors, you may be going about finding your ideal shade the wrong way. Test the product near your jawline, not on your hand, which is usually darker than your face.

☐ **BRONZER-AND-BLUSH DUO:** Where does the sun naturally hit your face: the forehead, the cheek-bones, the center of the nose? That's where you dust bronzer. Add blush for a touch of color on the apple of each cheek.

□ **TINTED LIP GLOSS OR MOISTURIZING CREAM LIPSTICK:** Something that's a shade or two lighter or deeper than your natural lip tone works with everything else in your makeup kit.

□ **CLEAR BROW GEL:** "When your brows are groomed, even if they're kind of overgrown, you will instantly look more pulled-together," says Davis.

Must-have tools

□ **EYE-SHADOW BRUSH:** No spongy applicator! Using one is like trying to re-create a Monet with a paint roller. Spring for a full, domed brush, which allows you to blend and pack color beautifully.

□ **EYELINER BRUSH:** You can use this thin, angled brush with a gel liner, a cream liner, or a cake liner or to smudge a penciled line. "I've even run this brush over the tip of an eyeliner pencil or over wet powder eye shadow; it allows you to apply a much softer line," says Davis.

□ **EYELASH CURLER:** This is how you achieve lashes with drama: Begin with clean, makeup-free lashes. (If you curl after applying mascara, the tool can stick to the makeup and yank out hairs.) Position the tool as close as possible to the base of your upper lashes and squeeze for a few seconds. Move the curler slightly outward, to midlash, and gently squeeze again for a second or two. For more drama, blast the curler with a hair dryer for a few seconds before you crimp. (It's like using hot rollers on your hair. But make sure to test the heat against your hand before curling!)

□ **CONCEALER BRUSH:** The bristles are flat and shaped like a thumb, with a tapered point to get into tricky corners around the nostrils and the lash line while providing a feather-light application to the delicate under-eye area and blemishes. "This brush prevents you from getting that caked-on look," says Davis. Choose synthetic bristles, which hold up better when you are using a wet or creamy product.

□ **POWDER BRUSH:** A not-too-large yet fluffy one can do triple duty: applying loose powder, bronzer, and blush. "Opt for a domed shape, so you can buff product into the skin well and it won't sit on the surface and look flourlike," says Davis.

NEVER PUT ON MAKEUP THE WRONG WAY AGAIN

Does concealer go on before or after foundation? And when does the eyeliner happen? For maximally gorgeous results, follow this sequence.

1 | EYES
(SHADOW, THEN LINER,
THEN MASCARA)

2 | CONCEALER

3 | FOUNDATION

4 | BRONZER

5 | LIPSTICK OR LIP GLOSS

6 | BLUSH

7 | BROW GEL

BEAUTY BLUNDER No.1: STREAKY FOUNDATION

FIX IT NOW: Mist the problem spot with water and blot with a tissue, lightly brushing outward from the center of the face.

AVOID IT TOMORROW: Spread moisturizer evenly over your face before applying foundation so it doesn't soak in unevenly and leave darker, heavier-pigmented spots.

The only 3 looks you need to master

Spend too much time on YouTube and you'll fall down a rabbit hole of doll-eye tutorials. Want some makeup advice you can use in the real world? Look no further.

Look No. 1: **Everyday pretty**

EYES: Using a neutral palette trio (or quad), apply the palest shade over the entire lid. Next, add the midtone shade from the lash line to the natural crease. Then line the lash line with the dark shade and blend it lightly into the crease. Line the upper rim of the eyes with a brown or bronze liner. Apply one coat of mascara.

FACE: Apply concealer to under-eyes and any dark spots. Smooth foundation over the entire face. Finish with powder.

LIPS AND CHEEKS: You want just enough blush or bronzer to give you a natural flush. Pick a lipstick that's darker than your natural lip color by two shades max. Always keep your lips and cheeks in the same color family—warm or cool—for a cohesive look.

HINT: HOW TO APPLY FOUNDATION SO IT DOESN'T LOOK LIKE YOU'RE WEARING A MASK

1 Put a dot of foundation on each cheek and your chin, nose, and forehead.

2 Blend from the center of your face outward, using a makeup wedge for the thinnest coating. You can also blend with just your fingers; your body heat will help the formula melt into your skin for a natural finish.

TIP: If your foundation tends to cake up, especially in the creases around your nose and under your eyes, smooth it out with a fingertip's worth of moisturizer.

Look No. 2: **Big night out**

EYES: Dazzle with a sultry, smoky eye shadow. Brush a midtone neutral, like taupe or pale gray, from the lash line to the natural crease. Choose a dramatic color shadow (maybe a metallic navy, gunmetal, or copper) and apply it across the top and bottom of the lash line and lightly smudge. Line the upper lash line and the lower inner rim of the eyes with an eyeliner in a darker, complementary color. Add two coats of mascara.

FACE: Apply concealer to under-eyes and any dark spots. Smooth foundation over the entire face, then add powder. Finish with a touch of highlighter.

LIPS AND CHEEKS: Because the eyes are so intense, your cheeks should be softly neutral. Lips, too, should be a nude or a neutral brown or pink shade.

HINT: HOW TO USE HIGHLIGHTER
TO GET A LUMINOUS GLOW
1 Form the letter C with your thumb and index finger. Place your thumb on your cheekbone and your index finger on your brow bone.

2 Remove your hand and apply a small amount of cream, liquid, or powder highlighter in the shape of that C.

3 Blend well with your fingers. If you're afraid that you've gone overboard, tone down the color by dusting a little loose powder on top.

TIP: To make close-set eyes look farther apart, dab a bit of highlighter onto the inner eye corners. If you want your mouth to appear more shapely, apply highlighter to the bow of your upper lip with a flat-tip brush. To make your face look slimmer, sweep a bit down the center of your nose.

Look No. 3: **Important interview**

EYES: Try the classic cat-eye, which opens up your eyes and looks sophisticated. Start by swiping a neutral eye shadow that's close to your skin tone across the whole lid. Then, using a liquid eyeliner in black or brown, draw a thin line along the lash line from the inner corner of the eye to the outer corner and extend just a bit upward. Finish with a coat of mascara.

FACE: Apply concealer to under-eyes and any dark spots. Smooth foundation over the entire face. Finish with powder.

LIPS AND CHEEKS: Go for a neutral brown or pink in a creamy or matte finish. Give cheeks a subtle flush with a warm pink blush.

HINT: HOW TO CREATE A SUPER-STRAIGHT LINE
WITH LIQUID OR PENCIL EYELINER
1 Dot liner between your lashes, working from the inner corner of the eye to the outer one.

2 Using light, feathery strokes, connect the dots. If you need to steady your hand, rest your elbow on the mirror or a table.

TIP: Set the liner (and mask any wobbles) by tracing over it with a shadow in the same color, using a thin, angled eyeliner brush.

BEAUTY BLUNDER No. 2: CLUMPY SPIDER LASHES

FIX IT NOW: If your lashes are stuck together in thick spikes and the mascara is still wet, take a dry toothbrush (that you no longer plan to use on your teeth, obviously) and brush it through. If your mascara is dry, use a slightly damp toothbrush. This will rewet the mascara and separate the lashes.

AVOID IT TOMORROW: First clean off excess mascara from the brush with a tissue, then apply three quick coats. If coats have time to start drying, they stick together.

TAKE IT OFF. TAKE IT *ALL* OFF.

Wear that gorgeous makeup to bed and your skin will pay the price the next day. (Hello, pimples!) And that's to say nothing of what waterproof mascara will do to those nice 300-thread count sheets. How to come clean.

1 | TACKLE EYE MAKEUP FIRST.
Soak a cotton pad with makeup remover. Hold the pad on the lid for five seconds to let the solvents break down the makeup. Then gently smooth the pad from the inner corner of the lid downward and outward to move makeup away from the tear duct, where it can cause infections. Continue folding the pad over, dousing it with remover as needed, and wiping until your eyes come clean. Use a tissue to remove the residue, moving it upward along the underside of the lashes and down over the top of the lashes.

2 | COVER YOUR FACE IN CLEANSER.
Using your fingers, massage a quarter-size amount of a cleanser (Cetaphil is a great choice) all over your face; you don't need to use water. Be sure to get the cleanser into your brows and the corners of your nose. Even if

you no longer see makeup, continue to rub your cheeks delicately in a circular motion. Sure, some of your makeup rubs off during the day, but the rest can seep into your pores, where it can foster blemishes. Rinse.

3 | CLEAN OFF LIP COLOR.
Generally, a facial cleanser will remove a conventional lip gloss or lipstick. But long-wearing formulas and lip stains call for a more ambitious remover, such as a repurposed eye-makeup remover. (What's gentle enough for the eyes is too mild for the lips.) Sweep a pad soaked in remover over your mouth and let the formula sit for a few seconds. Finish by drenching your face several times with lukewarm water. Blot dry with a towel.

Your killer-haircut cheat sheet

The No. 1 rule for beautiful hair is to work with, not against, your natural texture. Jen Atkin, the hairstylist for gorgeous head-turners (see Katy Perry), shares her favorite easy-to-execute looks.

Straight + short

WHAT TO TELL THE STYLIST: "I want a chin-length tapered bob that's a bit longer in front than in back." Undercutting hair in this way gives straight hair added volume, says Atkin.

WHY YOU'LL LOVE IT: It's neat and professional but with edge. Classic Victoria Beckham.

FOR SALON RESULTS AT HOME: Direct hair forward with a brush as you blow-dry.

Straight + long

WHAT TO TELL THE STYLIST: "I want graduated layers with blunt bangs." Atkin suggests, "Ask the stylist to add texture to the ends. This creates movement."

WHY YOU'LL LOVE IT: A face-framing style plays up your eyes and cheekbones and has an indie-darling vibe à la Zooey Deschanel.

FOR SALON RESULTS AT HOME: After blow-drying, finish with a shine serum for added luster.

Wavy + short

WHAT TO TELL THE STYLIST: "I want a tousled pixie—but not too short."

WHY YOU'LL LOVE IT: Messy in a good way, this Halle Berry–esque do gives body to fine hair.

FOR SALON RESULTS AT HOME: Allow hair to air-dry (yes!), then work in a texturizer, like a dry shampoo.

Wavy + long

WHAT TO TELL THE STYLIST: "I want a long shag that comes to a V in back."

WHY YOU'LL LOVE IT: You don't have to blow-dry to achieve beachy, Kate Hudson waves.

FOR SALON RESULTS AT HOME: Scrunch a flexible-hold hair spray onto dry ends for piecey texture.

Curly + short

WHAT TO TELL THE STYLIST: "I want a jaw-length blunt cut with long, side-swept bangs."

WHY YOU'LL LOVE IT: This Charlize Theron style is sexy and kind of retro, and it gives shape to curls.

FOR SALON RESULTS AT HOME: Prep damp hair with leave-in conditioner. Blow out bangs.

Curly + long

WHAT TO TELL THE STYLIST: "I want center-parted loose ringlets that fall slightly longer in back than in front, like Beyoncé." Atkin says, "Don't be afraid to layer your hair. This adds volume."

WHY YOU'LL LOVE IT: A precise part gives curls a modern twist.

FOR SALON RESULTS AT HOME: Use a dime-size portion of conditioner to define curls before air-drying.

BEAUTY BLUNDER No. 3: GREASY HAIR

FIX IT NOW: Spritz on some dry shampoo (such a lifesaver). Don't have any? Apply baby powder or cornstarch (an ingredient in many dry shampoos) at the roots.

AVOID IT TOMORROW: Don't use more than one styling product each day. The more you layer on, the slicker your hair gets 24 hours later.

IF YOU DO ONLY ONE THING...

"Don't wash your hair too often. I'm a believer in that; it's too drying. I would wait until your hair looks greasy to wash it."

SALLY HERSHBERGER, a renowned hairstylist (and the creator of the "Sally shag"), has her own salon and product line.

BEAUTY BLUNDER No. 4: UNEVEN LIPSTICK

FIX IT NOW: If the color of your lipstick is intact but faded, apply a clear-colored lip gloss on top. If the color is starting to flake off (which often happens with long-wearing lipsticks), apply a colored gloss that complements the lipstick and fills in bare spots.

AVOID IT TOMORROW: When your lips are soft and well conditioned, lipstick is less likely to look dry or attach to flaky patches. Keep lips moist by using a balm when you're not wearing lipstick, especially at night.

I will never have hair like Reese Witherspoon

*And that's fine. How some bad advice and too much pomade taught me who I really wanted to look like. (Spoiler alert: It was me.) By **Sarah McCoy***

WHEN I GRADUATED FROM COLLEGE, I carefully chose the style of my framed diploma: classic cherry with a chic black trim. It's funny to me now that at 22 I had such confident opinions on how to display a piece of paper but so little faith in myself.

My first job out of school was at a public-relations agency in Richmond. I rented a one-bedroom on the outskirts of the city, got my weekly groceries at the dollar store, and paid for my morning Starbucks in piggy-banked change—because my coworkers drank venti coffees and I wanted to show team spirit, even in our caffeine consumption.

A few weeks after I started, I had my first employee review of sorts. They said my work was great but there was a major issue: my public image. They'd decided I came off too young and girlie to be taken seriously. Part of the problem? My long, wavy hair.

"It's not personal," said a colleague only a year older than myself. "We're trying to help."

I have no idea how this advice was supposed to be helpful, but I nonetheless took it to heart. I was naive and scared of not living up to my cherry-wood diploma, of not paying my bills, of failure. Fear plus a mighty shot of *I'll-show-you* drove me straight to a local salon. I told the hairdresser I wanted a more business do. She showed me a photo of Reese Witherspoon's bob in the film *Sweet Home Alabama*. I couldn't imagine having that hairstyle. But, hey, Reese looked professional! Desperate, I let her razor off 12 inches.

Unfortunately, it slipped my mind that I have curly hair. The shorter I go, the more powerful the 'fro. Bless her heart—the stylist did the best she could, taming my cropped bangs with pomade and shaving the cork-screw curls from my neck. But in the end she was sweating and apologizing; I was crying and apologizing. It was a hair massacre.

I had achieved the goal of not looking young and girlie. But I didn't look sophisticated, either. I looked like a young woman who put more stock in other people's vision of her than what she knew to be true of herself.

It was a eureka moment. I went home, washed the gunk out, clipped back my sheared locks, and sent out my résumé. I vowed then to be taken seriously without compromising my personal style. Soon I was hired by a larger company that didn't care if I was a troll so long as my editorial copy was strong. They wanted the Sarah that earned that diploma—the hell with the pretty frame.

SARAH McCOY IS THE AUTHOR OF THE NOVELS *THE MAPMAKER'S CHILDREN* **AND** *THE BAKER'S DAUGHTER.*

THE HAIR NECESSITIES

You really don't need all the serums, spritzes, and stylers that have taken over your bathroom vanity. You just need this streamlined kit.

☐ **SHAMPOO AND CONDITIONER.** Whether you choose products that are color-protective (for tinted hair), hydrating (for dry), or deep-cleaning (for oily), you may have to switch formulas periodically. Your hair's needs are fickle and can change with the weather or even how much you've been heat-styling (a notorious moisture-zapper).

☐ **LEAVE-IN CONDITIONER.** While you may not require extra hydration daily, this styler can also double as a detangler and a heat protector.

☐ **DRY SHAMPOO.** Don't have time to shower? This oil-absorbing miracle worker instantly revitalizes greasy locks. It can also add body and texture to clean hair. Use a powder dry shampoo if your hair is medium to thick. An aerosol, which goes on much lighter and adds volume, is better for fine hair.

☐ **FLEXIBLE-HOLD HAIR SPRAY.** Forget the sticky, stiff stuff. New, lighter formulas keep your updo up, tame frizz, and give roots lift without giving you pageant hair.

☐ **A GOOD HAIRBRUSH.** Boar-bristle brushes are easiest on strands and great at redistributing natural oils throughout hair. However, they tend to be expensive. If they're out of your price range, look for a combination of boar and plastic bristles.

☐ **HAIR DRYER.** Invest in a good one. An ionic dryer with a high wattage (at least 1,200) will help reduce damage by speeding up drying time. And less damage equals a better chance of achieving that shampoo-commercial shine.

Be your own stylist

Reality check: Hauling your butt down to ShortCutz for a bang trim or a blow-out every two weeks is not going to happen. Save yourself the hassle (and beaucoup bucks) by following these DIY tips.

How to trim your bangs

1 Gather your bangs in your nondominant hand and hold a pair of haircutting scissors in the other.

2 Pull the hair down until your thumbnail rests vertically on the bridge of your nose with your thumb pointing up.

3 Trim right around the tip of your thumb. This will give you a flattering, gently rounded arc from temple to temple.

How to master a blow-out

1 Wash hair and prep it with mousse if you prefer volume, styling cream if you need hydration, or smoothing serum if you want sleekness. Comb hair to distribute the product evenly.

2 With your dryer set on medium heat and high speed, blow air all around your head to get the excess water out. When your hair is at least halfway dry, you're ready to start styling. Part your hair and secure the top layers with clips.

3 Attach the nozzle to your dryer, and turn the heat setting up and the speed of the air down. Start with the back section, using a large round brush. Here's the frizz-free technique: Slowly move the brush and the dryer together from roots to ends in one pass. Don't run it up and down the same length of hair or you'll cause the cuticles to open up. Work your way around your head. Unclip the top layers and repeat.

4 | To style the hair around your face, roll the layers forward on the brush as you dry. Be sure to keep a comfortable tension between your hair and the brush to achieve a sleek, flat-ironed effect. After your hair is totally dry, give it a blast of cool air to set the style in place. Finally, massage a pea-size amount of smoothing serum or styling cream into the ends to flatten flyaways, and pat the top of your head with your hands so that any residual serum will level the shorter, broken hairs that tend to stand up around the crown.

How to rock a messy bun

1 | Spray wet hair with texturizing spray and scrunch. Blow-dry hair using your fingers rather than a brush to create a tousled look.

2 | Gather hair into a ponytail just below the crown. Secure with an elastic. Don't worry if short pieces around the face come loose. (That's the messiness.)

3 | Split the ponytail into three sections. Working section by section, twist the hair and secure it to the scalp near the elastic with bobby pins. Let the ends stick out.

How to get pin-straight hair

1 | Start with dry hair. (Flat-ironing damp hair creates steam, which can cause hair to frizz or, in the worst case, scald your scalp.) Set your flat iron on the lowest temperature and attempt to straighten a section. If your hair isn't smooth after two passes, raise the heat.

2 | Move steadily and quickly. Hold your wrist still and, starting at the roots, draw the iron straight down a length of hair in one fast motion. You can singe your hair if you leave the iron in one spot for too long.

3 | Let the iron reheat between sections. Wait for three seconds after you finish one area before going to the next. Hair cools down the iron with each pass.

PORTION CONTROL: HAIR-PRODUCT EDITION

How much of this stuff should you actually be using?

SHAMPOO
A QUARTER-SIZE CIRCLE

DAILY CONDITIONER
A QUARTER-SIZE CIRCLE

LEAVE-IN CONDITIONER
A QUARTER-SIZE CIRCLE

GEL
A NICKEL-SIZE CIRCLE

MOUSSE
A GOLF BALL–SIZE BLOB

SHINE SERUM
2 PEA-SIZE DABS

STYLING WAX
A PEA-SIZE DAB

CONDITIONING MASK
A QUARTER-SIZE CIRCLE

Adventures in hair removal

The novelty wore off a long time ago. Let's get this over with, shall we?

Shaving

BEST FOR: Legs and underarms. Also the ideal method for the time-crunched, those with high klutz potential, and wimps.

STUBBLE-FREE FOR: One to two days.

GETTING STARTED: Shave at the end of your bath or shower. By then the warm water has softened stubble, making it easier to get a close shave. Lather up with a shaving gel or foam or a thick body wash. Avoid bar soap; it's too drying.

REMOVAL STRATEGY: For optimal silkiness, always go against the direction of hair growth. That means, for legs, you'll be moving the blade upward. For underarms, you'll have to shave up, down, and sideways, because the hair under your arms grows in many different directions. Use a razor two to three times at most before you change blades. A dull blade doesn't coast over skin, so it's more likely to cause nicks and cuts. Any drag is a sign that the razor isn't sharp enough.

MAYDAY! Run out of shaving cream? Use hair conditioner or expired sunscreen. If you cut yourself, apply pressure with a tissue for a minute or two until the bleeding stops. Dab on a protective ointment, like Aquaphor, to help the cut heal. Razor burn is the result of shaving too frequently or aggressively. To calm inflamed skin, apply a 1 percent hydrocortisone cream right after shaving.

FYI: If you're prepping your beach body, apply self-tanner after you shave. Otherwise you will shave off your "tan."

Waxing

BEST FOR: Bikini area and upper lip.

STUBBLE-FREE FOR: Three to six weeks. Since waxing removes hair deep down in the roots, this technique leaves you smoother to the touch longer, because waxed hairs grow back in with naturally tapered ends, which feel softer than the blunt ends of razor-cut hairs.

GETTING STARTED: Whether you go to a salon or do it yourself at home, hair needs to be at least ¼ inch long to give the wax something to grip. Lightly exfoliate the area with a gentle scrub and a wet washcloth 24 hours before waxing to remove dead skin. Taking aspirin or acetaminophen half an hour before waxing helps dull the pain. Home waxers can also step into a hot shower right before the treatment. Heat opens the follicles, which makes the hair easier to yank.

Don't wax just before or at the beginning of your period, when you may be extra pain-sensitive. Home waxers will run into fewer problems if they opt for a hard wax that's easy to heat up and requires no additional tools or muslin strips. Freshly waxed skin is more sensitive to sunlight, so avoid the sun for 24 hours.

FOR THE BIKINI AREA

1 Heat the wax until it has the consistency of honey. Test a drop on your wrist to make sure it's not too hot.

2 Before you attempt the tricky contours of the bikini line, practice on a large, flat area, like a forearm or a leg.

3 Tuck folded tissues around the elastic trim of your underwear to protect it from the wax. Sit on the floor with your knees slightly bent and legs turned outward.

4 Using a spatula, apply the wax very thinly and evenly, in the direction of hair growth, to an area of about two by five inches.

5 To minimize pain when you pull off the wax, brace your skin with your other hand. Pull parallel with and close to your body. Once the wax is off, press your hand into the skin to reduce the pain.

6 To stay ingrown-free after the hair starts to grow back in, use pads and toners that contain alcohol and salicylic acid. These can help because they lightly exfoliate the skin, preventing hairs from getting trapped.

FOR THE UPPER LIP

1 Think of your upper lip as divided into three sections—left, right, and center—and wax each part individually.

2 Using a spatula, apply the wax in the direction of hair growth, in inch-long sections.

3 Hold the skin at the outer corner of your mouth, then remove the strip by pulling up and toward your nose.

MAYDAY! Sticky leftover wax won't come off? Swipe the excess with a stick of deodorant, wipe it off with a soft cloth, and dust the skin with baby powder. To ease redness, soothe skin with an aloe-based moisturizer.

FYI: Yup, there is a chance that you could get burned or make a mess (or both), which is why most dermatologists recommend that you leave waxing to a pro. The downside: Professional sessions can cost you (from $15 to $100 each).

Depilatory cream

BEST FOR: Fine to medium hair, as found on the bikini line, stomach, arms, legs, toes, and upper lip. Don't bother if you have coarse hair; it won't be as effective.

STUBBLE-FREE FOR: Three to six days. Skin feels less prickly than it does after shaving, as the product dissolves hair below the skin, instead of slicing it off.

GETTING STARTED: Do a patch test (like on a hidden spot behind your ear) 24 hours beforehand, since the active ingredients can be aggravating.

REMOVAL STRATEGY: Smooth the product on and let it sit for a few minutes. Follow the package directions to a T (otherwise you may get major irritation), then gently wipe off and rinse.

MAYDAY! There are still a few hairs left. Whatever you do, don't reapply hoping to get rid of every last one. (Unless you're after the raw-and-blotchy look.) Instead use a razor or a tweezer to deal with the strays.

FYI: You must stand or sit perfectly still covered in goo while the cream works its magic.

Laser hair removal

BEST FOR: Those prone to ingrown hairs and people with dark hair and light to medium skin. Rather than uprooting hairs, lasers damage the growth mechanism by targeting the dark pigment in the hair follicles. This means they won't work as well on blond or white hairs or someone with dark skin.

STUBBLE-FREE FOR: It's complicated. Most women need several laser sessions at one- to two-month intervals to start noticing a slowing of hair growth. You can expect anywhere from 70 to 90 percent less hair after three to five laser treatments. The results may or may not be permanent; for some, hair grows back in months.

GETTING STARTED: Take ibuprofen beforehand, as the treatments can be uncomfortable. (Imagine an elastic band snapping against your skin over and over again.)

REMOVAL STRATEGY: For the best results, go to a facility that specializes in hair removal (not a nail salon) or see a dermatologist. Home devices have shown results on par with pro treatments, but you may need additional sessions, since at-home devices aren't professional-strength.

MAYDAY! If you have sensitive skin, apply a topical numbing cream as needed. Don't take a hot shower afterward; stick to tepid water to avoid further irritation. And avoid sun exposure for the next few days.

FYI: Professional sessions are expensive ($100 to $1,200 each, depending on the size of the area) but can save time, money, and distress in the long run.

IF YOU DO ONLY ONE THING...

"Get enough sleep. I need at least seven to eight hours to function. Because when I let that go, everything else goes, too. When I don't sleep, I don't eat right. I don't work out. Everything goes to hell."

AMERICA FERRERA starred in *Ugly Betty* and the *Sisters of the Traveling Pants* movies.

BEAUTY BLUNDER No. 5: CAKEY CONCEALER

FIX IT NOW: Take a tiny dab of moisturizer (the size of half a pea) and lightly pat it over the trouble spot with a finger. If you do this gently and don't rub, the moisture will smooth out lines and cracks without removing color.

AVOID IT TOMORROW: Thin out overly thick concealer that isn't spreading well with moisturizer and a concealer brush, which tends to pick up and apply less product than a finger.

Scrimp or splurge?

Admit it: The exotic list of ingredients and the promise of supermodel shine are tempting. But then you hear a little voice in your head (hey, is that you, Mom?) saying, "It's hype! You're paying for a pretty box." Some products are worth every dime; some not so much. How to tell the difference.

Shampoo = Scrimp

Springing for extravagant shampoo is essentially like watching your money go down the drain with the suds. However, if you've spent a small fortune coloring or highlighting your hair, you might want to go with the product that your hairstylist recommends.

Conditioner = Splurge

Yes, you rinse conditioner out, but these products are emulsions, which means they contain an oil or wax that doesn't mix with water. So whatever healthy ingredients are in them adhere to the hair and don't wash away.

Cleanser = Scrimp

Because the fancy-pants ingredients will be on your face for only two seconds—not long enough to be worth the expense. Have acne-prone or sensitive skin? Look for labels that say "gentle" or "noncomedogenic."

Day cream = Scrimp

Make sure it's the kind with sunscreen included; it should have broad-spectrum protection of at least SPF 15. You'll find an aisle full of worthy options at the drugstore.

Foundation = Splurge

Since the chances that your face may end up looking like an Oompa Loompa are high. Instead head to the department-store cosmetics counters, where you can try out not only shades but also formulas before you buy. Do you prefer lightweight and sheer? Or something with more coverage to hide acne?

Powder = Splurge

Unless you opt for a colorless translucent powder (in which case, you can totally go thrifty), you'll want to try this on before you buy, especially if you're using powder as an all-purpose foundation/concealer/makeup setter. A well-made one also gives you that flawless, practically Photoshopped look and will last longer, so you won't need to apply as much of it.

Powder blush = Splurge

The pigments in blush are very similar to those in eye shadow. The less expensive the product, the more likely it is that the pigments have been diluted with talc and other powder ingredients. Also, cheaper blushes have a tendency to leave streaks.

Eyeliner = Splurge

You don't want one with a crumbly tip that creates a shaky line. Generally, the more expensive the pencil, the softer the wax and the smoother the application.

Eye shadow = Splurge

Department-store–brand shadows adhere to the lids better, go on smoother, and offer richer colors than their drugstore counterparts. Certain pigments, such as deep blues and purples, are expensive, so companies that charge more can use more of them. But if you want to test-drive trendy shades, then, by all means, go economical.

Mascara = Scrimp

Bombshell: There isn't a lot of difference between high-end and low-end formulas. Because bacteria grow easily in mascara, you should trash a tube after three months—which is all the more reason to cut corners.

Lip gloss = Scrimp

No need to go all out if you want just a hint of tint and a bit of shine. And who are we kidding? Half of it will rub off on your coffee cup anyway.

Lipstick = Splurge

If it's your signature shade, don't cheap out. You'll get a creamier texture and possibly even extracts or vitamins that will prevent your pucker from becoming caked and flaky.

BEAUTY BLUNDER No. 6: PONYTAIL BUMP

FIX IT NOW: Camouflage a hair-elastic crimp by adding more texture. Apply a small amount of product (gel or hair spray—even baby powder or hand lotion will work in a pinch) and scrunch your hair from the roots to the ends.

AVOID IT TOMORROW: Use only cloth-covered elastics. Better yet, only use cloth-covered elastics on second-day hair. Bumps occur more easily on hair that is freshly washed and styled.

Salon drama, avoided

You went in for a cute blunt cut and came out feeling like Britney Spears midbreakdown. Do everyone a favor (yourself especially) and learn how to deal with salon-staffer mishaps. John Barrett, the founder of the John Barrett Salon, in New York City, explains.

WHAT TO DO WHEN...

You positively hate your haircut.

"Point out to the stylist what you're not happy with and he should try to modify the cut to your liking," says Barrett. Be specific—for example, the top is too puffy. It could be a simple tweak or just the way your hair was styled.

If you chicken out and squeak a feeble "It's great," you can still call once you're home. Odds are, the stylist will be happy to fix it. (After all, he wants to keep his clients happy.) If he is resistant, don't return. Next time, schedule extra time at the beginning of the appointment for a thorough consultation, says Barrett, who recommends bringing photos for inspiration.

To avoid confusion, don't talk inches. Have the stylist show you where he is going to cut and ask what the upkeep of the new do will be, including the products and the tools required as well as how long it will take you to re-create the look.

The facialist launches into a pushy upsell of, say, Himalayan cleansing milk, and you're broke (or just don't want any).

"Always be clear and up-front from the start of your service if you're certain you're not buying anything extra," says Barrett.

Curious but not able to splurge? Requesting sample-size products before committing is a good way to show interest without overpromising. For those times when you're trapped in the sales pitch, Barrett suggests whipping out this line to make your escape (at least for the time being): "I'm all set with products for now, but I'll be back to see you soon."

The waxer double-dips the spatula, the manicurist didn't sterilize the tools, or something else gross.

Gross isn't the word. Try *infectious*. In the case of the waxer, say, "I noticed you double-dipping." If she says, "It's OK. The heat will kill the bacteria," demand new wax and a new applicator—or leave.

Disease-carrying bacteria spores can survive at incredibly high temperatures. At the nail salon, you can put yourself at risk for all sorts of fungal attacks. If you didn't see the manicurist place the metal instruments into an autoclave (which looks a bit like a toaster oven and uses pressurized steam heat to sterilize) and the nonmetal instruments aren't soaking in a hospital-grade liquid sterilizer, alert the manager before your service.

Also, pay close attention to the soaking bowl. It should be glass, not plastic, which might absorb germs. "Whirlpool spas for pedicures are notorious in the business for being difficult to clean," warns Barrett.

Whether the salon uses bowls or spas, make sure you watch them disinfect the vessel before your manicure or pedicure. And when getting a facial, keep an eye out to see that the aesthetician washes her hands in front of you before starting. A makeup artist should also clean the brushes and shave the lipsticks after each use. If these sanitary precautions aren't taken, you have every right to voice your concerns, says Barrett.

You want to switch to a different stylist or manicurist but don't want to hurt anyone's feelings.

"The key to a tear-free transition is being as transparent and honest as possible," says Barrett. Explain exactly why you're looking to make a move, highlighting what you've loved about your current stylist and a few characteristics that you're looking for with your next experience. He should be able to handle that. Ultimately it's good for clients to switch stylists sometimes; it gives everyone a fresh perspective on your hair, which often leads to positive change. Or you can keep it simple: "Saying you want to 'mix things up a bit' could also work," says Barrett.

The stylist is trying to talk you into a look that is so not you.

If you've clearly explained what you wanted in the consultation and she's still not letting up, use your lifestyle as an excuse. Say, "I'm too busy to handle a big hair change right now." You may have to come to terms with the fact that this person isn't the right fit for you, and you should make a switch.

To dodge this dilemma in the future, pick a pro who has a personal style similar to your own. (In the age of social media, this shouldn't be a difficult assignment.) Since you'll be on the same wavelength, she'll be more likely to give you the look that you're after.

BEAUTY BLUNDER No. 7: THE FRIZZIES

FIX IT NOW: Add a little lotion to your palm and run it through your hair. You can remove static by passing a dryer sheet over your hair or running a brush spritzed with a little hair spray through it.

AVOID IT TOMORROW: Spritz on a leave-in conditioner before you go to bed if high humidity is predicted for the next day. The product will keep your hair from absorbing that atmospheric moisture, which can lead to fuzz.

CHAPTER 4

DRESSING LIKE A GROWN-UP

A closet full of leggings and tees isn't going to cut it now that more of your days are taken up with sales meetings and bridal showers. But you don't need to default to pantsuits and pumps just yet. Figuring out the right thing to wear isn't always cut-and-dried, but there are some simple guidelines you can follow.

Want to learn what's kosher to wear at your job? We'll tell you. Curious about how to garb yourself for tricky occasions (like, say, a beach wedding)? Read on. What's more, you'll find out how to save yourself from a variety of wardrobe woes, from nightmare bras to toe-mangling heels. Once you realize that you don't have to sweat these details, you'll have more time for important things, like color-coordinating your Instagram pics.

The cure for nothing-to-wear-itis

Your closet is packed—and yet it feels empty. Why? Sounds like you may be missing the crucial pieces that will get you through the week. Fashion designer Rebecca Taylor shares the essentials that every woman—regardless of shape or size—should have.

1 | Striped long-sleeve tee

If you don't already own one of these icons of French style, click "Add to cart" immediately. The humble sailor shirt has graced the backs of some of history's chic-est, from Coco Chanel and Pablo Picasso to Brigitte Bardot and Edie Sedgwick, and its popularity shows no signs of waning. But don't save this top for chill Sunday brunches. Use it as an interesting layering piece under a blazer at the office, too. (FWIW, it's true that horizontal stripes sometimes get a bad rap; however, thinner lines are pretty forgiving, especially when they're worn on your top half.)

2 | Menswear-style trousers

You'll be surprised how often you'll step into these dependable pants for work, formal parties, and other no-idea-what-to-wear occasions. Choose a wide-leg cut to balance curvy hips, or opt for a more tapered style with a flat waistband if you're fuller around the middle. You'll probably get the most wear out of a black pair, but a gray, navy, or even tweed or herringbone style can be just as functional, says Taylor.

3 | Gray cashmere cardigan

A long cardigan that hits past the hips can straddle the line between done-up (over an A-line dress) and downtime (with jeans and a tank), especially if it's in a sumptuous fabric. And because it's gray instead of black, you can pull it on any day of the year with any color without veering too Goth.

4 | Pointy red pumps

Fact: If you're wearing really fabulous footwear, the rest of your outfit can be so-so and you'll still look like you just stepped straight out of Pinterest. Why red? It adds the perfect pop to professional neutrals (say, navy pants) without sacrificing corporate polish. Plus, a candy-apple hue plays well with tons of other colors, from Kelly green to pale pink to aubergine.

5 | Floral printed blouse

Choose something silky and lush, says Taylor. Pair it with jeans on Saturday night. Then, come Monday morning, whip it out again to add much needed dimension to work separates, like a blazer and a pencil skirt.

6 | Skinny jeans

Even a slightly tapered or straight-leg cut will give you the effect of skinnies without making your bottom half look like a lightbulb. Select a clean, dark rinse for optimum day-to-night wearability and you'll be able to pair them with nearly everything else on this list.

7 | Leather jacket

Think of the last, oh, 60-odd years: When hasn't a black motorcycle jacket been in style? That's why it's one of the smartest buys you can make. Not only is the jacket the epitome of cool but it also lends said coolness to whatever it associates with, whether that's blue jeans, a sheath dress, or cigarette pants. However, for a version with the most legs, you might want to go easy on the zippers and buckles.

8 | Crisp white shirt

This wardrobe chameleon can look no-nonsense when paired with tweed trousers or lavish with a holiday taffeta skirt. "Accessories play a big part in keeping your look fresh," says Taylor, who recommends jazzing up a plain button-down with a big, bold necklace or a brightly colored pair of sandals. Beware of frumpy fits, though—the silhouette should be tapered to a woman's body even if it's a looser "boyfriend" cut. And cop some attitude: Push up your sleeves; roll up your cuffs; pop a collar.

9 | Classic sneakers (like Vans or Converse)

The beauty of these kicks? You can be comfortable without fear of being mistaken for a power walker. And they make everything a little more fun—from your witty-sayings T-shirt collection to a polished maxi dress or even cropped pants and a schoolboy blazer.

10 | Little black dress

No list would be complete without this fashion superstar. Opt for the sleekest, simplest shift you can find in a lightweight wool, silk, or synthetic blend. (It tends to look expensive even if you bought it for less than the cost of a Bikram class.) Plus, this silhouette will always and forever have that elegant-minimalist thing going for it, which means you won't have to keep replenishing your closet season after season. And what versatility: "You can wear an LBD with fashion-forward sneakers for a sporty-luxe look or with studded heels for a more refined vibe," says Taylor.

Scrimp or splurge?

Casual dress = Scrimp

You can find tons of cute styles for peanuts. And sundresses rarely last more than a few summers anyway.

Tees and tanks = Scrimp

These take a lot of wear and tear, so you'll need to replace them fairly often. And the white ones are notorious for underarm stains.

Jeans = Depends

What makes for an amazing pair? A great fit. And premium denim brands put more research into making sure their cuts look and feel like a second skin. That said, if you can rock Old Navy jeans, don't bother paying more.

Black pants = Splurge

Choose a well-tailored pair with slim or straight legs in a seasonless fabric (try lightweight wool or a synthetic blend) and they'll be able to withstand twice-a-week wearings.

You love trading cheapo scores from Forever Teeny-bopper. But your (limited) cash might be better used on clothes that will go the distance—or at least last until your 10-year college reunion. Here's when to pinch pennies and when to pony up the Benjamins.

Dark suit = Splurge

Invest, especially if you need to wear it for work, in which case, it's worthwhile to cough up extra for both the matching skirt and pants for optimal mixing and matching. Even if your job is more laid-back, it's wise to have a classic suit stowed away that can be busted out for an unexpected interview, meeting, or funeral.

Work dress = Splurge

A knee-length dress in a neutral or jewel tone can also be a default outfit for any occasion, so you'll want one or two that will last for years.

Work shoes = Splurge

A well-made leather pair will hold up to daily pavement pounding. (Your orthopedist will thank you.)

Party heels = Scrimp

Unless you plan on living it up like Carrie Bradshaw seven nights a week, you probably won't get that much wear out of satin stilettos. So go cheap. Besides, one splash of pomegranate martini and they're toast.

Evening clutch = Scrimp

Again, chances are, you won't use it too often. And you really need to buy only one in a metallic shade, which means it will go with almost anything.

Formal dress = Scrimp

Head straight to the sale rack. Evening events last only a few hours, and you may not have an opportunity to recycle it around a different crowd.

Tights = Scrimp

Even if by some miracle the tights don't run or rip, they'll eventually sag. And while that $40 pair may hold up longer, cheaper ones will be easier to replace.

Exercise clothes = Splurge

Better-quality fabrics can be more breathable and reduce chafing. Plus, the sweat-wicking properties of high-tech fabrics may help you put pedal to the metal in spin class.

Raincoat = Depends

You can easily score a water-resistant model for less. But if you're after an iconic, *Casablanca*-esque trench, spend away, since that silhouette is trendproof.

Winter coat = Splurge

Obviously, if you live in the frost belt, a quality coat is a no-brainer. But also think of it this way: Outerwear is what most people will see you in, as you'll wear it every day for four (or more) months.

**IF YOU DO ONLY
ONE THING...**

"Remember this:
High heels hurt, and it never
gets easier. You know
what really helps? Toe pads.
I highly recommend them."

JESSICA ALBA has appeared in dozens of films, and she is the founder of the Honest Company, a line of eco-friendly goods.

Your office dress-code decoder

Even Fortune 500 execs need help with their wardrobes. Enter Lauren A. Rothman, the author of Style Bible: What to Wear to Work *and the founder of Styleauteur, a fashion-consulting firm in Washington, D.C. She offers her real-world advice, sized to fit every workplace.*

THE BIZ: **Law, consulting, or accounting**

WHAT TO WEAR: No surprises here. These sectors are conservative, and a timeless dark suit is par for the course. Go for one that includes wide-leg trousers and a shawl-collar or peak-lapel jacket so you'll look modern. And though you may not yet be able to shell out for high-end designers, don't settle for pieces that look cheap—buy the best you can afford. (Remember: These staples won't go out of style anytime soon.) "Dressing up, even if you're just starting out, also makes it hard for others to determine whether you're an assistant or a manager," says Rothman.

THE BIZ: **Banking or financial services**

WHAT TO WEAR: Formality is expected, but unique touches are encouraged. Stock your closet with black, charcoal, and navy suits, but consider introducing pops of color with a pair of closed-toe red suede pumps or a teal silk blouse. Another tip: Spend money on a quality handbag, which carries the most executive cachet.

THE BIZ: **Public relations, marketing, or advertising**

WHAT TO WEAR: These are creative jobs that are often in corporate settings, and your dress should mirror that balance. There's no need to don a suit, but if you choose to, the cut should be feminine and incorporate trendy accents so it doesn't look too staid. When schmoozing with clients, lighten up with a more playful color, whether pale (blush pink) or bold (cobalt blue). Lean toward traditionally professional staples with an unexpected twist, like a jacket with exaggerated shoulders or a pencil skirt with an exposed zipper.

THE BIZ: Sales, real estate, or customer service

WHAT TO WEAR: "You are essentially the visual representation of the brand to its customers," says Rothman. Invest most in external items—a tailored coat, polished shoes, classic sunglasses, a structured tote bag—because that is how you'll often greet clients. And since your bag may well end up being your cubicle on the go, it will need to be roomy yet look neat and refined. Aside from that, follow the corporate or business-casual dress code the rest of your company follows.

THE BIZ: Government, nonprofit, policy research, teaching, or social work

WHAT TO WEAR: Business casual tends to be the norm, but err on the side of more buttoned-up out of respect for your organization. Plus, "looking polished helps young women maintain an air of authority," says Rothman. She recommends a sheath dress and a belted cardigan, paired with pointy-toe flats and a necklace, to strike the right note, whether you're around officials, parents, or kids. And keep low necklines and short hemlines in check.

THE BIZ: Media, design, fashion, or entertainment

WHAT TO WEAR: While black is frequently the backbone of creatives' wardrobes, feel free to experiment and express yourself, so long as you don't overdo it. Pick one trend and pair it with more minimalist staples. Try mixing prints—say, color-block pants with a clean white button-down and a scarf with a tiny pin-dot pattern. And since there's a chance that you'll be on your feet a lot, whether you're merchandising displays or attending events, it's smart to rely on walkable shoes and stretchy fabrics that move with you.

THE BIZ: Information technology

WHAT TO WEAR: Most of your job takes place behind the scenes, so you won't need to go all out. "Still, when everyone else will likely be sporting sneakers and hoodies, it may do you well to up the ante a little with a long tunic and dark jeans tucked into riding boots," says Rothman. Keep a blazer or a nice cardigan on the back of your office door if you get the opportunity to hobnob with your company's founder or an important investor. If you're part of an IT department within a larger corporation, you don't need to dress up as much as other employees do, but you don't want to stick out as the computer geek, either.

THE BIZ: Retail

WHAT TO WEAR: If your job is at a clothing store, there's no question what you'll be wearing. However, if your gig is at a store that doesn't specialize in apparel, the safest bet is business casual: tailored pants and an on-trend blouse or a simple, professional shift dress. Also, be sure to opt for comfy flats with arch support, since you don't have a lot of (sitting) down time.

Is this appropriate for my office?

First figure out which workplace type most accurately describes your own, whether formal (corporate law) or chill (um, cannabis retail...). Then find out if your fashion choice—bare legs? cropped pants?—will fly.

	A CORPORATE OFFICE	A BUSINESS-CASUAL OFFICE	A CREATIVE OFFICE
JEANS	Not a chance.	If and when denim is allowed (most likely on Fridays), a sleek, dark pair is the way to go.	Skip weird washes and extreme distressing, but thumbs-up to colored or printed denim. Always dress jeans up with a nice top or blazer.
CROPPED PANTS	A pair made of suiting fabric that hits right at the ankles may be doable on laid-back days.	Go for it, but follow the criteria at left.	All good. Just stay away from casual cargoes.
LEGGINGS	Nope.	Still no.	Only wear them dressed up and as a layering piece with a long jacket or a tunic that covers your derriere.
SHORTS	Never.	Probably not, even on a summer Friday.	Rock on, but stick to a tailored knee-length pair with a silky top and a jacket. Pair anything shorter with tights.
STRAPPY TOPS AND DRESSES	Sleeveless dresses and those with thick straps might be fine. Just keep a cardigan handy.	See the advice at left. Flutter or cap sleeves are OK, too.	Avoid straps so thin that you need to wear a strapless bra.
BARE LEGS	Depends. Don't go sans hosiery until you see someone senior doing it.	Usually OK, but opt for shoes with more coverage instead of sandals.	Absolutely—nude hose can make you look stodgy. Still, don't go au naturel with a miniskirt.
OPEN-TOE SHOES	Doubtful, but classic slingbacks and peep-toes might be fine.	Yes, but the more covered up, the better. And avoid backless footwear that flaps noisily when you walk.	Go ahead—straps and all. But reserve flip-flops (especially rubber ones) for the beach.

Good-bye to muumuu

When I was 25, I wore the same thing every day for an entire season. I have some regrets about this. By **Jessica Grose**

DURING THE SUMMER OF 2008, I lived in one dress. It was a black baby-doll style that hit my legs at midthigh. It had fluted cap sleeves, a cotton eyelet overlay, and a gauzy base layer. When I bought the dress, I thought it was adorably mod, something that Mia Farrow would have worn in the 60s. After several weeks of donning it without washing it—it had to be dry-cleaned, which seemed like a lot of work and money—it was less Mia Farrow and more Edie Beale.

I worked from home, writing for the women's website Jezebel. In a lot of ways, it was a dream job. I got to write for a big audience, and my boss and coworkers were strong, smart women who taught me a lot, not just about work, but about how to be a person. In other ways, it was less glorious. I woke up around 7 A.M. and rolled from my bed to my couch, where I began working immediately, without even brushing my teeth.

I could have just stayed in my pajamas. But I put on the muumuu to delineate my work self from my leisure self. Since the job could be emotionally intense—it involved an endless stream of anonymous commenters ready to critique any misstep—I came to think of my muumuu as a kind of musty, dark armor. I could put it on and be able to withstand any cyber insults.

The problem with wearing only the muumuu (the smell aside) was that when I got a slightly more corporate job at the web-site Slate, I had to learn how to dress like a professional adult. The place didn't have a clear dress code. So I had to figure out a style that seemed appropriate and fit my needs as a twentysomething who wanted to look cute when she got on the subway in the morning. I also had to let go of the muumuu, which had morphed from armor to security blanket.

Sartorial missteps were made. I recall a frantic trip to Urban Outfitters upon realizing, halfway through a workday, that the dress I was wearing was on the wrong side of transparent. But by the time I had been at Slate for a year, I'd figured out the work clothes that were right for me: fitted cotton dresses and ankle boots, which were easy to throw on and looked reasonably authoritative. I also learned to face the world of anonymous critics by making sure that my writing had the strongest possible arguments, not by wearing a magical garment. I still have the muumuu, but it's been relegated to the back of my closet as a swimsuit cover-up. And it's been thoroughly dry-cleaned.

JESSICA GROSE IS THE AUTHOR OF THE NOVEL
SAD DESK SALAD.

What to wear, everywhere

No, you don't have to don black for a funeral or a suit for a job interview. Those rules are, we're happy to say, completely outmoded. Before your next special occasion, glance over these guidelines and banish all that getting-dressed stress.

THE OCCASION: A shower, a baptism, or another religious ceremony

THE SAFE BET: A pretty daytime dress or a feminine jacket-and-skirt/pants combo. If the event is held at a religious institution, the outfit needs to be somewhat modest. That means nothing low-cut or clingy. (If you've never been to a particular house of worship, it's a good idea to double-check its conventions.) The dress code for a Bar or Bat Mitzvah can be determined by the party held afterward: If it immediately follows the service, you'll wear the same thing to both, so put on a cocktail dress, but cover up with a jacket or a wrap at the temple.

THE OCCASION: A job interview

THE SAFE BET: Suits are still a good choice at large, traditional companies. However, in many creative or artistic fields, it can be a plus to shake things up with a knee-length sheath dress or a circle skirt with a blouse and a cropped jacket. Avoid jangly jewelry and anything overly trendy. (Stow the leopard-print pumps at home.)

THE OCCASION: A business dinner or a work holiday party

THE SAFE BET: A neutral suit or a sheath dress paired with a sparkly necklace or a colorful pair of heels. (It's still OK to carry your everyday bag.)

If your office is casual, kick up your usual look with a skirt rather than pants, a blouse in place of a tee, and pumps over flats. Either way, always keep your hemline around the knee and your neckline conservative. (You are still working.)

THE OCCASION: **A funeral or a wake**

THE SAFE BET: A pantsuit or a knee-length dress with a cardigan. What's most important is to convey the somberness of the event, which can be accomplished with toned-down clothing in dark neutrals, like navy, charcoal, forest green, or, yes, black, or a dark and discreet pattern. Jewelry should be quiet and classic—think pearl studs.

THE OCCASION: **A wedding**

THE SAFE BET FOR A BLACK-TIE WEDDING: A tea- or floor-length dress. (Old Hollywood glamour, not Disney Princess.) Heels are a must.

THE SAFE BET FOR A BLACK-TIE–OPTIONAL WEDDING: The above dress is preferred, but a knee-length cocktail dress is acceptable as long as it's awards-show fancy and you gussy it up with shimmery jewelry. Heels are still a requisite.

THE SAFE BET FOR A COCKTAIL OR SEMIFORMAL WEDDING: A little black dress (black *is* OK to wear to a wedding!) or a sophisticated, colorful party dress, two inches above the knee, max. It's also perfectly acceptable to splash out in dressy separates—say, brocade cigarette pants topped with a beaded shell. Heels are encouraged.

THE SAFE BET FOR A BEACH WEDDING: A flowy maxi or a printed sundress in pastel or tropical shades. Ditch the heels, which will sink into sand. Beaded sandals are a better choice.

THE SAFE BET FOR AN OUTDOOR WEDDING (SAY, IN A PARK OR A FIELD): A colorful shift or a flared silk dress with bold jewelry. Again, heels could sink into grass. Go with embellished wedges or flats.

THE SAFE BET FOR A CITY HALL OR VEGAS WEDDING: A dress would be nice, but you can probably come as you are. Seriously. You're lucky just to be invited.

WHAT TO DO WHEN YOU STILL HAVEN'T GOT A CLUE

Say the invitation offers no heads-up on attire. You have two choices: Ask the host what she is wearing, or play detective.

INSPECT THE INVITATION. If the invitation is engraved, letterpressed, or embossed on nice card stock, the host is probably spending time and money on the event. Acknowledge her efforts with a cocktail dress. When dealing with Evites or store-bought cards, look for hints in the design. An invitation with quirky graphics and bright, bold text implies a more hang-loose event than one with silver script bordered by rose petals.

BE MINDFUL OF THE THEME. If this is an annual event for a charity or an organization, check out what has been photographed and documented online to guesstimate your getup.

NOTE THE TIME. Generally, parties after 5 P.M. mean more elegant looks, whereas daytime functions tend to be low-key.

SCOPE OUT THE LOCATION. A party at someone's house will probably be more relaxed than one at a venue. If it's at a catering hall or a restaurant, browse the website to gauge its chichi quotient. Outdoor shindigs tend to be less formal than indoor functions. Country-club protocol, however, leans toward sundresses, not jeans.

Never again wonder: Bra, or medieval torture device?

Susan Nethero, the founder of Intimacy, a nationwide chain of lingerie boutiques, offers her best tips for finding the just-right bra— one that will make you appear taller, slimmer, and blessed with book-on-your-head posture.

Get sized by a professional fitter.

Ideally do this once a year or any time you've experienced bodily changes—for example, a weight gain or loss of 10 pounds or more, an increase or decrease in exercise, hormonal fluctuations, the use of birth control, pregnancy, or nursing. Each of these can affect the size, the shape, and the perkiness of your breasts.

Don't be swayed by looks alone.

It's better to buy a quality model that will hold up day after day. And if you are larger than a C cup, you'll need stronger materials, seaming, and side panels, which also raises the price tag considerably.

Test that the band is snug.

Ninety percent of support should come from the bra's band. When you're trying on a style in the dressing room, make sure that the bra fits firmly. You should be able to squeeze only one finger underneath the band when it's fastened on its loosest hooks. This way, when the bra gives over time, you will be able to tighten it.

Assess the bra's lift factor.

Look at your profile in a mirror. Your bustline should hit midway between your elbow and your shoulder.

Make sure your breasts are positioned within the frame of your torso.

In other words, not spreading out toward the armpits. But don't smush them together, either. There should be one inch of space between your breasts.

Check that the underwire is comfortable.

Most complaints are due to improper cup and band size. If the wire is jabbing your breasts, you may have to go up a cup size. If the wire digs into your midriff, you may have to go down a band size.

Look for back fat.

No worries—it's not a sign that you should lay off the doughnuts. But it does mean that the band is too loose, causing the bra to ride up your back, pushing any soft tissue into a bulge in the process. The bra should be totally level from front to back.

Step away from minimizer bras.

These compress breast tissue, which increases the surface area of your breasts and makes your whole body seem wider. If you want to make your large chest appear smaller, select a seamed bra that offers amazing lift and side support, and you'll get a sleeker-looking torso, too.

Have a minimum of five everyday workhorses.

And make sure you rotate your bras so that you don't wear the same one two days in a row. Spandex needs time to bounce back into shape to prevent stretching out.

Don't buy a wimpy sports bra.

Sidestep all those popular crop top–style picks. Better models come in bra sizes (not S, M, L) and encapsulate each breast separately, either through the use of seaming or underwire to reduce breast bounce and minimize the stress on ligaments. Also make sure the one you buy is engineered for the type of exercise you do. A bra labeled "low impact" provides just enough support for yoga, walking, and Pilates; "medium impact" is ideal for the elliptical, hiking, and cycling; and "high impact" is best for running, Zumba, and anything aerobic.

IF YOU DO ONLY ONE THING...

"Tell yourself, *I don't look fat.* Growing up in the fashion business, the motto was 'You can never be thin enough,' and I think, as a teen, that was hard for me, because I had boobs and hips. But it's not just that industry; the whole world goes through stages of idolizing certain body types. At one time, the ideal was Twiggy; at another, Marilyn Monroe; and right now it seems to be a very boyish body, which is unattainable for a lot of girls. Just try to be the best version of yourself that you can be."

EMMY ROSSUM got on your radar as Christine in the film *The Phantom of the Opera* and has since starred in many movies and TV shows.

Style secrets you don't want to learn the hard way

These five axioms will help you save face (and money) time and again.

Style secret No. 1: Don't wear a white bra under a white shirt.

It may seem counterintuitive, but layering white on white is like shining a spotlight on your demi cups. If you want your unmentionables to stay that way, stick to a bra in a color that is close to your skin tone—whether that's blush, beige, tan, or brown—and it will vanish under pale clothing. This tip also holds true for the undies you sport under white and light pants, dresses, and skirts.

Style secret No. 2: Killer shoes don't have to kill your feet.

Why settle for bandaged toes when you can learn what makes for a pair that masterfully combines comfort and fashion?

RULES FOR ANY SHOES

• Buy footwear with leather or rubber soles for optimum shock absorption.

• Avoid synthetics. Opt for pairs with leather, suede, or fabric uppers. These materials breathe. (Fewer blisters, less stink.)

• To prevent squashed-toe syndrome, make sure the toe-box area is wide enough for the broadest part of your foot. Go sole to sole—line up your bare foot against the bottom of the shoe—to check that your foot fits within the borders of the shoe.

RULES FOR HEELS

• Hold the shoe at the heel and the toe area. The sole should be flexible enough to bend at the front of the arch yet have a stiff bottom through the arch.

• Choose a pump with a heel that is directly underneath the center of your heel. If it is too far forward or at the back of the shoe, you'll have balance problems.

• Press the ball area. It should have a little give or a slightly padded feel.

• Look for a stacked heel that has a broad heel tap (base), which is more stable.

RULES FOR FLATS

• Try to push in the area that cups your heel. If that collapses to touch the insole, the shoe is not supportive.

• Hold a shoe at each end and attempt to twist it. If the shoe bends too much, it won't be supportive.

• If you have high arches, look for a flat with a teeny bit of a heel, which provides relief from foot pain.

• Avoid annoying slippage and cuts on your heel by finding a shoe with a back that holds your foot securely.

Style secret No. 3: You can suss out top-quality bargains in a store. (Even if you can't so much as sew on a button.)

How to tell if that garment is a legitimate score or a dud? Run it through the **SPIFFY** checklist.

• **S**titches and seams should be small and straight—no loose or jumbled threads. Give buttons and zippers a firm tug to ensure that they're secure.

• **P**rints, like plaids, stripes, and color blocking, should line up perfectly at the seams. Uniform, graphic patterns are also nearly impossible to mess up, unlike splashy florals and abstract designs, which have the potential to look like a Regretsy reject.

• **I**nterior lining should lie flat, without bubbling or poking out from underneath.

• **F**ibers look and feel most rich when they're natural—think cotton, silk, and linen. However, synthetics are better than ever these days; just test if the material is a lint magnet by rubbing it with a fluffy white knit.

• **F**aux shouldn't look fake. Synthetic patent leather and mock crocodile can pass for the real deal. Microsuede doesn't look like suede up close, so it's doable for shoes, but not bags. Pleather, on the other hand, works for shoes and bags if it is distressed and has some heft. A dead giveaway of bad fake leather? It's very smooth and lightweight.

• **Y**ank the material to test the resilience: Pull the fabric across its width and length. Lesser-quality materials will sag, an effect that will become more pronounced after multiple wearings.

Style secret No. 4: Be nitpicky in the changing room.

You want so badly for it to be perfect. The cut and the color are exactly what you've been searching for, and the price tag says "30 percent off." But if the fit is wonky, the piece is going to end up in the back of your closet until donation day. Before you buy, check yourself out from all angles—and be your harpiest, most persnickety self. Why? Because every last thing that only slightly bothers you about an item in the changing room will eventually drive you insane.

Pay attention to the following:

SHOULDERS: The seams should align with the tips of your shoulder bones.

BUST: The garment should lie flat against your body without pulling, puckering buttons, or bubbles of excess fabric.

WAISTBAND: If it bunches up when you add a belt, it's too big. Muffin top? It's too small. Find a happy medium.

RISE: If the crotch is snug or droops low, the item goes into the "no" pile.

THIGHS: The fabric ought to hug curves smoothly, not pinch the backs of the legs.

Next, stand up straight and assess the **LENGTH**. In general, shirts should fall between your waist and hips; long sleeves, at the wrist bones. Pants should brush the tops of the shoes you plan to pair them with (or be alterable).

Then evaluate the **GIVE** factor of stretchy clothing, particularly jeans. Wear them for 10 minutes or so while you're trying on tops. If they get saggy, go down a size.

Finally, determine their real-life **WEARABILITY**. Bend over and sit down in skirts and pants. Do they ride up, pull down, or dig in? For jackets and tops, try these moves: "Give yourself a hug," then lean over to "pick up the groceries" and reach up to "change a lightbulb." The garment shouldn't feel constricting or expose your midriff.

Style secret No. 5: **A tailor can (usually) make it all better.**

As for all those so-so items lingering in your closet, there is still hope. Alterations can make the average piece outstanding for a relatively low cost. Keep in mind: You have more leeway to take a garment in than to let it out.

These alterations yield the highest payoff:

LOWERING THE HEM. The most flattering and classic skirt hemline is at the knee. If you have two inches folded at the hem, a tailor will be able to extend the length by an inch.

NARROWING A BODICE. There shouldn't be excess fabric under the arms or the bust.

STITCHING UP BULGING POCKETS. Have the linings removed and the slits stitched shut for a stream-lined look.

SHORTENING PANT HEMS. They should stop just short of kissing the floor.

TAKING IN A SAGGY WAIST. You should be able to slide only two fingers inside the band.

TACKING UP LONG SHIRT CUFFS. Full-length sleeves should hit your wrist bones.

However, you'll want to skip these pricey fixes: a droopy crotch, too-big shoulders, and any problem in an area with a zipper or pleats. These will require a complete overhaul, which in the end will cancel out any money you're saving.

PRESSING MATTERS

For a wrinkle-free work wardrobe, strike while the iron is hot.

BUTTON-FRONT SHIRT
STEP 1: Iron the underside of the collar, working from the center to the points. Flip over and repeat on the outside.

STEP 2: Secure one shoulder over the nar-row end of the board and iron from the yoke to the center of the back. Repeat on the other shoulder.

STEP 3: Lay a sleeve flat on the board with the buttons or cuff-link holes facing up. Iron the inside of the cuff, then flip the sleeve over and do the outside of the cuff. Next, iron the sleeve, beginning with the button side. Repeat on the other sleeve.

STEP 4: Iron both front panels, then flip the shirt over and iron the back. With the placket, be careful to iron between the buttons so you don't damage them.

PANTS
STEP 1: Turn the pants inside out, lay the pockets flat on the board, and iron.

STEP 2: Turn the pants right-side out and slip the waistband around the small end of the board. Rotate the pants around the board as you iron. Iron lightly over the outside of the pockets to avoid creases.

STEP 3: Place one pant leg on top of the other, inseams aligned. Fold back the top leg and iron the inside of the bottom leg to the crotch; flip the pants over and iron the outside. If you prefer no crease, iron out to the edges of the legs, but not over them.

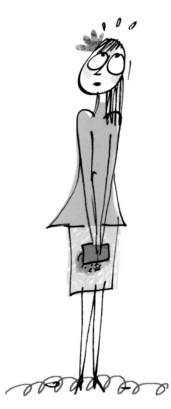

Scuff happens. So do stains, static cling, and an assortment of other mishaps. Have to just get out the door anyway? Then try our nifty half-assed solutions (a.k.a. cover-ups). Time for a real, expert-approved fix? Then go for the full monty.

Fashion faux pas, averted

ANNOYING PROBLEM: Your jeans stink like last night's fajitas.

THE HALF-ASSED APPROACH: Try this refreshing trick used by many owners of vintage-clothing stores. Mist the garment with one part vodka and two parts water and let dry as you put on your makeup. Naturally scentless, vodka helps to deodorize. If that sounds like a bad use of good booze, hanging the jeans up in the bathroom as you take a steamy shower also helps.

THE FULL MONTY: Add ½ cup baking soda (to absorb odor) and 1 cup distilled white vinegar (to destroy bacteria) to the regular wash cycle.

ANNOYING PROBLEM: *Blerg*, static cling!

THE HALF-ASSED APPROACH: No Static Guard? No sweat! You can pat yourself down with a fabric-softener sheet or run a wire hanger over the spots where your clothing tends to bunch. And if a skirt rubbing against tights is causing the clinging, lightly spray the tights with aerosol hair spray.

THE FULL MONTY: Use fabric-softener sheets in the dryer or add ½ cup distilled white vinegar to the rinse cycle. The acidic vinegar removes soap residue and softens the fabric, thus cutting down on friction in the dryer and minimizing static. But the number one thing that you can do to prevent those electrical charges? Change your shoes. Rubber-soled shoes help create static. That's because rubber is such a poor conductor, the electricity is stored up in your soles. Switching to leather soles will keep the electricity moving through you instead of building up and can drastically reduce static cling.

ANNOYING PROBLEM: Hanger dimples on your favorite crewneck.

THE HALF-ASSED APPROACH: A blast of steam from a steamer or an iron will knock them flat in seconds. (Just be careful not to spill any water if you're using an iron.)

THE FULL MONTY: Let's be clear: No wire hangers! They can leave unwanted puckers at the shoulders of sweaters and other garments. Swap them out for padded hangers, or better yet, fold all your knit pieces.

ANNOYING PROBLEM: You found your sleekest pumps. They look sad and scruffy.

THE HALF-ASSED APPROACH: Use a black permanent marker to fill in obvious scuffs on black leather or roughed-up heels. Remove white salt stains with an old T-shirt dipped in vinegar. To polish up leather, er...well, without the polish part: Give footwear a wipe with a clean microfiber cloth—the same kind you use to dust bookshelves.

THE FULL MONTY: Dab scratches with a little distilled white vinegar to swell the abrasion. (Think of it as collagen for leather.) Let dry, then buff the item with colorless shoe polish. To make footwear last for the long haul, ask a cobbler to attach rubber sole protectors; they'll extend the life of the soles tenfold. Finally, apply a waterproofing spray to suede and leather shoes and boots before the first wearing and at the start of every season.

ANNOYING PROBLEM: You stepped on your pant cuff and ripped the hem. Because of course.

THE HALF-ASSED APPROACH: You can reattach a falling hem in seconds with a little double-stick tape. Duct tape will work, too, if that's all you have.

THE FULL MONTY: Not much of a seamstress? Use iron-on fusible binding tape (like Stitch Witchery). Turn the garment inside out and iron any wrinkles. Cut a strip of Stitch Witchery to the same length as the diameter of the pant cuff. Place adhesive-side down between the hem fold and the pant fabric. Cover with a pressing cloth, and press with an iron for a few seconds (or as long as the fusible-tape instructions recommend for the fabric).

IF YOU DO ONLY ONE THING...

"Don't wear Doc Martens with bike shorts."

ROSE BYRNE is a star of film (*Bridesmaids*) and TV (*Damages*), and you've probably streamed something with her just this month.

In case of fashion emergency

You need to be prepared for anything. Jacqui Stafford, a celebrity stylist and the author of The Wow Factor, *comes to the rescue with the most important items to stash.*

IN YOUR CLOSET

☐ **NEEDLES AND THREAD.** Because buttons fall off.

☐ **STRAPLESS BRA.** So you can comfortably wear daring necklines.

☐ **DOUBLE-STICK TAPE.** Use it to keep wrap dresses and button-down shirts from gaping open.

☐ **SHAPEWEAR.** Even if you hit the treadmill four times a week, you'll need an extra layer to smooth you out under filmy or clingy dresses and skirts.

☐ **LINT ROLLER.** To remove errant fuzzies, courtesy of Fluffy or your fluffy mohair throw.

☐ **PILL REMOVER.** It will keep the sweaters from last year (and the year before that) looking brand-new.

☐ **FABRIC SPRAY.** Febreze—a busy (or lazy) woman's best friend.

IN YOUR HANDBAG

☐ **BANDAGES.** To salve the blisters from those gorgeous sky-high heels you just had to wear.

☐ **SAFETY PINS.** Attach a few to your key ring and you'll have a quick save if you split a seam.

☐ **SPARE EARRING BACKS.** Those little suckers are so easy to lose, and gorgeous statement sparklers can make or break an outfit. (You can also use a pencil eraser in a pinch.)

☐ **GUM OR MINTS AND FLOSS.** To give you a selfie-perfect smile and coffeeproof breath IRL.

IN YOUR DESK

☐ **DEODORANT WIPES.** You'll need these when the heat is on as you're running from meeting to meeting.

☐ **STAIN-REMOVER STICK.** For latte dribbles and salad-dressing splatters.

☐ **TRAVEL-SIZE PERFUME.** Give yourself a quick spritz before you go from desk to dinner.

☐ **HAND MIRROR.** To check up on your smile. You don't need to show your boss that you ate tabbouleh for lunch.

☐ **WRINKLE-RELEASER SPRAY.** Because sitting all day can leave your pants with some nasty creases.

CHAPTER 5

FEEDING YOURSELF (AND OTHERS)

Remember the nursery rhyme "Old Mother Hubbard"? No? Well, here's a quick recap: Her cupboards were bare, blah, blah, blah, her dog dies, comes back to life, and at one point plays a flute (look it up)—all because she didn't have some basic pantry staples on hand. The lesson? Things get weird when you rely on pizza delivery every night. Whether you love to cook or you see a frying pan solely as a weapon, this chapter will give you something to chew on. We'll help you stock your cabinets, your fridge, and your bar—and show you how to shop seasonally and avoid rookie mistakes.

You can't cook without...

...these staples. Keep them stocked and behold the opportunities.

IN THE PANTRY

☐ Balsamic vinegar

☐ Brown rice

☐ Canned beans (like garbanzo, cannellini, and black beans)

☐ Chicken broth

☐ Honey

☐ Jarred marinara sauce

☐ Pasta

☐ Quinoa

☐ Red wine vinegar

☐ Rolled oats

☐ Soy sauce

☐ Tomato paste

☐ Vegetable oil

☐ White rice

☐ White wine vinegar

FOR BAKING

☐ All-purpose flour

☐ Baking powder

☐ Baking soda

☐ Brown sugar

☐ Granulated sugar

☐ Unsweetened cocoa

☐ Vanilla extract (go for pure, not imitation, which often has additives and an unnatural flavor)

IN A COOL, DARK SPOT

☐ Garlic

☐ Onions

☐ Potatoes

IN THE REFRIGERATOR

☐ Butter

☐ Dijon mustard

☐ Eggs

☐ Maple syrup

☐ Milk

☐ Parmesan

☐ Plain yogurt

☐ Lemons

IN THE FREEZER

☐ Assorted vegetables (like peas, corn, and spinach)

☐ Bacon (if you don't eat it in a few days, the freezer is the best place to keep it fresh)

☐ Bread (ditto)

☐ Nuts (they'll go rancid in the pantry)

☐ Shrimp

☐ Strawberries or mixed berries (for smoothies)

IF YOU DO ONLY ONE THING...

"I have found it nothing short of lifesaving to know how to make a satisfying and modest meal from a starkly empty pantry and a panic-inducingly bare fridge. To open a can of white beans and a can of tuna; to paw desperately through the crisper and find a soggy, rotten onion with a still-viable heart, plus an otherwise limp head of celery with still-crisp interior leaves; and to make an acceptable, aesthetically pleasing meal from such dregs has brought me a very, very long way. And with your last $9, gleaned from coins from the laundry jar, you can buy a drinkable bottle of cheap Cava to take the edge off."

GABRIELLE HAMILTON is a double threat: the chef-owner of the restaurant Prune, in New York City, and the author of *Blood, Bones and Butter: A Memoir.*

The spice-rack starter kit

There are 11,452 spices in that aisle of the grocery store. But you need only 12 or so to make your dishes sing.

1 | BLACK PEPPER. Yes, freshly ground pepper really does taste better. So buy some peppercorns that come with a built-in grinder (which can be refilled repeatedly, by the way) and play restaurant waiter at home.

2 | CAYENNE PEPPER. Some say this hot, spicy pepper can help your body detox. And maybe that's true. But Master Cleanse aficionados aren't the only ones who benefit from this staple—so do lovers of barbecue rubs and veggie dishes with a kick.

3 | CHILI POWDER. Sure, you could mix up your own blend of dried chilies, cumin, coriander, and oregano before the next Super Bowl party. Or you could just buy a jar.

4 | CINNAMON, GROUND. *Mmm*—this aromatic staple adds warmth to cookies and cakes and earthiness to stews.

5 | CUMIN, GROUND. A mellow, intensely flavorful spice, ground from a small seed. Delicious in Mexican, Middle Eastern, and Indian cooking, especially curries.

6 | CURRY POWDER. Up to 20 spices—including coriander, cumin, and turmeric—can make up this popular Indian blend. Look for a Madras variety, which brings the heat.

7 | GINGER, GROUND. This spice has a more intense and astringent taste than fresh ginger.

8 | KOSHER SALT. Forget the salt from the shaker; this is your go-to for seasoning everything from chicken to salad dressing. It's coarser than regular table salt, which makes it easier to pinch and sprinkle, and it dissolves fast.

9 | NUTMEG, WHOLE. A warm, delicate spice frequently used in savory winter concoctions (roasted squash, spinach casserole) and baked goods. Use a microplane to grate it as needed.

10 | OREGANO, DRIED. A member of the mint family (who knew?), this robust herb adds a wallop of flavor to everything from spaghetti with marinara sauce to pizza to grilled tilapia.

11 | RED PEPPER, CRUSHED. Use these flakes of crushed red chilies *sparingly* to spice up pastas and stir-fries and to add zing to pizza.

12 | SEA SALT. These big, flaky crystals should be a final touch on just-cooked foods. Take a pinch and crush the crystals between your fingertips over vegetables, fish, or (bliss) warm chocolate chip cookies.

Heavy metals: a beginner's guide

You don't have to have a lot of pots and pans— just the main players for pasta, scrambled eggs, and catching drippy roof leaks.

Pasta pot

WHY YOU NEED IT: Besides the fact that spaghetti is your signature dish? This is going to be your biggest pot—your go-to for dinner-party quantities of pasta, soup, and anything else that might require a large surface area and tall, straight sides. Its round base conducts heat up the sides while insulating the bottom to ensure that your sauce or stew doesn't burn.

WHAT TO LOOK FOR: First, you do not need a pot the size of a Fiat with a colander insert. (Buy a separate colander.) A 6- to 12-quart size is ideal. It's large enough to hold rice and beans for four but small enough to be carried easily from stovetop to sink even when full. Don't skimp by buying a pot with a thin bottom. Thickness equals a longer life and a good transfer of heat. The bottom should be thicker than the sides. (A hefty bottom prevents scorching.) Stainless steel is your best bet. In addition to being durable, it tends to be lighter than other materials—something that you can appreciate when the pot is full of scalding water.

Saucepan

WHY YOU NEED IT: This is your equal-opportunity pot, a midsize workhorse with tall sides and a thick base that's ideal for making everything from hard-boiled eggs to chocolate sauce.

WHAT TO LOOK FOR: The pan should feel a bit weighty (at least two or three pounds), but not so heavy that you need bulging biceps to lift it when it's full. Make sure the handle is secure; it should be soldered or riveted to the base. A long handle—12 to 16 inches—is best, since it gives you more leverage and keeps your hands farther away from the action. The handle should be heatproof; before you buy, make sure it is. Get a tight-fitting lid to contain sauce splatters. (This may be sold separately.) Consider a pan with flared sides, called a Windsor pan. The sloping sides help facilitate evaporation and make it easier to stir sauces while you're reducing them.

Frying pans (regular and nonstick)

WHY YOU NEED THEM: The wide surface of these pans (also called skillets or sauté pans) browns and crisps, making them good for searing salmon, pan-roasting chicken, stir-frying vegetables, and sautéing almost anything.

WHAT TO LOOK FOR: You're going to need two of them—one stainless steel and one nonstick. The untreated surface works better for browning meat and caramelizing onions. (A nonstick surface prevents that yummy, sticky crust from forming.) But when you want your grilled cheese or omelet to slide out of the pan without using a ton of oil? That's when you need the slick coating. Buy pans that are 10 to 12 inches in diameter so that ingredients aren't crowded together.

Casserole dish

WHY YOU NEED IT: Because it's not just for casseroles. This is your brownie pan, your lasagna pan, and your chicken Parmesan holder. You can also nestle a whole chicken or a pork loin in it for roasting.

WHAT TO LOOK FOR: The standard 9 by 13 inches with slightly curved corners and sides about 3 inches high. Glass, ceramic, and aluminum are all good choices for material. Short handles on each side aren't necessary but can make gripping the pan with oven mitts a little easier.

Rimmed baking sheet

WHY YOU NEED IT: You can use it for cookies and so, so much more. Also called a sheet pan or a jelly roll pan, this is what you'll use for roasting a bunch of asparagus, chicken thighs, or salmon filets.

WHAT TO LOOK FOR: Baking sheets are typically aluminum. Choose one that feels thick and sturdy, not flimsy, and has short sides (about one inch) all around. It helps to have two if, say, you're roasting a big batch of vegetables or you want to make several dozen cookies. Be sure that a full pan will fit in your oven. If you have a small oven, consider buying half-sheet pans, which are smaller but still fit 3 to 4 chicken breasts or some potato wedges.

EXTRA CREDIT:
Dutch oven

WHY YOU NEED IT: Well, technically, you don't. Dutch ovens are more expensive than run-of-the-mill pots, but they're useful (and, let's be honest, pretty). A Dutch oven is perfect for braising a tough, inexpensive cut of meat—in effect self-basting the meat until it's fork-tender. It also makes a nice presentation for soups and stews, since you can take the pot straight from stove to table. One less dish to wash!

WHAT TO LOOK FOR: Make sure it's cast-iron. The finish will be either matte black or colorful and enameled—guaranteed to match your apron/dish towels/typography print hanging above the sink. Sizes vary, but if you're going to invest in a Dutch oven, buy one that's big enough to fit a medium-size roast—something similar in size to your pasta pot.

Choose your tools wisely

In an ideal world (or perhaps the one conjured up by the CB2 catalog), you would have every kitchen doohickey your heart desires. In this world, you have a limited budget—and limited (if any) drawer space. So opt for the ones that you can't get through a week of dinners without.

☐ **BOX GRATER.** Whether you're grating cheese for quesadillas or carrots for cake, a sturdy, stand-up box grater with various-size holes will come in handy. Watch your knuckles!

☐ **CAN OPENER.** Find a model that cuts around (not into) the edge of the can so there are no scary or scarring sharp edges left behind.

☐ **COLANDER.** Choose one with short, heat-safe handles on each side, so you can shake the water from spaghetti without oven mitts. Also good for rinsing lettuce for salad (especially since salad spinners are space hogs).

☐ **CUTTING BOARDS.** Buy two: one synthetic, for handling raw chicken and stinky garlic (synthetic is easier to clean), and one wood. A wood cutting board is less likely to dull knives, wipes up with soap and water, and looks spiffy.

☐ **MEASURING CUPS, DRY.** A simple, solid stainless-steel set will see you through years of baking adventures. Avoid the cutesy (and not as accurate) ones shaped like cupcakes or cats.

☐ **MEASURING CUP, LIQUID.** Get a 2-cup (1-pint) measuring cup made of tempered, microwave-safe glass, and use it for everything from melting butter to measuring oil for brownies.

☐ **MEASURING SPOONS.** Again, metal ones are easy to work with. Look for a set with slender mouths, which are more likely to fit into little spice jars.

☐ **MEAT THERMOMETER.** Determining if your chicken is fully cooked is really hard without

X-ray vision. Fortunately, a thermometer can solve the mystery. Get a digital model; it's easier to read than a dial.

☐ **MICROPLANE.** This long, slim tool takes up almost zero space and is indispensable for zesting a lemon or grating nutmeg.

☐ **PEELER.** A swivel or Y-shape peeler will strip apples or cucumbers equally well, so pick the design that you prefer. Get one with a comfy grip.

☐ **SPATULA, METAL.** Opt for a model with a 6-inch metal surface that's flexible, so it can slide under cod fillets, flip pancakes or fried eggs, and lift delicate cookies in one piece.

☐ **SPATULA, NONSTICK.** Don't scrape the bottom of a nonstick pan with a metal tool; it will scratch the coating. Instead, use a flexible nonstick version.

☐ **SPATULA, RUBBER.** Yet another spatula? Yes, sorry. A large one is perfect for scraping down frosting from the side of a mixing bowl.

☐ **SPOON, METAL.** For stirring stews, scraping up burned bits from the bottom of a pan, spooning juice over a roast, or scooping macaroni and cheese. Find one that feels sturdy and looks streamlined enough to use as a serving spoon.

☐ **SPOON, SLOTTED.** Is the penne cooked? Well, you'll need to fish one out for taste-testing. That's what a slotted spoon is for—not to mention removing blanched vegetables from hot water and serving fruit salad without too much juice. Look for one with a wide head.

☐ **SPOONS, WOODEN.** These are both strong (you can mix thick batters) and gentle (they won't scratch nonstick surfaces). Get two: one round and one with a flat or squared edge for scraping the edges of pans.

☐ **TONGS.** These babies pinch, poke, flip, and toss hot food. Nonstick tips are gentler to food and pans.

☐ **WHISK.** Choose wire, rather than less sturdy silicone versions, for whisking dressings, stirring batters, and whipping cream.

☐ **WINE OPENER.** A no-nonsense tool with a fold-out foil cutter, a corkscrew, and a notched lever to help lift out the cork. Classic and cheap.

SHARP ADVICE ON KNIVES

For starters, you need just three. And none should take a huge cut of your budget. You can find a good chef's knife (the big one, which you'll use most often) for less than $25. Look for stainless steel with a plastic or wood handle.

CHEF'S KNIFE. This is the all-purpose knife that you'll use for everything from slicing skirt steak to chopping onions. Like a reliable pair of walking shoes, it should feel comfortable—weighty in your hand but not too heavy to maneuver. An 8-inch blade is the most manageable and versatile.

PARING KNIFE. The cute one! This has a small (3- to 4-inch) blade that you'll use for coring a strawberry, slicing limes for gin and tonics, and peeling an apple slice.

BREAD KNIFE. Also known as a serrated knife, this blade (about 8 inches) is narrow and rectangular—no pointed tip—with a scalloped edge that can grip the crust of bread and saw through more cleanly than a smooth blade. You'll also need it to cut through the slick skins of tomatoes.

8 KITCHEN GADGETS YOU REALLY DON'T NEED

You're smart. You can find another way to get the avocado out of the peel.

ICE CREAM SCOOP. Mint chocolate chip tastes just as good scooped with a spoon.

MINI CHOPPER. It has a lot of parts that are a pain to clean, and it takes up valuable space. Use your chef's knife to chop onions.

MEAT TENDERIZER. Excellent at getting out stress but not essential. The bottom of a heavy saucepan works just as well (for the stress, too).

MANGO SLICER. It's big, bulky, and unnecessary. You can peel a mango with a paring knife or a peeler and slice the flesh off in slabs around the big, flat pit.

AVOCADO SLICER. See above (big, bulky, unnecessary). You can halve an avocado and remove the pit with a chef's knife; use a spoon to scoop out the flesh.

APPLE CORER. A stray seed or a tough piece of core won't hurt you. Use a knife.

MELON BALLER. Honestly, your friends won't be offended if your fruit salad contains cubes instead.

MORTAR AND PESTLE. Think you're going to grind your own spice blends? You're not.

Kitchen secrets: How to avoid common cooking mistakes

You navigated the crowded grocery store, splurged on the lamb, and narrowly avoided your ex in the cereal aisle. Don't let that hard work go to waste by overcrowding your frying pan. Study these scenarios to hone your, er, chops and be a more confident cook.

THE MISTAKE: Overcrowding the pan

WHY IT'S BAD: Most of us pile chicken breasts into one skillet or heap oven fries onto a single baking sheet if we're in a hurry or we want fewer dishes to wash. But when a pan is stuffed, the heat that rises from the cooking surface becomes trapped under the food and creates steam, making oven fries limp and preventing chicken breasts from getting that desirable caramelized crust.

DO THIS INSTEAD: To help ingredients brown (which gives food flavor and locks in moisture), make sure the pieces aren't touching one another in the pan. Patting damp food dry with a paper towel before cooking also helps. Don't have a large enough skillet or baking sheet? Cook in batches, keeping the first batch warm on a plate tented with foil while you prepare the second. Or use two skillets or baking sheets. (Switch the position of the baking sheets in the oven halfway through the cooking time.)

THE MISTAKE: Choosing lean ground beef

WHY IT'S BAD: Nothing is sadder than a dull, dry burger or meatball, which you're virtually guaranteed to get if you use lean beef. Fat bastes the meat as it cooks, keeping it moist. When you opt for 90 percent lean ground beef, there's less of the good stuff to make the food tasty.

DO THIS INSTEAD: Go with ground chuck, which is typically 80 to 85 percent lean. And don't worry about the extra fat. A lot of it—as much as 15 percent—will drain off during cooking. So the 80 percent beef you start with can end up being closer to 90 or 95 percent lean, as long as you drain the fat from the pan. And as the fat drains, it loosens the interior structure of the meat, so you end up with a less dense and therefore more tender burger.

THE MISTAKE: Overmixing doughs and batters

WHY IT'S BAD: Going whisk crazy on flour activates the gluten, a protein that gives baked goods a firm and elastic structure—delicious in a chewy pizza crust but less so in a birthday cake.

DO THIS INSTEAD: Go slow and gentle. When adding dry ingredients to cookie and cake batters, use the lowest speed on an electric mixer or mix by hand until just combined. A few lumps in the batter are fine. For piecrust, whether you use a food processor or mix by hand, work the dough as little as possible. Visible bits of butter and streaks of flour are what you want.

THE MISTAKE: Cooking with a cold pan—and cold oil or butter

WHY IT'S BAD: A hot pan and oil bond to create a surface that's virtually nonstick. If neither is hot enough, those sautéed vegetables will adhere to the pan like glue, leaving you with a tough scrubbing job later on.

DO THIS INSTEAD: Heat an empty pan for at least 1 to 2 minutes. The pan is ready when you can hold your hand about 3 inches above it and feel the heat radiating from the surface. Then add the fat. Oil will shimmer when it's hot; butter should melt and foam. One exception: If you're using a nonstick pan to brown delicate foods, add the oil or butter before turning on the heat, since some nonstick pans release fumes when they're heated up empty for an extended period.

THE MISTAKE: Searing meat over heat that's too low

WHY IT'S BAD: A good steak-house sear requires a burst of heat so that the proteins in the meat cook quickly. If you keep your burner on low to medium, the inside of the steak will be done at the same time as the outside, with little browning.

DO THIS INSTEAD: Crank the heat up to medium-high or high and let the pan sizzle for a couple of minutes before putting the meat in.

THE MISTAKE: Adding garlic too early

WHY IT'S BAD: Garlic browns in less than a minute. If you add it to the pan with, say, chicken breasts, which need about 15 minutes to cook through, the garlic will scorch and turn bitter long before the meat is finished.

DO THIS INSTEAD: Whenever possible, use slices of garlic or smashed whole cloves, which are less susceptible to burning than minced garlic. (Use the minuscule pieces for sauces and salad dressings.) And add the garlic near the end of the cooking process. (The exceptions: long braises, stews, and sauces. The liquid will keep the garlic from scorching.) If a sauté recipe asks for garlic to be added at the beginning, have the remaining ingredients prepped so that you can add them quickly, before the garlic starts to burn.

THE MISTAKE: Tossing cooked pasta with oil to prevent sticking

WHY IT'S BAD: If you intend to add sauce, the oil will keep it from adhering to the noodles. Period.

DO THIS INSTEAD: To stop cooked pasta from clumping, toss it with a little sauce immediately after draining. Or, if you won't be serving the pasta for 15 minutes or more, rinse it under cold water to remove the starch. Then, just before sitting down to eat, reheat the pasta directly in the pot of sauce.

THE MISTAKE: Turning meat too often or too soon

WHY IT'S BAD: Think of a wet sponge. The more you squeeze, prod, and touch it, the more liquid you expel. A pork chop is a lot like this. Also, if you don't leave the meat in one place long enough, it can't brown. You'll wind up with a tough, gray chop and a wet pan.

DO THIS INSTEAD: Be patient. If you're not sure whether a chop is ready to be flipped, nudge it or use tongs to lift a corner. It will release from the pan when the outside is sufficiently browned. If it sticks, let it continue to cook undisturbed and try again in a minute or so.

4 OOPS! THAT ARE NO BIG WHOOP

If you burn the tofu stir-fry, then, yes, dinner is toast. But in other cases, a cooking oops is easy to erase.

1 | YOU DIDN'T PREHEAT THE OVEN. You'll have to tack on a few extra minutes of cooking time, but the taste won't suffer much. Don't try this when baking, though. Cakes and cookies must go into a hot oven to rise properly.

2 | YOU COARSELY CHOPPED INSTEAD OF FINELY DICING. You can get away with this as long as you cook everything long enough. Keep in mind that big chunks will change the way a dish looks.

3 | YOU DIDN'T LET THE MEAT REST BEFORE CARVING IT. Most chefs don't recommend slicing a roast right out the oven, but doing so won't destroy a meal. You will, however, end up with a lot of juice on the cutting board and a slightly gray dinner. When meat rests, the temperature equalizes and the juices spread throughout the meat. For cuts like pork chops, which are sliced on the plate, resting isn't such an important issue, since a few minutes usually elapse before you sit down at the table to eat.

4 | YOU MEASURED DRY INGREDIENTS IN A LIQUID MEASURING CUP. The volume of a cup of liquid is 8 fluid ounces, and so is a cup of flour. The difference is that dry ingredients, like flour and sugar, mound. Dry measuring cups can be filled, then leveled off with a knife. But the line on a liquid measuring cup is below the rim, so you can't even out the top, which makes it harder to get an exact measurement for dry items. Using a liquid cup for dry ingredients generally won't ruin a dish. The exception is baking, which requires precision.

10 recipes anyone can make

You binge on episodes of Barefoot Contessa *and devour blog posts at* Breadtopia. *But when it comes to your own kitchen, you're cowed. Here are a few simple recipes to help you stop treating cooking like a spectator sport and get in the game yourself.*

1 | A TASTY SMOOTHIE
Creamy mango shake
TOTAL TIME: 5 MINUTES | SERVES 1

Puree 1 cup **frozen mango chunks,** ½ cup of both **low-fat or skim milk** and **plain yogurt,** 1 tablespoon **agave nectar,** and a pinch of both **ground ginger** and **salt** in a blender until smooth.

2 | A HEALTHY BREAKFAST
Oatmeal with blueberries, sunflower seeds, and agave
TOTAL TIME: 10 MINUTES | SERVES 1

Prepare 1 serving **quick-cooking or old-fashioned rolled oats.** Top with ½ cup **blueberries** and 1 tablespoon **sunflower seeds.** Drizzle with 1 tablespoon **agave nectar.**

3 | A GRAB-AND-GO SNACK
Avocado toast
TOTAL TIME: 5 MINUTES | SERVES 1

Top 1 slice toasted **whole-grain bread** with ½ sliced **avocado** and **salt.** Mash lightly with a fork. Drizzle with ½ tablespoon **olive oil** and ½ teaspoon **lemon juice.** Sprinkle with **red pepper flakes.**

4 | LUNCH AT YOUR DESK
Chopped salad with lemon-pepper buttermilk dressing
TOTAL TIME: 20 MINUTES | SERVES 6 (LEFTOVERS!)

Whisk together ¼ cup **buttermilk,** 2 tablespoons **mayonnaise,** 1 teaspoon finely grated **lemon zest,** 1 tablespoon **lemon juice,** 1 tablespoon chopped **chives,** 1 tablespoon chopped **parsley,** and **salt** and **pepper.** Combine 1 chopped small head **romaine,** 4 **radishes** (cut into wedges), 1 pint halved **cherry tomatoes,** 1 chopped **bell pepper,** ½ sliced small **red onion,** ½ chopped **cucumber,** and ½ cup **garbanzo beans or shredded, cooked chicken.** (If toting this to work, stow dressing separately to avoid wilted greens.)

5 | LUNCH AT HOME
Butternut squash and bean tacos
TOTAL TIME: 25 MINUTES | SERVES 4

Cook 1 **butternut squash** (cut into ½-inch pieces), ½ teaspoon **ground cumin,** and **salt** and **pepper** in 2 tablespoons **olive oil** in a large skillet over medium heat until almost tender, 11 to 13 minutes. Add 1 15.5-ounce can **black beans** (rinsed) and ¼ cup water. Cook until warm, 1 to 2 minutes. Divide the squash mixture, ½ sliced small **red onion,** and 4 ounces crumbled **goat cheese** (about 1 cup) between 8 warmed **corn tortillas.** Serve with torn **parsley** and **lime wedges.**

6 | DINNER WITH YOUR PICKY ROOMMATE
Bucatini with marinara and ricotta
TOTAL TIME: 20 MINUTES | SERVES 4

Cook ¾ pound **bucatini.** Cook 2 chopped cloves **garlic** in ¼ cup **olive oil** in a large pot over medium heat until fragrant, 15 seconds. Add 1 28-ounce can **whole peeled tomatoes** (crush them by hand first); add **salt** and **pepper.** Cook, stirring occasionally, until thickened, 14 to 16 minutes. Toss with the pasta. Serve with **ricotta** and **basil leaves.**

7 | DINNER WITH YOUR CLEANSE-CRAZY PAL
Kale, lemon, artichoke, and caper fish packet
TOTAL TIME: 30 MINUTES | SERVES 4

Place 4 cups packed torn **kale;** 4 6-ounce pieces **boneless, skinless cod, salmon, or bass;** 1 sliced **lemon;** 1 cup halved **artichoke hearts;** ¼ cup **olive oil;** and **salt** and **pepper** on 4 large pieces of foil, dividing evenly. Fold the foil over and seal to form packets. Bake, on a baking sheet, at 425° F until the fish is opaque throughout, 12 to 14 minutes. Open the packets and top with **capers.**

8 | DINNER WITH YOUR PARENTS
Roast chicken with vegetables and pesto
TOTAL TIME: 1½ HOURS | SERVES 4

Toss 4 pounds **bone-in, skin-on chicken pieces** (about 8 pieces), 1 pound small **carrots** (peeled and halved) or other root vegetable, 3 tablespoons **olive oil,** and **salt** and **pepper** on a large rimmed baking sheet. Roast at 400° F until the vegetables are tender and the chicken is cooked through and registers 160° F, 50 to 65 minutes. Serve with **pesto** (store-bought is fine).

9 | DINNER WITH YOUR SIGNIFICANT OTHER
Pork cutlets with sautéed mustard greens
TOTAL TIME: 30 MINUTES | SERVES 4

Combine 1 chopped **cucumber,** 1 sliced **red chili,** 2 tablespoons **rice vinegar,** 1 teaspoon **sesame seeds,** 1 tablespoon **canola oil,** and **salt.** Pound 4 **boneless pork cutlets** (about 1 pound total) to a ¼-inch thickness. Season with **salt** and **pepper.** Dip in 2 beaten **large eggs,** then in 1 cup **all-purpose flour,** then in 1 cup **panko bread crumbs.** Fry, in batches, in 4 tablespoons **canola oil** in a large nonstick skillet over medium heat until golden, 2 to 3 minutes per side. Transfer to a plate; reserve the skillet. Add 1 bunch stemmed and torn **mustard greens** and 2 tablespoons water to the reserved skillet. Cook, tossing, until just wilted, 2 to 3 minutes. Toss with the cucumber mixture. Serve the pork with the salad.

10 | DINNER WITH BENEDICT CUMBERBATCH (HIM ON THE LAPTOP, YOU ON THE COUCH)
Classic margherita pizza
TOTAL TIME: 40 MINUTES | SERVES 4 (OR 1 IF YOU'VE HAD THAT KIND OF WEEK)

Shape 1 pound **pizza dough** (at room temperature) into 4 rounds and place on 2 oiled baking sheets. Brush with 1 tablespoon **olive oil.** Dividing evenly, top with 1 cup **marinara sauce,** 8 ounces sliced **fresh mozzarella,** 1 ounce grated **Parmesan** (about ¼ cup), and **salt** and **pepper.** Bake at 450° F until golden, 16 to 18 minutes. Drizzle with **olive oil.** Top with **basil leaves.**

The microwave is sexier than you think

If you've used this magical appliance only to nuke leftover kung pao, it's time to heat things up.

USE IT TO...

1 | SOFTEN BUTTER
Place cut-up butter in a microwave-safe bowl. Microwave on low (power level 3) in 20-second intervals, checking in between.

2 | MELT BUTTER
Place cut-up butter in a microwave-safe bowl. Microwave on medium (power level 5) in 30-second intervals, checking in between.

3 | MELT CHOCOLATE
Place chopped chocolate in a microwave-safe bowl. Microwave on high (power level 10) in 30-second intervals, stirring in between.

4 | SOFTEN CREAM CHEESE
Place cut-up cream cheese in a microwave-safe bowl. Microwave on high (power level 10) for 15 to 20 seconds.

5 | SOFTEN ICE CREAM
Remove the top and the liner (if any) from the carton. Microwave on high (power level 10) in 10-second intervals, checking in between, until the ice cream reaches the desired consistency.

6 | SOFTEN BROWN SUGAR
Place sugar in a microwave-safe bowl and sprinkle with 1 teaspoon water (regardless of the quantity of sugar). Cover and microwave on low (power level 3) in 1-minute intervals, tossing in between, until soft, 4 to 5 minutes.

7 | WARM TORTILLAS
Wrap tortillas in a damp paper towel. Microwave on high (power level 10) for 40 seconds.

8 | WARM MAPLE SYRUP
Place syrup in a microwave-safe measuring cup. Microwave on high (power level 10) in 15-second intervals, checking in between.

9 | TOAST FRESH BREAD CRUMBS
Spread ½ cup fresh bread crumbs on a microwave-safe plate. Microwave on high (power level 10) in 1-minute intervals, tossing in between, until beginning to turn golden, 2 to 3 minutes.

10 | TOAST COCONUT
Spread ½ cup shredded coconut on a microwave-safe plate. Microwave on high (power level 10) in 1-minute intervals, tossing in between, until beginning to turn golden, 2 to 3 minutes.

11 | TOAST PINE NUTS AND SLICED ALMONDS
Spread nuts on a microwave-safe plate. Microwave on high (power level 10) in 1-minute intervals, tossing in between, until beginning to turn golden, 4 to 5 minutes.

12 | COOK BACON
Sandwich 6 slices of bacon between 2 double layers of paper towels. Place on a microwave-safe plate. Microwave on high (power level 10) until cooked through, 4 to 5 minutes.

13 | STEAM ASPARAGUS AND GREEN BEANS
Place 1 pound of trimmed asparagus or green beans in a microwave-safe baking dish with 1 tablespoon water. Cover and microwave on high (power level 10) until tender, 3 to 4 minutes. Uncover immediately.

14 | STEAM CARROTS
Place 1 pound thinly sliced carrots in a microwave-safe baking dish with 1 tablespoon water. Cover and microwave on high (power level 10) until tender, 4 to 6 minutes. Uncover immediately.

15 | STEAM ARTICHOKES
Place 2 trimmed artichokes in a deep microwave-safe baking dish with 1 tablespoon water. Cover and microwave on high (power level 10) until tender, 10 to 12 minutes.

16 | COOK WINTER SQUASH
Cut squash in half lengthwise and scrape out seeds. Place cut-side down in a microwave-safe baking dish. Microwave on high (power level 10) until tender and easily pierced with a paring knife, 10 to 13 minutes for a medium (3-pound) butternut or spaghetti squash; 6 to 8 minutes for a medium (1½-pound) acorn squash. Let stand for 5 minutes.

17 | BAKE A POTATO
Rub a potato with olive oil and place on a microwave-safe plate. Microwave, uncovered, on high (power level 10) until tender and easily pierced with a paring knife, 12 to 14 minutes.

18 | COOK CORN ON THE COB
Place unshucked corn on a microwave-safe plate. Microwave on high (power level 10) for 6 minutes. Let stand for 5 minutes. Carefully remove husks and silk.

19 | POACH SALMON
Season pieces of skinless salmon fillet with salt and pepper and place in a shallow microwave-safe baking dish with 2 tablespoons white wine vinegar or rice vinegar (to add flavor) and enough water to reach halfway up the fish. Cover and microwave on high (power level 10) until the fish is opaque throughout, 3 to 4 minutes. If the fish is not fully cooked, microwave, covered, on high in 45-second intervals. Remove from liquid and serve.

20 | COOK RICE
In a microwave-safe baking dish or medium bowl, combine 1 cup long-grain white rice, 2 cups water, and ½ teaspoon salt. Microwave, uncovered, on high (power level 10) until the rice is tender and the liquid is absorbed, 15 to 18 minutes.

21 | MAKE POPCORN
Place ½ cup popcorn kernels in a large microwave-safe bowl with 1 tablespoon olive or canola oil. Cover with a microwave-safe plate and microwave on high (power level 10) until the majority of the kernels have popped, 3 to 5 minutes.

IF YOU DO ONLY ONE THING...

"Learn how to cut an onion. If you know how to do that, you have the basic skill to cut just about anything. When you have your knife skills down, cooking becomes faster, easier, and more pleasurable."

ELLIE KRIEGER is a cookbook author, most recently of *Weeknight Wonders: Delicious Healthy Dinners in 30 Minutes or Less.*

Your seasonal guide to (almost) everything

Strawberries? Check. Sweet potatoes? Check. Squash? Three kinds. Buying produce when it's in season means it tastes better and usually costs less. This list gives you the dirt on when things grow—plus learn how to choose the best specimens, store them, and use them up.

Arugula

WHAT TO LOOK FOR: Fresh arugula has long, firm, bright green leaves. Larger leaves are more peppery than small ones. Holes, tears, and yellowing edges are signs arugula is past its prime. If you can, buy bunches with the roots intact; this helps retain freshness.

HOW TO STORE: If the roots are still on, wrap the stems in a moistened paper towel and place in a plastic bag in the vegetable drawer. Keep loose leaves in the clamshell packaging or a plastic bag.

FRESH IDEA: Arugula tends to be gritty, so rinse the leaves thoroughly. The greens are at their best in salads: Drizzle with extra-virgin olive oil and lemon juice and top with shaved Parmesan, salt, and pepper.

Basil

WHAT TO LOOK FOR: Look for whole, smooth leaves that are aromatic, bright green, and free of black spots.

HOW TO STORE: Basil does best at room temperature. Trim the bottoms of the stems (or don't, if the roots are still attached) and place in a few inches of water in a sturdy glass, vase, or jelly jar—as you would a bunch of flowers. Keep out of sunlight.

FRESH IDEA: Mix chopped basil leaves and fresh lemon juice into mayonnaise. Serve with grilled shrimp, roasted potato wedges, or cut-up raw vegetables.

Beets

WHAT TO LOOK FOR: Smooth, blemish-free dark red or golden yellow skins. If you want to cook any attached leaves, make sure they're bright green.

HOW TO STORE: Before you refrigerate, separate the beets from the leaves. To keep the beets dry, store them and the leaves, unwashed, in separate plastic bags in the vegetable drawer.

FRESH IDEA: Small, young beets are revelatory when grated raw in salads. (Beet juice can stain, so now is the time to pull out that apron.) Steam, boil, or roast them at 400° F for 45 minutes; slice and top with goat cheese, olive oil, and balsamic vinegar.

Bell peppers

WHAT TO LOOK FOR: Red peppers are mature green peppers. Yellow and orange peppers are different, sweeter varieties. You want shiny, unblemished, wrinkle-free skins, regardless of color.

HOW TO STORE: Refrigerate peppers, unwashed, in a plastic bag in the vegetable drawer. Keep them dry, as moisture will eventually cause them to rot.

FRESH IDEA: Peppers are delish grilled, baked, or sautéed. Roasting makes them smoky. Insta-dinner: Cook a box of couscous and stir in 1 diced bell pepper, a can of chickpeas, 2 tablespoons extra-virgin olive oil, 2 tablespoons red wine vinegar, and salt and pepper.

Berries

WHAT TO LOOK FOR: Blackberries and raspberries should have a rich hue; blueberries should be a little frosty white. Check all fruit for mold, and inspect containers for stickiness or stains.

HOW TO STORE: Place unwashed raspberries and blackberries in a single layer on a plate, cover loosely, and store in the refrigerator. Blueberries are sturdier, so leave them in their container.

FRESH IDEA: For a sweet-tart breakfast: Top a small dish of fresh ricotta with a mix of blueberries, blackberries, and raspberries; drizzle with honey; and sprinkle with toasted almonds.

Chard

WHAT TO LOOK FOR: Chard is typically classified by the color of the stems—red, white, green, or rainbow (a combination of colors). Look for crisp, crinkly green leaves; avoid ones with spots or holes. The smaller the leaves, the sweeter the taste.

HOW TO STORE: Refrigerate chard, unwashed, in a plastic bag in the vegetable drawer.

FRESH IDEA: Stir chard into stews and soups, or blanch or sauté it, like spinach. Bear in mind: Small leaves can be cooked with the stems attached. Larger leaves have tougher stems, so separate them and give the stems a few minutes' head start when cooking.

Corn

WHAT TO LOOK FOR: Pull back the husk (just a bit) to check the quality of the ear. The kernels should be closely spaced, firm, and round. Look for grassy green, tightly wrapped husks. The silk should be glossy and pale yellow, the stem moist.

HOW TO STORE: Refrigerate ears unshucked in a bag.

FRESH IDEA: If the corn is very fresh, try tossing raw kernels with tomatoes, Feta, extra-virgin olive oil, vinegar, salt, and pepper for a simple side dish.

Cucumbers

WHAT TO LOOK FOR: Firm, dark green ones with no wrinkles or spongy spots. No matter the variety, smaller cucumbers contain fewer and tinier seeds.

HOW TO STORE: Because cucumbers keep best in temperatures just over 40° F, place them in a plastic bag on a shelf toward the front of the refrigerator, which tends to be warmer.

FRESH IDEA: Thinly slice 2 regular cucumbers (peel waxed cukes; lightly scrub unwaxed ones) and toss with 3 tablespoons rice vinegar, 2 tablespoons chopped cilantro, 2 teaspoons sesame oil, and a pinch each of sugar and salt.

Eggplant

WHAT TO LOOK FOR: Size matters. Eggplants are tastiest when they weigh less than 1½ pounds. Look for a smooth, shiny dark purple skin (a dull exterior indicates overripeness) and a green stem with leaves clinging to the top.

HOW TO STORE: Refrigerate in a plastic bag in the vegetable drawer.

FRESH IDEA: For an easy starter, brush ½-inch-thick slices with olive oil and grill for 2 to 3 minutes per side. Layer with sliced fresh mozzarella and top with extra-virgin olive oil, balsamic vinegar, salt, and pepper.

Stone fruits

WHAT TO LOOK FOR: Gently squeeze plums, peaches, and nectarines; they should yield slightly. Look for richly colored plums with no brown spots. Peaches and nectarines should have no green or wrinkly patches.

HOW TO STORE: Ripen stone fruits at room temperature, stem-ends down. A sweet, flowery smell means that peaches and nectarines are ripe and should be refrigerated, unwashed, in a plastic bag. Ripe plums have dull skins.

FRESH IDEA: Slice a peach or nectarine in half, coat it with butter and sugar, and grill for 2 to 3 minutes per side. Serve with ice cream and you've got a killer dessert.

Summer squash

WHAT TO LOOK FOR: Select brightly colored yellow squash and zucchini less than 8 inches long. Larger squash can be bitter.

HOW TO STORE: Refrigerate yellow squash and zucchini, unwashed, in a plastic bag in the vegetable drawer.

FRESH IDEA: Slice them thinly, sauté with chopped onions and fresh thyme, and serve with grilled steak.

Tomatoes

WHAT TO LOOK FOR: A deep color and firmness, with a little give. If they're missing that sweet, woody smell, leave them behind. Check grape tomatoes for wrinkles, a sign of age.

HOW TO STORE: Keep tomatoes at room temperature on a plate; never store them in a plastic bag. If you want to speed the ripening process, put the tomatoes in a pierced paper bag with an apple, which emits ethylene gas, a ripening agent.

FRESH IDEA: In a large bowl, combine chopped tomatoes, thinly sliced garlic, olive oil, salt, pepper, and a pinch of crushed red pepper. Let sit at room temperature, stirring occasionally, for at least an hour. Toss with cooked pasta and chopped fresh basil. Dinner, done.

FALL

Apples

WHAT TO LOOK FOR: You want bright color, a shiny skin, and zero bruises. If you think the apple is shiny because it's waxed, flick the skin close to the stalk. A dull sound means an apple is ripe; a hollow sound means it's overripe.

HOW TO STORE: Apples do well in the fruit drawer of the refrigerator. At room temperature, they ripen quickly and become mealy.

FRESH IDEA: Homemade applesauce is the greatest: Core and roughly chop the fruit; leave the skins on. Add about ½ cup water and a small pinch of salt for every 4 to 6 apples. Simmer, covered, until very soft. Stir in cinnamon to taste.

Broccoli

WHAT TO LOOK FOR: Tight, compact florets that are dark green; the stalks should be slightly lighter in color. Yellowing broccoli is old and won't taste good.

HOW TO STORE: Refrigerate broccoli unwashed (moisture speeds decay) in a plastic bag in the vegetable compartment.

FRESH IDEA: For a surprising slaw, combine chopped raw broccoli and red onion with a dressing of mayonnaise, sour cream, cider vinegar, and honey.

Brussels sprouts

WHAT TO LOOK FOR: Firm, compact heads with clean stem ends. They should be no larger than one inch in diameter. Any bigger and they'll taste cabbagey.

HOW TO STORE: Keep them unwashed (moisture speeds decay) and tightly wrapped in a plastic bag in the vegetable compartment of the refrigerator.

FRESH IDEA: Need something to serve with your pork chops? Halve the sprouts and sauté them in olive oil over medium heat until tender, 7 to 10 minutes. During the last minutes of cooking, toss in 1 large clove of garlic, thinly sliced, and a handful of golden raisins.

Butternut squash

WHAT TO LOOK FOR: Pick a squash that is rock-solid and heavy for its size. A matte skin is ideal; a shiny finish is a sign that the squash wasn't ripe when it was picked.

HOW TO STORE: Protect butternut squash from light and heat by storing it in a cool, dry place (not in the refrigerator).

FRESH IDEA: Halve, seed, and roast butternut squash at 400° F, cut-side down (to keep it from drying out). When it's tender, scoop out the flesh and mash it with butter, a little nutmeg, salt, and pepper. A satisfying main.

Cauliflower

WHAT TO LOOK FOR: Compact white florets and bright green leaves. Avoid anything with a yellowish tinge or tiny spots of black mold.

HOW TO STORE: Refrigerate it unwashed in a plastic bag in the vegetable compartment.

FRESH IDEA: For a quick Monday-night dinner, toss cauliflower florets with olive oil, salt, and pepper and roast at 400° F until tender (about 25 minutes); let cool. Serve on salad greens with sliced red onion, crumbled Feta, chopped almonds, and your favorite vinaigrette.

Grapes

WHAT TO LOOK FOR: Plump, unblemished pretties firmly attached to a flexible stem. When ripe, green grapes should have a yellowish cast; red and purple ones should have no green. Buy organic if possible. Conventionally grown grapes can have a high amount of pesticide residue.

HOW TO STORE: Store grapes unwashed in a ventilated plastic bag in the refrigerator. They will shrivel and even start to ferment (not in a good way) at room temperature.

FRESH IDEA: A simple dessert: Fill a prebaked tart shell with vanilla pudding. Sprinkle with red and green grapes and chill. Dust with confectioners' sugar before serving.

Leeks

WHAT TO LOOK FOR: White bottoms and bright green leaves. Avoid those with very dark green tops or rounded (rather than flat) bottoms, which can be signs that the vegetable is overgrown, old, or both. Smaller leeks are the most tender.

HOW TO STORE: Before storing, cut off and discard the tops, but keep the roots intact. Stow tightly wrapped in a plastic bag (to contain the aroma) in the refrigerator.

FRESH IDEA: Leeks tend to be sandy, so wash them well just before cooking. Try them braised: Halve them lengthwise and put them in a pot with enough chicken broth to reach halfway up their sides. Dot with butter and simmer, covered, until tender, about 10 to 12 minutes.

Mushrooms

WHAT TO LOOK FOR: Smooth, dry skins and tightly closed caps. Avoid any that are wrinkled, spotted, or slimy—all signs of age.

HOW TO STORE: Mushrooms need to breathe. Place them, unwashed, in the refrigerator in a paper bag or wrapped in a damp paper towel. Store them whole, not sliced, for the longest shelf life.

FRESH IDEA: Wipe mushrooms with a damp paper towel just before using. Never soak them or they will become mushy. For a quick, healthy side, cut them into quarters and sauté in olive oil until golden brown, 4 to 6 minutes.

Pears

WHAT TO LOOK FOR: Unlike most fruits, pears ripen best off the tree, after they've been picked. Buy specimens that are smooth, free of bruises, and firm. An unripe pear has a bright and shiny skin; a ripe one looks matte.

HOW TO STORE: Stand pears, unwashed, on their bottoms and let them ripen at room temperature. To speed up the process, place them in a paper bag until the flesh on the neck gives a little when pressed. Refrigerate ripe pears.

FRESH IDEA: For a sweet treat, poach them. Peel 4 ripe pears and simmer them gently in 1½ cups red wine and ¾ cup sugar until tender, about 25 minutes.

Potatoes

WHAT TO LOOK FOR: Few eyes or green patches—those are signs of prolonged exposure to light.

HOW TO STORE: Place them in a paper bag and stow in a well-ventilated, cool, dark place. Just don't forget about them, because after a few weeks they can start to reek.

FRESH IDEA: Peeled potatoes turn brown when exposed to the air, so prepare them just before using. For creamy mashed potatoes, simmer peeled and quartered potatoes until tender, 15 to 20 minutes. Drain and mash with butter, milk, and sour cream. *Mmm.*

Sweet potatoes

WHAT TO LOOK FOR: Look for small to medium ones; large ones can be tough. You want a smooth, evenly colored skin without cracks or wrinkles.

HOW TO STORE: Keep them in a well-ventilated, cool, dark place, like a pantry or the bottom shelf of a cabinet (not on top of the fridge).

FRESH IDEA: It's simple to bake them: Prick the skin with a fork, cover with foil, and place in a 400° F oven until tender, about 1 hour. Serve drizzled with maple syrup.

SPRING
Asparagus

WHAT TO LOOK FOR: Firm, straight stems and tightly closed buds. Avoid spears that are shriveled or wet or that have thick, woody stalks.

HOW TO STORE: Wrap the cut ends in a damp paper towel and store in a plastic bag in the refrigerator.

FRESH IDEA: Rinse to remove sand from the tips. Snap off or trim the bottoms (no need to peel). For an easy lunch, boil asparagus, then run under cold water to cool. Drizzle with olive oil and fresh lemon juice and sprinkle with chopped hard-cooked eggs and chives.

Baby lettuce

WHAT TO LOOK FOR: Be sure the leaves are whole and unbroken, with no signs of wilting or browning. Avoid loose leaf lettuces that appear wet; they decay quickly when moist.

HOW TO STORE: Keep unwashed greens in a plastic bag in the vegetable drawer. Don't place them near apples or pears; they give off ethylene gas, which turns lettuce brown.

FRESH IDEA: Don't get complicated. Simply dress with extra-virgin olive oil, salt, and pepper to let the flavor shine.

Cherries

WHAT TO LOOK FOR: A uniform color; a deeper red equals a sweeter taste. An exception is Rainier cherries, which have a creamy yellow and red exterior. Be sure that the fruit is plump and firm, with unblemished, glossy skins.

HOW TO STORE: Keep cherries unwashed in a bowl or an open plastic bag in the refrigerator.

FRESH IDEA: Pit them and toss them with fresh mint, then serve over vanilla ice cream for dessert.

Green beans

WHAT TO LOOK FOR: Smooth, bright green beans with velvety skins. Bend one in half to make sure it snaps; a bit of moisture at the breaking point shows freshness. If you can see the beans clearly through the pods, they were picked past their prime.

HOW TO STORE: To keep green beans moist, refrigerate them in a tightly sealed container.

FRESH IDEA: Drizzle them with sesame oil, soy sauce, and red pepper flakes and roast at 400° F for 10 to 15 minutes for a savory side.

Peas

WHAT TO LOOK FOR: Ripe snow peas should be light green and almost translucent, with tiny seeds. The pods of garden peas should be glossy, crunchy, sweet, and full of medium-size peas. Sugar snaps should be bright green with plump pods.

HOW TO STORE: Keep all varieties unwashed and loosely wrapped in plastic in the vegetable drawer. Leave garden peas in their pods until you're ready to use them.

FRESH IDEA: Snow peas and sugar snap peas can be eaten whole after removing the stems and the strings. Garden peas should be shelled and blanched in boiling water just until they turn bright green (1 to 2 minutes). Try them smashed with olive oil, dill, goat cheese, and black pepper and spread on toast.

Radishes

WHAT TO LOOK FOR: No cracks, a firm texture, and crisp, bright leaves (if they are still attached).

HOW TO STORE: Remove the leaves. Refrigerate radishes in a loosely closed plastic bag.

FRESH IDEA: Just before using, trim the stems and the root ends and wash. Make like the French and snack on this: halved radishes served with soft unsalted butter and sea salt.

Scallions

WHAT TO LOOK FOR: Bright green tops and firm, white bases. A no-no: wet, wilted tops.

HOW TO STORE: Keep bunches unwashed and wrapped in a plastic bag in the vegetable drawer.

FRESH IDEA: Wash just before using and trim the roots. They're great grilled whole: Season with olive oil, salt, and pepper and cook until tender (about 4 minutes).

Spinach

WHAT TO LOOK FOR: The crinkly leaves of savory spinach are more flavorful (though a bit tougher) than the flat-leaf variety. Whichever kind you choose, look for a deep, dark color and unbroken leaves with no signs of wilting or yellowing.

HOW TO STORE: Refrigerate spinach unwashed and loosely wrapped in a plastic bag.

FRESH IDEA: Chop off the root ends and thick stems, then swish the leaves in a bowl of cold water to rinse. Serve it raw, tossed with boiled egg, walnuts, oil, and vinegar.

Strawberries

WHAT TO LOOK FOR: Shiny, bright red, and fragrant = good. Bruised, withered, or brownish = bad. Also opt for smaller ones, since big berries tend to be less juicy.

HOW TO STORE: Wrap the container of remaining unwashed berries loosely in a plastic bag or paper towel and store in the refrigerator.

FRESH IDEA: Wash the berries and trim off the caps just before using. Top with freshly whipped cream. Or sprinkle with sugar and balsamic vinegar and serve with sliced pound cake.

WINTER
Acorn squash

WHAT TO LOOK FOR: A thick, hard skin and firm flesh. Look for one that is 6 to 8 inches in diameter, heavy for its size, and free of cracks and soft spots. (A lighter squash has less moisture and can taste drier.)

HOW TO STORE: Keep a whole acorn squash in a cool, dark, dry place. Leave the stem on until you're ready to cook. Cut squash should be covered with plastic wrap and refrigerated.

FRESH IDEA: Cut the squash in half, scoop out the seeds and strings, and place the pieces cut-side down on an oiled baking sheet. Bake at 400° F until tender, about 30 minutes. Turn over, add a pat of butter and 1 teaspoon brown sugar to each side, and bake for 10 minutes more.

Cabbage

WHAT TO LOOK FOR: Tightly packed, crisp-looking, shiny leaves ranging in color from green to almost white. Avoid cabbages with yellow leaves, a strong smell, or a woody, split core.

HOW TO STORE: Keep a whole head of cabbage unwashed in a plastic bag in the refrigerator. Sliced pieces should be sprinkled with a few drops of water, placed in a plastic bag, and refrigerated.

FRESH IDEA: You can't go wrong with homemade cole slaw. Shred 1 head of cabbage and toss it with ½ cup mayonnaise, ¼ cup sour cream, 2 teaspoons pepper, ½ teaspoon kosher salt, a pinch of sugar, and 2 tablespoons cider vinegar.

Citrus fruits

WHAT TO LOOK FOR: Ripe grapefruit and oranges are plump, firm, and heavy for their size, with shiny skins. Clementines should have a thin, glossy, deep orange peel; avoid clementines that feel hollow or dented. Lemons should be firm and heavy, with smooth (not pitted) skins.

HOW TO STORE: Grapefruit, oranges, and lemons last longest when wrapped in a plastic bag and stored in the vegetable drawer. Clementines are best kept in the refrigerator or in a cool, dry spot in a mesh bag or a basket so air can circulate around them.

FRESH IDEA: Try broiling citrus: Sprinkle the unpeeled fruit halves with brown sugar, then broil until the sugar is melted.

Collard greens

WHAT TO LOOK FOR: Brightly colored, plump, and crisp bunches. A strong odor means the greens are past their prime.

HOW TO STORE: Stow unwashed and wrapped in damp paper towels in a plastic bag in the vegetable drawer.

FRESH IDEA: For a super side: Sauté ½ sliced red onion in oil until soft. Add 1 bunch chopped collards and cook until almost tender. Stir in 2 teaspoons each brown sugar and cider vinegar and cook until tender.

Fennel

WHAT TO LOOK FOR: Big, round, clean bulbs with a bit of sheen. They should be white, with no cracks or browning. Larger bulbs are usually more tender than long, slender ones. Crisp stalks with bright, feathery greenery (called fronds) are a sign of freshness.

HOW TO STORE: Keep bulbs tightly wrapped and unwashed in a plastic bag in the vegetable drawer.

FRESH IDEA: Sprinkle cut fennel with lemon juice to prevent it from discoloring. For a salad, toss 2 thinly sliced bulbs with 2 tablespoons each lemon juice and olive oil, 1 ounce shaved Parmesan, and a little fresh thyme, salt, and pepper.

Kale

WHAT TO LOOK FOR: Richly colored, frilly, dark green leaves that have a little spring to them. Skip those that are yellowing or wilted.

HOW TO STORE: Keep kale unwashed in a plastic bag in the coldest section of the refrigerator, which is usually the back.

FRESH IDEA: Try adding 2 cups chopped leaves to a pot of soup. Simmer until tender, about 4 minutes.

Radicchio

WHAT TO LOOK FOR: A full, heavy head with crisp, richly colored leaves. Pass over smaller heads that feel light. Their compact size is often the result of having been repeatedly stripped of damaged outer leaves.

HOW TO STORE: Keep fresh heads unwashed in a plastic bag in the vegetable drawer.

FRESH IDEA: Grill it: Halve 3 heads and brush with olive oil. Season with salt and pepper. Cook over high heat until slightly charred. Drizzle with balsamic vinegar.

That's the spirit

*A tribute to the first truly adult drink of my life. By **Rosie Schaap***

I'D MADE MARTINIS for years before I ever tasted one. I tended bar when I was in college and always had at least a few regulars who were devoted martini drinkers. They were older, sharp, and dryly funny, with an urbane, seen-it-all manner I found immensely appealing.

Lacking any inherent sense of how a martini ought to taste, I'd mix their drinks to their specifications. They usually asked for dry martinis, so I'd make like Winston Churchill and just nod at the vermouth bottle in the bar while stirring the gin until it was bracingly cold, straining it into a cocktail glass, harpooning a few olives with a toothpick and lowering it in.

By 25, I was firmly a beer-and-whiskey girl. That felt just right to me: honest and unfussy but assertive. Which is interesting, because in most other respects I didn't feel so confident. I was teaching English in New York City, plus working in a library— and nursing a broken heart. I didn't feel quite up to the task of being a professional, grown-up person or of overcoming a soured relationship.

One night, after I'd already spent a few hours at my usual bar drinking Guinness, I said good night to the other regulars and headed home. It was late, and I was tired. But when I hit West Broadway, the bright red neon that spelled out ODEON above a bar and restaurant at the corner was a beacon: "Don't go home," the sign seemed to say. "Come here."

I wasn't sure I belonged there. The other customers looked glamorous—like they'd just come from a party in a nearby loft or a performance-art event. Still, I claimed a seat at the bar. I hadn't thought about what I wanted to drink when the bartender asked me. As if compelled by some force outside myself, I blurted, "I'll have a martini." I didn't say gin or vodka. I didn't say olives or twist. I knew that whatever materialized in front of me would be just right. And it was: cold and clear and crisp, rendered with care.

That martini made me sit up a little straighter. It made me feel more self-possessed than my whiskey and beer. I felt as though I'd crossed an invisible border into adulthood, in a true and delicious way. I hadn't seen it all yet, but maybe I would. And I told the handsome bartender about my heartache, too. "I don't doubt for a sec that you'll move on," he said with a big smile. And that was true, too.

ROSIE SCHAAP IS THE AUTHOR OF *DRINKING WITH MEN*, A MEMOIR.

Wine 101

You've waited long enough—and read almost the entire chapter. It's time we turned to wine. Devon Broglie, the master sommelier and associate global beverage buyer for Whole Foods Market, teaches you how to choose the right one.

How to decide "by the glass"

• Avoid famous names. It's not that the heavyweights aren't good—but because they're in high demand, restaurants tend to mark them up.

• If you can swing it, opt for the second or third cheapest offering on the menu, not the cheapest. When a restaurant is putting together its list, it needs one low option. But that's not necessarily the one they put a lot of thought into. It's simply the least expensive that's drinkable, says Broglie. "The second and third cheapest are the wines that the sommelier had to search out," he says. "They're usually pretty fun, a blend of value and quality."

• Drink where you eat. A rule of thumb is wine and food from the same place tend to go together: Chianti with Italian food, an Argentinian Malbec with a big steak, a Loire Valley wine with French chèvre. That being said, if you love only Pinot Noir, don't feel pressured to order Chianti with your veal scaloppine.

How to select a bottle

• Know what you like. (See the following page for some guidance.)

• Look at the label. "The person making the wine also signs off on the label. I find that the outside is a good representation of what's inside. Old school–looking labels tend to be on old-school wines. Flashier labels tend to be flashier wines," says Broglie, who has done blind taste tests on this theory. "If the label resonates with you, you'll probably like the wine."

• Ignore the year. Unless you're buying at a high price point, it doesn't matter.

• Opt for the top you prefer—cork or screw top. Your dad might have told you that screw-top bottles are cheap or tacky, but that idea is outdated. Broglie says a cork is preferable for a wine that is meant to age. Otherwise there isn't much difference.

WHICH PINOT IS WHICH?

The varietals you're most likely to encounter—and how to tell them apart.

WHITE

CHARDONNAY: Very popular. A full-bodied wine. French Chardonnays are slightly crisper (think green apple). California versions are more ripe and juicy (more pineapple or mango).

SAUVIGNON BLANC: Generally, there's a grapefruit flavor to this wine. In France, it's more tart. In the U.S. and New Zealand versions, you find more melon and tropical notes.

PINOT GRIGIO: When you see this name, the wine should hail from Italy. A Pinot Gris, which is similar, can be from the United States, France, or other locales. Medium-bodied, peachy, and ripe, it falls between Chardonnay and Sauvignon Blanc in terms of acidity.

RIESLING: "Wine novices love Riesling because it's a little sweet, and wine experts love it because it has incredible balance and complexity," says master sommelier Devon Broglie. Stick with German bottles, where Riesling (pronounced *Reez*-ling) originated; look for the term *kabinett* or *spätlese* on the label.

RED

CABERNET SAUVIGNON: The most structure and body you'll find in a red wine, with a more tannic (or astringent) finish, which is why you typically drink it with heavier dishes and red meat. French Cabernets will probably hail from Bordeaux (Broglie likes the Medoc region). For U.S. picks, look for Cabernets from California's Napa or Sonoma Valley.

MERLOT: A bit less tannic than Cabernet, Merlot hails from the same places. France and California are the big producers.

PINOT NOIR: Pinot Noir is lighter and more medium-bodied compared with Cabernet and Merlot. It can be exciting and complex but can also cost more. France, California, and Oregon produce excellent bottles.

MALBEC: Lush like Merlot and full-bodied like Cabernet, without being too tannic or bitter. Argentina makes some of the best versions.

ROSÉ

Done right, a rosé should be dry, light, crisp, and refreshing—a perfect warm-weather drink. Rosés from the Provence region of France are popular, as are Pinot Noir rosés from California. Bonus: They're usually inexpensive.

BUBBLES

Champagne comes from the Champagne region of France—and nowhere else. The specific way it's made adds to the steep cost. Spanish Cava uses the same method but is much cheaper because it doesn't have the fancy rep. Prosecco tends to be lighter, sweeter, and more effervescent. Stick with Italian ones from the Valdobbiadene region.

The cheapster's guide to cocktails

There's a middle ground between vodka soda and the $18 artisanal potion you drank at that speakeasy last weekend. These classic recipes fall squarely in that zone. Each serves 4.

Gin and tonic

Stir 1 cup (8 ounces) **gin** and 3 cups **tonic** together in a pitcher. Serve over ice with a squeeze of **fresh lime** and a few slices of **cucumber.**

Gimlet

Combine 1 cup (8 ounces) **gin or vodka** with 1 to 2 cups **Rose's sweetened lime juice.** (This is typically a strong drink with a 1:1 ratio; adjust as desired.) Serve over ice with **lime wedges.**

Whisky sour

Combine ⅔ cup **simple syrup,** ¾ cup (6 ounces) **bourbon,** ½ cup **fresh lemon juice,** and ½ cup **fresh lime juice** in a pitcher. Serve over ice with **maraschino cherries.**

Dark and stormy

Combine 2 cups (16 ounces) **dark rum** (such as Gosling's Black Seal) and 3 cups **ginger beer** (such as Barritt's or Gosling's) in a pitcher. Serve over ice with **lime wedges.**

Rum punch

Combine ½ sliced **fresh pineapple,** 2 tablespoons **fresh orange juice,** 2 tablespoons **simple syrup,** 3 tablespoons **fresh lemon juice,** ¼ cup **brandy,** ½ cup **rum,** 2 cups (16 ounces) **apple cider.** Chill at least 4 hours before serving.

Bloody Mary

In a large pitcher, combine 3 cups **tomato juice,** ¾ cup (6 ounces) **vodka,** ⅓ cup **fresh lemon juice,** 1 to 2 tablespoons **prepared horseradish,** 2 teaspoons **Worcestershire sauce,** 1 to 2 teaspoons **hot sauce** (such as Tabasco), ½ teaspoon **celery salt,** and ¼ teaspoon **black pepper.** Divide 4 **celery stalks** and 4 **pepperoncini peppers** among the glasses and serve over ice.

Mimosa

Pour ¾ cup (6 ounces) cold, **fresh orange juice** into 4 Champagne flutes, dividing evenly. Top with ½ cup (4 ounces) cold **Champagne or sparkling wine.**

HOW TO MAKE SIMPLE SYRUP:
Whisk together 1 cup sugar and 1 cup warm water until the sugar is dissolved. Chill until ready to use.

IF YOU DO ONLY ONE THING...

"Remember—cooking is about three things: patience, practice, and persistence. In my early 20s, my cooking was fast, haphazard, and experimental, which made it fun for sure. But it was only when I learned to slow down, read, and think things through, build layers of flavor and stop touching my food so much, that I discovered how complex and deeply rewarding—how scientific but also how magical—cooking can be. And it was only by practicing these newly acquired skills over and over again that I was truly able to cook calmly and with total confidence, no matter the dish or the challenges it posed."

GAIL SIMMONS, a special-projects director for *Food & Wine* (which is owned by *Real Simple*'s parent company, Time Inc.), famously judges chefs on *Top Chef.*

CHAPTER 6

SPENDING AND SAVING THE RIGHT WAY

When it comes to your weekend plans, YOLO is a decent motto. When it comes to your money, though, it is an epically bad idea. Especially since (unless you're one of those irritating tech prodigies who sold her e-commerce start-up for billions) you probably don't have that many dollars and cents to play with. And for that you can blame your so-so salary, your sky-high rent, and your debts. That iTunes habit isn't helping, either.

What's more, this may be the first time in your life you've been 100 percent in charge of spending and saving money. You don't want to screw it up. So where can you learn how to smarten up your approach to money—from buying insurance to developing savvy habits that will last you from here to retirement? Turn the page.

The moneyphobe's glossary of financial terms

Don't skip ahead! You need to learn money jargon for lots of reasons, not the least of which is to feel confident and conversant with the people (accountants, bank representatives) who help manage your money. So pin your eyes open—Clockwork Orange–style if you must—and take in this info.

ASSETS: Anything that has monetary value. Think bank accounts (checking and savings), a house, a car, antiques, jewelry, cash, stock holdings, and mutual funds.

BONDS: A conservative type of investment. Bonds are, in essence, a loan from you to a government entity (federal, state, or local) or a business. In return, you most likely receive regular payments, plus interest—a.k.a. a steady stream of income.

CAPITAL GAIN: The increase between the cost of what you paid for, say, a stock, a mutual fund, or a bond when you bought it and its price when you sell it. When you make money by selling an investment for a higher amount than what you paid for it, in most situations you owe what is called capital gains tax.

CAPITAL LOSS: The opposite of a capital gain. The silver lining: Up to a certain amount of capital losses can be deducted on your taxes.

CREDIT BUREAUS: These organizations each keep a credit report on you. There are three major ones: Equifax, Experian, and TransUnion.

CREDIT REPORT: A compendium of financial facts about you. It lists all the credit cards you've had, any loans you've had, when you took out loans or opened lines of credit, your payment history, the amounts of your outstanding balances, and any bankruptcies, tax liens, or court rulings against you. A thrilling read? No. But it's really important because you won't be able to get credit cards or loans—or possibly even a job, depending on where you apply—unless your credit report is clean. You're entitled to a free credit report once a year from each of the bureaus. Go to annualcreditreport.com. And don't just Google these words, since there are a lot of bogus sites that look similar.

CREDIT SCORE: A three-digit number that lenders (for example, banks and credit-card issuers) use to determine your creditworthiness. It is a numerical representation of what's on your credit report and is calculated using information from each of the major credit bureaus. A score of 700 or higher is generally considered good.

DIVIDEND: A portion of earnings that is paid to a stockholder. You can usually choose to receive your dividend payment via direct deposit or have the money reinvested.

EARNINGS: The dollar amount of profit that a company earns. You'll often hear earnings described as "strong" or "weak," and they're usually quoted as dollars (or cents) per share. As in: *In the first quarter of 2015, Mega Corporation reported earnings of 78 cents per share.*

ELECTRONICALLY TRADED FUND (ETF): An assortment of stocks, bonds, and commodities, this investment is often a low-cost alternative to a mutual fund (see definition below).

GROSS INCOME: Your total income (your earnings and investment income) before subtracting taxes (state, federal, local) and any tax deductions.

INDEX FUND: A specific type of mutual fund or ETF that attempts to replicate the movements (ups and downs) of a specific portion of the stock market, such as the S&P 500, the Dow Jones Industrial Average, or the FTSE 100.

LIABILITY: Any debt that you owe, such as a car loan or credit-card debt. Long-term liabilities are debts that are paid over years or even decades; current liabilities are paid in full within a year.

MUTUAL FUND: This is a type of investment in which a pool of assets (stocks, bonds, cash) are lumped together and managed by investment professionals. Active mutual funds (the most common kind) aim to outperform index funds—in other words, make more money when the stock market is up and minimize losses when the market is meh.

NET WORTH: The amount that all your assets are worth once all your liabilities have been subtracted. Let's say you own an apartment that's worth $100,000, a car that's valued at $7,000, and $2,200 worth of investments. However, you have an $85,000 mortgage and a $5,000 student loan. Your net worth is—*bum-da-da-dum!*—$19,200.

PROFIT: The amount of money that a business makes after deducting all of its expenses (paying salaries, the cost of office space, employee-sponsored health insurance, staplers, etc.).

REVENUE: The amount of money that a company or the government brings in through its business.

REVOLVING BALANCE: The amount of spending on your credit card that goes unpaid from month to month. The larger your revolving balance is, the more you'll owe in interest.

STOCKS: A share in the ownership of a business. When it comes to buying stocks, there are two types available for purchase—common, which gives you voting rights even if you own just a single share, and preferred, which usually does not permit you to vote at shareholder meetings but entitles you to a bigger piece of the profits and earnings. Purchasing shares of individual stocks is considered riskier than owning bonds or mutual funds.

TARGET-DATE RETIREMENT FUNDS: A specific type of mutual fund in which a portfolio manager automatically adjusts the funds' holdings (and thus your risk) based upon how close you are to retirement. If you want to have investments but want them to be as low-maintenance as possible, these are the funds for you.

4 important questions
to ask before picking a bank

Back in college, when you got a checking account, you weren't picky. (They were giving away free totes!) But you're going to start having real money soon, so it would be best if your bank actually met your needs (besides your need for a free tote). Galia Gichon, the founder of the education firm Down-to-Earth Finance, helps you narrow the search.

1 | What matters to you the most about a bank?

Determine your top priority: Is it having a smartphone app that allows you to deposit checks instantly? Then narrow your search to national banks with the dough to put behind this type of service. Or are you more interested in doing business with an institution that shares your values or isn't "too big to fail"? "If you like to support local businesses or consider yourself socially minded, having a checking account at a local bank or a credit union is a great way to put your dollars into your activism," says Gichon.

2 | What are the bank's maintenance fees?

Once upon a time, nearly all checking accounts were free. Nowadays, if you're not careful, the cost of simply having one can reach triple digits annually. But here's the bottom line: You should never have to pay for a checking account. With most national banks and many local ones, you can avoid this maintenance charge if you meet certain requirements each month, such as direct-depositing a predetermined amount (typically $500 to $1,000 on a monthly basis) from the get-go, maintaining a minimum balance ($1,500 to $2,000), or making a certain number of purchases with your debit card. Don't assume that the biggest banks offer the best deals. "You can often negotiate to get this fee waived at small credit unions and savings and loans," says Gichon.

3 | Does the bank have handy ATM locations?

Ideally, pick a financial institution that has ATMs close to both your home and your workplace. Otherwise, every time you use a machine that's not affiliated with your bank, it will cost you a minimum of a few bucks per withdrawal. But if you rarely use cash, you may not need to choose the bank with an ATM just around the corner.

4 | Will your accounts be insured by the FDIC?

Regardless of where you do your banking—both checking and savings—make sure that your accounts are backed up by the Federal Deposit Insurance Corporation (FDIC). This means that if your bank goes under (and some did after the economic meltdown in 2008), your money will be returned to you—up to $250,000 total.

IF YOU DO ONLY ONE THING...

"Find something you believe in and invest in it. It's emotional investing, but you win either way: financially, if the project or cause takes off, or in other ways, by having the satisfaction that you supported something that touched you. It's much easier these days to find those sources of inspiration. And you only need to contribute a small amount."

AMANDA DRURY is a news anchor for CNBC.

WHERE TO STASH YOUR RAINY-DAY CASH

This one's a no-brainer. Just head online.

Chances are, you'll want a brick-and-mortar bank for your checking so you can easily hit up ATMs. But consider putting your savings into an online bank, such as Ally, American Express Personal Savings, or Capital One 360. (Choose one that can be linked to your checking account and lets you make transfers for free.) Since these banks don't have the expense of operating physical branches, they can offer you higher interest rates than those with physical locations. Also, since it's slightly more difficult to get to the money (it can take a couple of days to transfer money from an online bank), you will be less likely to dip into your savings when you want to make a withdrawal from the ATM but don't have the funds.

The truth about your credit cards

MYTH: You need only one.

FACT: More like two (not counting store cards). Ideally, your main card should be a rewards card that you use to charge everything, racking up points in the process. (Be sure that you pay the bill in full each month to avoid interest charges.)

The second card should be a backup, to be used primarily for emergency expenses. For example, your brakes go out and you must replace them stat. In case you ever need to carry a balance, make sure the card has a low interest rate (look for an APR in the midteens) and a high limit, such as $5,000 or more. Then use this card once a month. One idea: Set up one of your recurring bills, like electric, on auto pay to keep the account active, says Gerri Detweiler, the director of consumer education for the personal finance website Credit.com. Otherwise the issuer may close the account.

If you already have more than two credit cards, don't fret. Keep the accounts, as long as you're using them responsibly—meaning, you pay the balance every month and use less than 10 percent of your total available credit. But if you have a hard time keeping track of balances, due dates, and terms and conditions, then you might want to reduce the number you carry to two.

Befuddled by the best plastic practices—and all that fine print? In plain English, here's what you need to know.

MYTH: Moving a balance from, say, your Mastercard to a new Discover with a lower interest rate saves you money.

FACT: It seems as if 80 percent of your snail mail is made up of credit-card solicitations. And while the cover letters make it sound like balance transfers are awesome for everyone, that's not quite so.

On the pro side of balance transfers: You will reduce how much you owe each month, save money on finance charges, pay less in interest charges, and overall make your financial life simpler. The cons: Transfer fees could cost you as much as 5 percent of the balance. So moving $5,000 from card A to card B would cost you $250. Plus, the sweet deals, like zero-percent balance transfers for 18 months, are typically reserved for those with a spotless credit history.

Before applying for a new card that you plan to transfer a balance to, find out these important pieces of information from the issuer's website or a company representative.

- How long the introductory-interest-rate period lasts
- How much you need to pony up each month to pay off the balance before that time ends
- The balance-transfer fee
- The penalties you'll incur for late or missed payments
- Whether the "teaser rate" applies to new purchases

MYTH: Paying an annual fee is a waste of money.

FACT: Surprise, surprise: A card can be worth the cost. Before you sign up for one, however, do some math to see if the benefits pay for, or exceed, the yearly charge. Say an airline-sponsored card charges a $100 annual fee but allows cardholders to check one bag for free on every flight. If you take a few round-trip flights a year, you will come out ahead.

MYTH: There's no harm in signing up for store cards.

FACT: Who says no to a discount—especially when your closet is chock-full of concert T-shirts and you need a work wardrobe à la Olivia Pope? That's exactly what retailers count on when they offer promotions, discounts, rewards programs, zero-percent financing, and other perks if you open a card account with them. Some store cards can be worth having, but don't sign up for every one you're offered—that will put you at risk of racking up debt. "Get them only from the one or two stores that you frequent the most; otherwise you may lose track of when the various bills are due," says Bill Hardekopf, the chief executive officer of LowCards.com, a credit-card comparison site.

This rule of thumb especially holds true if you're in the market for something big that requires financing, like a new car. Why? Each application for a new credit card triggers an inquiry on your credit report. Opening several accounts in a short period of time makes you look like a risky borrower and could reduce your credit score by up to 30 points. As a result, you might only qualify for a loan with so-so terms.

If you're the type who never pays her credit-card bill in full, always say no to store credit cards. They usually charge interest rates that exceed 20 percent, compared with 14 percent and up for regular cards.

MYTH: One missed payment won't damage your credit score.

FACT: *Welll*, yeah, it actually could. Your score could plummet more than 100 points—especially if you had a great one (700 or higher). That's because the higher it is to begin with, the harder the fall. "Someone with a lower score is already seen as a risk, so their messing up is almost expected. As a result, they would potentially lose only 60 to 80 points," says Liz Weston, the author of *Your Credit Score.*

If making the payment totally slips your mind until the next month's statement arrives, there's not a lot you can do. Except set up automatic bill pay. Which, if you haven't done it already, you should get on it. Go ahead—we'll wait.

MYTH: Persuading your issuer to reduce your fees or increase your credit limit is like convincing Justin Bieber to put his shirt back on.

FACT: It's possible to do. Say you want a lower interest rate. Call customer service, mention that you've received a couple of the attractive competing offers, then tell the representative that you would like to remain a loyal customer but that you are weighing your options. Then ask, "What can we do to work this out?" instead of "What can you do for me?" "Using 'we' when you're talking about a solution creates a sense of working together toward a common goal," says Noah Goldstein, an associate professor of management and organization at the UCLA Anderson School of Management. Keep in mind, however, that if you've practiced poor behavior (maxing out your card, habitually skipping payments, or having poor credit), your issuer probably won't do you any favors.

MYTH: There's no difference between using a debit card and a credit card.

FACT: Debit cards have their benefits: Unless you overdraw, you can't spend more than the amount that's in your bank account, and you don't have to worry about late fees or interest rates.

Credit cards, however, are generally more consumer-friendly. According to federal law, a credit-card user will pay, at most, $50 if fraud occurs on a card. (Even better, many issuers offer zero liability, meaning you won't pay a penny.) In sharp contrast, a debit-card user can be on the hook for $500 if she doesn't report the unauthorized transactions within two business days of learning about them, according to the Federal Trade Commission. And if more than 60 days go by before the bank is informed of the fraud? Say *auf Wiedersehen* to all that money.

Use plastic for all online purchases and for all big-ticket items (sofas, coffeemakers, trips to Bermuda), since your credit-card company will refund your money if the item you purchased was misrepresented. This won't happen with a debit card. Additionally, when you use a debit card for certain types of purchases—those in which the final purchase price is unknown at the exact time of the swipe, like filling your tank with gas or making hotel reservations—the merchant can place a hold on your account and reserve more money for itself than you actually spend, says Linda Sherry, a spokesperson for the San Francisco–based watchdog group Consumer Action. Example: A gas station might freeze $100 (even though you bought only $20 worth of gas) for several days. If you need that money, you'll be out of luck until it removes the hold.

MYTH: With a "cash back" credit card, you basically get paid for shopping.

FACT: Alas, there's no (totally) free lunch—or Kate Spade trench. Yes, rewards-card issuers promise to give you back a percentage of your credit-card purchases every month—sometimes after you earn a preset minimum, ranging from $20 to $100. You receive the cash back in the form of a check, a credit toward your balance, or a gift card.

However, there are a few catches: You'll need a gold-plated credit score (720 or higher) to qualify for the cards with the best rewards, like those that offer 1 to 1.5 percent cash back on all purchases or up to 6 percent back in bonus categories, like dining or at designated retailers. Cards with the most lucrative rewards levy an annual fee of $50 to $100; their interest rates are higher on average than those for standard cards; and some issuers cap how much cash back you can accrue in a year. These cards can pay off if you are spendy in categories that offer cash back, like gas and clothing, says Beverly Harzog, a credit-card expert. But if you usually carry a balance, she says, "opt for a low-interest card or you'll spend more on interest than you'll ever get in cash back."

The cost of living

I was terrified of spending a dime. Then I figured out a new way to tally my own personal balance sheet.
By **Cristina Henriquez**

I CAN'T REMEMBER exactly how it started. $1.09 for a bar of soap. $7.99 for disposable razors. $22 for a wool winter coat from the thrift store. All of it felt like too much. I remember so vividly standing in the aisle of Walgreens, picking up a bottle of shampoo and putting it back again, having a conversation in my head that went something like this.

"Shampoo! Old friend!"

Put it back. You don't need shampoo.

"Oh, really? You need to wash your hair, don't you?"

But you don't want to spend money.

"But it's only $1.89."

But you don't want to spend money.

"Relax. It's OK. You can afford $1.89."

I left the store without the shampoo.

It was never really about the money, of course. I had just graduated from college and had walked at last into the wide-open world, which felt enormous and overwhelming. I had a job as an administrative assistant where I earned not very much, but enough to get by. Enough, certainly, to purchase shampoo. But I was scared of so much back then. Sirens blared near my apartment on the South Side of Chicago; cats clawed at each other in the alleyway as I tried to sleep; the radiators hissed and knocked. I was terrified that my boss would discover I had no idea what I was doing and expose me for the imposter I was. I was terrified that anyone would discover me at all, actually, not only at work but in life, and terrified, too, that they wouldn't. The bounds of the world felt so impossibly beyond me—and they were. I couldn't control almost anything—but I could control my money.

I sewed skirts with their uneven pleats and serpentine zippers. I gave myself haircuts, hoping no one would notice the blunt ends. I packed my lunches, said no to going out with friends, hoarded prepaid phone cards to keep from paying for long distance.

When my money anxiety got so bad that I had a panic attack, I sought out a therapist. Strangely, I remember almost nothing about the sessions—I went to only a few—but whatever happened must have helped.

Slowly, I found my bearings. The world was still huge, but within it I found a space that felt manageable and safe. Gradually, my fears diminished. The sirens, I told myself, meant someone was getting help; the radiators provided comfort through the long winters; I got better at my job. I learned to focus not only on the money I was spending but also on what I was getting for it in return. It was a lesson about the world: What you give, you get back.

From that point on, I went to Walgreens as often as I needed. I walked through the aisles and bought the razors, the soap, and, yes, the shampoo.

CRISTINA HENRÍQUEZ IS THE AUTHOR OF THE NOVELS *THE BOOK OF UNKNOWN AMERICANS* AND *THE WORLD IN HALF.*

Health insurance: A primer

In the immortal words of R.E.M., everybody hurts... sometimes. Which is why everybody needs insurance, regardless of her age or how many SoulCycle classes she rocks each week.

Stuff happens. And by stuff, we mean the flu, a sprained ankle, an errant bike messenger who zooms into your crosswalk at the exact moment you step off the curb. If you don't have insurance, even a small medical mishap can become a financial catastrophe. You are probably covered in one of three ways: through your parents' insurance; through your employer; or independently. Whichever situation applies to you, here's what you need to know.

If you're on your mom or dad's plan

You're good to go until the age of 26, at which point you will need to obtain it through your employer or purchase it yourself.

If your employer provides health insurance

Go ahead and select a plan offered by your employer. In general, if you are healthy and don't suffer from any chronic illnesses, you can consider a plan that has a lower monthly premium and a higher deductible. Just remember that if you do get sick or have an accident, you may need to cough up a lot out of pocket. This type of policy often has a health-savings account (HSA) attached to it, which allows you to set aside pretax dollars to be used for medical expenses. If the funds aren't spent during the calendar year, they roll over to the following year.

However, if you have a chronic illness or want the peace of mind of knowing that you have lower copays and deductibles, opt for a plan that charges more money up front.

Once you make your choice, be aware that you are committed to that plan until your company's next annual open enrollment period (typically in the fall), unless your job is terminated.

If you need to purchase insurance on your own

Head to HealthCare.gov, the federal health insurance marketplace, which presents all your insurance options in one place and in easy-to-understand language. (If your state runs its own marketplace, the federal site will redirect you there.) You'll see all the various plans that are available; the monthly cost, copays, deductibles, and out-of-pocket maximum costs of each plan; prescription-drug restrictions; the provider network; and whether you're eligible for a subsidy to help reduce your monthly expenses or cost-sharing reductions, which will lower your deductibles, copays, and coinsurance.

If you're worried that you will sign up for a junky policy, fret not. All individual plans sold through the marketplaces must meet minimum-coverage requirements established by the Affordable Care Act (ACA)—including emergency services, prescription drugs, rehabilitative services, lab work, and pediatric care. The ACA also prohibits insurance companies from denying you coverage because of preexisting conditions, and it kills all lifetime dollar-amount limits on necessary benefits, like hospitalizations. It also allows you to receive a number of preventative-care services—vaccines, blood pressure checks, depression screenings, a yearly physical, and in most cases contraception—for free, even if you haven't met your insurance deductible. Some also offer dental and vision coverage. All individual plans must include maternity coverage, too. And while that may not matter to you today, in a few years you might think differently.

Finally, when shopping the marketplaces, understand that all policies are categorized into four types—bronze, silver, gold, and platinum. A bronze policy, for example, may have a lower premium but could charge higher cost sharing or a higher deductible, whereas a platinum policy will probably have a higher premium but lower cost-sharing expenses. Regardless, the benefits are the same across all four tiers, protecting you from all sorts of medical-related financial worries.

MONEY-SAVING SECRET
EATING OUT? BE THE ONE WHO ORDERS FIRST

HERE'S WHY: According to research from the University of Illinois at Urbana-Champaign, peer pressure strongly influences your meal choice, even more so than price or calorie count.

"People eating together may not choose the exact same entrée, but they tend to pick dishes that are in a similar category," says Brenna Ellison, an assistant professor of agricultural economics and the study's author. So if your GF orders the expensive beef tenderloin, you're more likely to pick something of similar quality, like rack of lamb, even if that means you won't be able to pay your Visa bill for the month.

To keep dining-out expenses from eating up your budget, speak up first when the waiter takes your order, says Ellison. If you're planning to order only an entrée (saving money by skipping an appetizer or dessert), stick to that, even if your friend opts for a feast. Or scout the online menu and make a decision before you ever sit down.

How much insurance does one woman need?!

You already know you've got to have medical coverage, plus renter's or homeowner's insurance. But it seems as if there are about 5,000 other policies, from car to flood to (meow) pet. So, are they must-haves, or can you live without them?

GET IT

Auto insurance

If you drive, this coverage is a must. And it's illegal to drive without it in nearly every state. Your liability policy will include bodily-injury protection, uninsured- and underinsured-motorist coverage, and property-damage coverage. You should have at least $100,000 worth of coverage per person and $300,000 per accident for each of these types of coverage, says Jeanne Salvatore, a senior vice president of the Insurance Information Institute (III), an industry organization.

If you bought a new car and you financed the purchase, expect your lending institution to require comprehensive and collision coverage as well. If you have owned your vehicle for a while or paid cash for it but can't afford to replace it or pay for extensive repairs (some idiot runs into you or a tree falls on the windshield), elect to have this protection. Just cut your comprehensive and collision premiums by taking the highest deductible that you can afford. You'll save about 40 percent on the total cost by upping your out-of-pocket deductible from $250 to $1,000.

Disability insurance

More than one in four of today's 20-year-olds will become disabled at some point during his or her working life, according to the Social Security Administration. And by "disabled," we're not talking about broken legs. We're talking about people sidelined for weeks, months, or years by conditions ranging from depression to cancer. Yet fewer than half of workers in their 20s and 30s have disability insurance.

If you're lucky, your boss offers long-term disability insurance that pays 60 to 70 percent of your gross income if you're unable to work because of injury or illness. If your coverage falls short (which it's very likely to, particularly if you work for a small business), you can buy a supplemental plan on your own or through your employer that will cover up to 70 percent of your earnings. (Sorry, there are no plans that replace 100 percent of your income.)

If you have to find your own disability coverage, look for a guaranteed-renewable or noncancellable policy. While these options differ slightly, insurers in both cases must continue coverage without messing with your benefits—provided that you pay your premium on time. (However, your rates can still go up with guaranteed-renewable coverage.) To find a policy, check with the companies that sell health insurance in your state and make sure that the policy covers both accidents and illnesses. Costs vary widely, depending on your health, occupation, and level of coverage, but your monthly premium could be as low as $20 a month.

Renter's or homeowner's insurance
(See page 22 for details.)

EH, IT DEPENDS
Flood insurance

After shelling out for your first home, you don't want to see it or its contents submerged under inches (or—ack!—feet) of water. However, if a megastorm strikes your area, not only will you be left with a pile of waterlogged wreckage but, potentially, you'll be underwater financially as well. That's because homeowner's insurance generally excludes losses from floods.

If you have a federally backed mortgage on a house in a government-designated flood zone, you must obtain flood insurance. (Lenders will inform you if your home falls into that category.) And if you live within a mile or two of a body of water, even a small lake, it's generally a good idea to get flood insurance, which costs an average of $650 a year.

Life insurance

Single? Feel free to skip it. But if someone else relies on your income—a spouse, a new baby, or an aging parent—you should sign up. The insurance money will go directly to your bene-ficiaries tax-free if you die, helping to protect them from financial misfortune. At the very least, buy a policy that's equal to five to eight times your annual salary.

There are two types of life insurance: term and whole life. You want to sign up for term, which charges an annual premium over a predetermined time frame, rather than a whole life policy, which is (a) more expensive and (b) confusing—so much so that it's not worth explaining here. Also, sign up for the longest term possible (30 years is usually the max) to get the cheapest rate.

Pet insurance

You would do anything for Buster and Mittens. And that devotion costs you just over $500 annually, according to the U.S. Bureau of Labor Statistics. Which is why you might want to consider pet insurance, especially if you don't have money set aside for routine vet bills and the occasional "my Schnauzer ate a sock" visit to the doggie ER. Coverage can significantly reduce the price of many treatments and surgeries (with some policies reimbursing up to 100 percent of the cost), and you can choose any licensed veterinarian you wish.

Comparing policies side by side is difficult (these things never seem to be written by humans), so be aware that most plans will not cover charges related to a preexisting condition, such as diabetes or the hip dysplasia afflicting your Lab. And the issuer could drop your coverage or raise your premium unless you have a plan that specifically offers "continuing coverage." But if you're worried about how you'll pay the bill if your pooch gets sick, opting for a plan with a high deductible and a low monthly premium that will cover catastrophic events can be worth it.

Travel insurance

Getaways don't always go off without a hitch, as anyone who has been waylaid by a tropical storm knows. Travel coverage can soften the (financial) blow, since a comprehensive package—which costs 4 to 10 percent of your prepaid, nonrefundable trip expenses—will reimburse you for unexpected hotel stays, medical emergencies, charges for interrupted or canceled trips, and lost or damaged luggage.

Consider buying travel insurance any time you're required to make a big deposit—like $1,000 or more—or prepay for travel services that come with a big cancellation penalty. (We're looking at you, airlines!) Compare rates from independent insurance providers online and buy a policy within 7 to 21 days of your first trip payment. Note: If you decide to forego the coverage, you may still have a minimum level of protection through your homeowner's or renter's insurance or the credit card you used to book the vacation.

SKIP IT
Cell-phone insurance

After shelling out several hundred dollars for an iPhone, you don't want to be forced to buy a new one if you drop it in the toilet or if it gets stolen. These plans, however, aren't worth the dough you have to spend on them. Here's the reason: The replacement model provided to you might be a refurbished (not new) one, and it might be a completely different device than your original. And on top of the $8 to $10 you spend monthly on your policy, you will also have to pay a deductible of about $200. Bad deal.

Flight insurance

Even though plane crashes dominate news headlines when they occur, the chances of being a victim of one are close to zero. So go ahead and say no to this coverage—it pays only in the highly unlikely event that you are injured or killed in an airline accident. A life insurance policy is a much better buy. Or consult your credit-card issuer to see if it automatically provides flight insurance

when you charge a ticket. Discover, for example, provides up to $500,000 of flight accident insurance when you purchase an airline ticket with its card.

Rental-car insurance

At the rental counter, you'll be offered collision coverage—and a loss-damage waiver. Oh, and uninsured-motorist protection, too. Pass on all of these if you have a policy for your own wheels. Most regular car insurance protects you when you drive a rental, not just when you're in your trusty Civic. Additionally, some credit-card companies automatically offer insurance when you use their cards to pay for a rental. So tell the rental-car guy with his high-pressure sales tactics to back off, you're good to go.

IF YOU DO ONLY ONE THING...

"Acquire a savings habit. I wasn't born with one! When I was 30, a friend twisted my arm and forced me into the company retirement plan. It's amazing how easy savings become once they're taken out of your paycheck automatically."

JANE BRYANT QUINN is the author of *Making the Most of Your Money* and tons of other books about personal finance.

Budgeting for people who hate budgets

Here are three clever strategies that can help you achieve financial balance, and not one of them involves spreadsheets. Adopt them and you'll find it relatively easy to spend less.

Strategy No. 1: **Hide your dough.**

It's harder to spend what you don't have access to. Set aside a percentage of your pay in savings before it ever hits your pocketbook. Have your employer withhold money from each paycheck for your retirement account. (Turn to page 149 for details on the different types.) If you use direct deposit—and you should—you can also request to have most of your paycheck funneled into a checking account and the remainder into a savings account.

Another easy option is to have an automatic withdrawal that transfers money from your checking to savings. (How much is ultimately up to you.) Schedule this transaction for a day or two after you're paid so that the money goes away before you're aware of it—and you're not tempted to spend it on a new pair of yoga pants. Focus on fully funding your emergency account (a.k.a. your savings account) so that it has enough cash on hand for six months' worth of your most vital expenses (housing, transportation, food, utilities). Once you've achieved that, set aside at least $25 per paycheck to bulk up your savings even further.

Strategy No. 2: **Tally up those bad buys.**

In college, coffee not only woke you up for that 8 A.M. chemistry class but also sustained you during too-numerous-to-mention all-nighters.

Now, though, that venti-a-day habit is instead more likely to produce what's referred to as the "latte effect." This is the phenomenon whereby you fritter away small amounts of money on frivolous things and are barely aware of the cumulative cost until you add it all up. (This is why one classic piece of financial advice is "Brew at home.")

To eliminate—or, more realistically, reduce—mindless expenditures, look at your credit-card and bank statements several times a year. For each purchase, ask yourself, "Do I regret buying that?" You may be shocked to realize that you spent a disturbing amount on extra moves in Candy Crush. Then keep a list of any purchases that make you wince on your smartphone. Seeing where you spend too much can help prevent you from making the same mistakes again.

Strategy No. 3: Set aside a little extra for those long-term goals.

Maybe you wish that you could afford a new tablet. Or you're hoping to ditch that secondhand sedan for a new one. One easy move can make it more likely that you'll succeed: creating a new savings account with a name that specifically refers to your goal (such as "Elinor's Tablet Fund"). "Saving money is an abstract concept, but doing this taps into the emotional part of your brain," says Brad Klontz, Psy.D., a financial psychologist and a coauthor of *Mind Over Money*. Increase your resolve by posting photos that symbolize your goals somewhere you'll see them daily—like on the refrigerator or your work computer. When you save toward a clear goal that you genuinely want to achieve, you're more motivated—and less likely to feel as if you're doing without.

Only 40+ years to retirement!

You're a long way from 65. But the reality is, now that you're earning, you should be investing in your retirement. Go ahead—your future self will thank you.

"One of the biggest factors in determining how secure you will be in retirement can be how much you save and how early. By funding your retirement early on, you give that money more time to grow," says Alexa von Tobel, the CEO and founder of LearnVest.com, a financial planning and education website.

Sure, you may pooh-pooh the idea, especially considering how urgent your current expenses are and how many eons it will be before you qualify for AARP. But consider this: If you start saving a small percentage of every paycheck now, you could have a million (or even more!) by the age of 70. Wait until your 40s, however, and you may have to go back to eating ramen noodles in your golden years.

YOUR OPTIONS

NOTE: You may qualify for one or, at most, two of these types of accounts.

401(k)

WHO IT'S FOR: People currently working for a public or private company or a small business that offers a 401(k) plan.

ANNUAL CONTRIBUTION: Up to $18,000 a year.*

TAX STATUS: A regular (not Roth) 401(k) is a tax-deferred account, so you won't pay any taxes (federal or state) on your contributions or earnings until you withdraw the money during retirement.

403(b)

WHO IT'S FOR: Public-education employees, those who work for nonprofits, and clergy.

ANNUAL CONTRIBUTION: Up to $18,000 a year.

TAX STATUS: See 401(k). Basically the same rule applies.

Traditional IRA (individual retirement account)

WHO IT'S FOR: Anyone with taxable income who is younger than age 70½. It can be used in addition to a 401(k). There are no income limits for a traditional IRA.

ANNUAL CONTRIBUTION: Up to $5,500 a year.

TAX STATUS: Depending on your annual income and whether you have access to an employer-sponsored 401(k), you may be able to receive a tax deduction. Taxes are paid when you withdraw the money during retirement.

Contribution limits can fluctuate from year to year. Check irs.gov for the most recent figures.

Roth IRA

WHO IT'S FOR: Those whose annual gross income is less than $116,000 ($183,000 for joint filers).

ANNUAL CONTRIBUTION: Up to $5,500 a year.

TAX STATUS: You pay taxes (state and federal) on your contributions now. When you withdraw the money during retirement, all earnings are tax-free.

SEP IRA

WHO IT'S FOR: Those who are self-employed or who are small business owners.

ANNUAL CONTRIBUTION: Up to 25 percent of net earnings, with a maximum of $53,000.

TAX STATUS: Contributions are usually tax-deductible. A SEP IRA is a tax-deferred account, so you won't pay any taxes until you withdraw the money during retirement.

HOW MUCH TO CONTRIBUTE

If the financial pros had their way, you would max out your retirement account every single year—regardless of whether you have an individual account or an employee-sponsored one. But if that's not possible (don't feel bad—it's a pipe dream for 98 percent of us), try to contribute up to your employer's match, if one exists. For example, if your company offers a dollar-for-dollar match for up to 5 percent of your salary and you make $50,000 annually, if you contribute $2,500 to your 401(k), the company will add $2,500 to your savings. Nice.

If you can't survive on a paycheck that's that much smaller, start by putting $50 or even $25 a month into your retirement account, then increase your contributions later on. Or try setting aside 1 percent of your paycheck now and upping it to 2 percent in six months or a year. (Some retirement accounts offer the option of automatically increasing your contributions by 1 percent each year.)

HOW TO KNOW WHERE TO PUT YOUR MONEY

With 401(k)s and 403(b)s, you are typically restricted to a predetermined list of mutual funds, stocks, and bonds provided by your employer. Even given those constraints, you can have a diversified portfolio.

One way to achieve that goal is to employ the "rule of 120." Start by subtracting your age from 120. The number you get represents the percentage of your retirement savings that you should consider investing in stocks and mutual funds. (Generally, the younger you are, the riskier your investments should be.) So if you're 27 years old, you should invest 93 percent of your retirement savings in mutual funds and stocks. Once a year, do a check-in with your investments and make sure that your portfolio hasn't fallen out of balance. (Put an alert on your phone's calendar so you don't forget.) Don't keep noodling with your portfolio. "If you reallocate your savings too frequently, you may rack up unnecessary transaction fees and taxes," says von Tobel.

And if you don't have an employer-sponsored retirement account, where do you even start? If you feel clueless about all things Wall Street, consider working with a certified financial planner. Planners are either fee-based, meaning they charge a consultation fee and then possibly a commission, or fee-only, meaning they charge by the hour, by a percentage of assets managed, or by a flat fee or a retainer and do not earn fees directly from the companies they recommend.

You can also invest on your own through low-cost providers, such as Fidelity, Vanguard, and TD Ameritrade. They offer lots of investment options without the sky-high transaction fees . required by some brokerage houses. If you're not sure what to invest in, consider a target-date retirement fund. These mutual funds put investing on autopilot, since they automatically reallocate your holdings based on how close you are to retirement. If you're decades away, your portfolio is mostly stocks and mutual funds; as you near retirement, the allocation shifts toward bonds. Or consider an electronically traded fund (ETF), another low-cost investment option.

The 5-minute guide to your taxes

After a frigid winter, you welcome spring. The one dark cloud? Tax season. Allow us to answer some of the head-scratchers that accompany this grim occasion.

Should I DIY my taxes?

Well, how complicated is your financial life? In the previous year, if you held several jobs, earned investment income, were self-employed (either part-time or full-time), received an inheritance, or lived in several states that collected income tax, you have a fairly complex tax situation. Verdict: Hire a tax pro.

But if you have a salaried job and receive W-2 income (meaning your employer withholds money from your paycheck) and you rent (so you don't have any housing deductions), your taxes are pretty basic. So take a stab at figuring them out yourself. That being said, if you wake up in the night freaking out that the Internal Revenue Service (IRS) is going to come after you, use a tax preparer for peace of mind.

Speaking of which, how do I decide which type of tax professional to hire?

If you don't have too many variables, using a franchised tax service (such as H&R Block) is a good option. But if your situation is complicated in any way, hire an enrolled agent or a certified public accountant (CPA). All CPAs must complete a rigorous accounting education and be licensed in the state in which they work, giving them the ability to prepare taxes. (Although doing so isn't their only focus.) Enrolled agents, on the other hand, specialize solely in taxes. Licensed by the IRS, they must demonstrate that they are competent in all areas of taxation.

To find someone to take your case, ask your friends or family for recommendations. Hopefully, they will be able to suggest people whom they have confidence in and also give you a ballpark idea of how much the tax prep will cost. If they don't have any suggestions, go to the American Institute of CPAs (aicpa.org) or the National Association of Enrolled Agents (naea.org) to find someone locally.

If I do my taxes myself, should I use tax-prep software?

Yes. The software will walk you through the entire process by asking you questions that have tax implications. (For example: Do you have a student loan you're paying off?) Then it directs you toward the forms that might be involved with your situation. "Not everyone is going to be a tax geek, but these programs do help you to learn a little about how taxes work and how to plan better," says Kay Bell, the founder of the tax blog Don't Mess With Taxes. For many years, TurboTax ruled atop the Iron Throne of tax-preparation software, but now all the programs (including TaxAct.com, FreeTaxUSA.com, and HRBlock.com) are fairly comparable. Many have mobile-optimized sites and apps that will let you do your taxes on your phone.

For tax purposes, what receipts do I need to hold on to all year?

Keep receipts for medical expenses, charitable gifts, unreimbursed work expenses, educational or tuition expenses, tax-return–preparation expenses, and, if you're self-employed, business-related expenses (office supplies, mileage for work travel) for the previous calendar year. Keep them in a folder—physical or digital—so that they're easy to locate.

How long do I need to keep tax returns and the receipts associated with them?

You've deposited your refund, but that doesn't mean you should toss your returns and background documentation into the recycling bin just yet. The IRS has the right to review your return for up to three years, so you want to keep all your receipts as proof in case the tax agency hits you with an audit. (Chill: Only 1 percent of taxpayers are audited each year.) Hang on to your returns forever. They don't take up much space (none, if you save them digitally), and if a lender ever asks to see them, you won't have to request a copy from the IRS, a process that could take some time.

3 SUPER-COMMON TAX-RETURN ERRORS

Clocking in at 73,954 pages, the Internal Revenue Code is more than twice as long as *Les Misérables* and three times the size of *The Complete Works of William Shakespeare*. No wonder people often screw up. Learn from their foibles.

MISTAKE NO. 1: OMITTING INCOME

Perhaps you worked part-time as a sales clerk to earn some extra money. Maybe you nannied for a few months until you landed your first job post-grad. When you have numerous sources of income, it's easy to forget about something. "But regardless of how much or how little you earned, you must declare it as income on your taxes, even if you were paid in cash," says Cindy Hockenberry, the manager of the Tax Knowledge Center, an educational division of the National Association of Tax Professionals. Fail to do so and the Internal Revenue Service (IRS) could want even more money, in the form of penalties, in addition to what you already handed over. Stay organized by keeping a folder on your desk and place all tax paperwork (W-2s, 1099 forms, applicable receipts, pay stubs) inside it.

MISTAKE NO. 2: MISSTATING YOUR SOCIAL SECURITY NUMBER

Significant others may come and go, but this series of nine digits remains steadily by your side throughout your entire life. Although you can probably recite your identification number in your sleep, you may rush through and enter it incorrectly on your return. Double check—or triple-check—that you didn't transpose digits or leave one number out before submitting. Getting it wrong could mean a longer wait for your tax refund.

MISTAKE NO. 3: OVERVALUING NONCASH CHARITABLE GIFTS

Impressively, you've made a massive donation to charity and even remembered to pick up a receipt. Good job. But before you declare on your taxes that your trash bag of discarded clothes was worth $2,000, consider this: There are all sorts of deduction rules from the IRS that must be followed. (For example, that interview suit you bought for $250 may get you only $6 to $25 in deductions.) For a complete list of guidelines, check the Donation Value Guide at the Salvation Army's website (satruck.org). It's unlikely that you'll be hit with a penalty for overvaluing donations, but the IRS might adjust your return. So you could end up with a smaller refund or a larger tax bill than you anticipated.

How to go to your friends' weddings—without going broke

Get this: The average guest spends $592 per wedding, according to American Express. If you can't afford that kind of outlay, join the club. Learn how to get through wedding season sans bankruptcy.

The shower

Abby Larson, the founder and editor of the wedding blog Style Me Pretty, suggests "scouring a flea market for gorgeous vintage barware that any bride would love. Think ice buckets, Champagne saucers, trays, and cocktail shakers." Etsy and other online marketplaces can also be great, affordable resources for unique, personalized pottery and other serving pieces.

The engagement party

Consider a stock-the-bar gathering, where guests bring their favorite liquor or beverage that can be enjoyed by guests at the party and by the couple thereafter. Or throw a fancy potluck. "Guests bring their favorite dish and a handwritten recipe card that is tucked into a pretty box and gifted to the couple," says Larson. There's no need to spend more than $20 or so, says Kellee Khalil, the CEO and founder of Lover.ly, a wedding-inspiration website.

The bachelorette party

Ask each guest to contribute, say, $25, then "pool it to buy some fun party decor and a seriously wow-worthy lingerie gift for the guest of honor," says Larson. Increase the fun factor by having everyone bring a bottle of bubbly in a pretty shade of pink.

SAVING ON THE WEDDING GIFT
Remember thoughtfulness above all else.

While the average wedding gift costs between $75 and $150, according to data from TheKnot.com, nothing says that you need to give cash or even a gift that expensive. Khalil suggests "buying something small but special, like a vintage map of the couple's hometown or a locally made serving tray." Or if you have a particular skill, offer to help with the wedding (like putting together gift bags for the hotel rooms of out-of-town guests). You can also give cash if that's customary with your crowd. But include a personal note with a suggestion for how they could use the cash (couples' massage on their honeymoon).

Look for registry items in low-cost places.

Just because the happy couple registered at Saks doesn't mean that you have to buy their salad bowl there. Look for the item at a more affordable store or website and get it there. Then notify the store where they are registered to have the gift list updated to avoid duplicates. Note, however, says Khalil, "that buying a different version of something they registered for is a faux pas."

SAVING ON WEDDING ATTIRE
If you're in the wedding party

Ask the bride if you can do your own hair and makeup. The day-of glam-fest is often seen as a bonding event for the bride and her maids, but it can be stressful if you have to pay for it (on top of the dress, the shoes, and so on). "Consider presenting the bride with a few options: You could find your own stylists who are less expensive, you could do your own, or she could help cover the cost. She'll appreciate having a say in whatever alternative you end up with," says Khalil.

If you're not in the wedding party

See page 89 for cost-saving sartorial suggestions.

MONEY-SAVING SECRET
WEAR HEELS

HERE'S WHY: According to a study published in the *Journal of Marketing Research,* stabilizing your body can lead you to curb an overspending habit.

How does this work? Imagine a woman shopping while wearing stilettos. As she walks, she must exert effort to remain balanced. Crazy as it sounds, that leads her to be aware, if only subconsciously, of the principle of balance. And that in turn leads her to make more middle-of-the-road buying decisions. So a big spender will be inclined to buy more midpriced goods instead of deluxe items. (Conversely, a penny-pincher may drop a bit more cash than usual.) "Because you're balancing yourself, you'll find a more balanced product appealing," says Jeffrey Larson, an assistant professor of marketing at Brigham Young University, in Provo, Utah, and one of the study's coauthors.

Use this wacky bit of trivia to your benefit. The next time you're shopping online, say, and you want to avoid the urge to go for broke, lean back in your chair. In this case, what may be crummy for your posture may be terrific for your bank account.

CHAPTER 7

TAKING CARE OF YOUR HEALTH

You are young. You want to set the world on fire, burning brighter than the sun (h/t fun.).

So you have to take care of yourself. We chatted with some of the best researchers and clinicians to put together this head-to-toe guide. From stocking your medicine cabinet to maximizing your workouts to navigating birth control, here's the information you need to be the healthiest person you can be—now and for decades to come.

Your get-healthy, stay-healthy calendar

Turns out, it doesn't take that much to take care of yourself. Chances are, you're doing a lot of this stuff already (and Mom is patting herself on the back). But to help you keep it all in check and on schedule, we present this TLC timeline.

EVERY DAY

☐ **FLOSS AND BRUSH,** in that order, so bacteria and food particles have already been whisked away by the floss before you pull out the brush. Can't manage to do both? Then floss; it's more crucial.

☐ **APPLY A BROAD-SPECTRUM SUNSCREEN** with an SPF of 30 or higher. It will protect you against cancer-causing UVA and UVB rays. "An SPF 50 blocks 98 percent of UVB rays, while an SPF 30 blocks 97 percent," notes Barbara Gilchrest, a professor of dermatology at the Boston University School of Medicine. "These are not meaningful differences, particularly given that no one applies sunscreen in amounts that actually give the stated degree of protection."

☐ **DO AEROBIC EXERCISE** at moderate intensity for at least 30 minutes. Just five days a week is fine. Even 20 minutes on three days a week is OK, as long as you work up a serious sweat.

☐ **EAT PLENTY** of fruits and vegetables. A 25-year-old female who exercises at least 30 minutes a day should eat two cups of fruit and three cups of veggies daily.

☐ **TAKE 1,000 TO 1,200 MILLIGRAMS OF CALCIUM** and 600 to 800 international units (IU) of vitamin D daily if your doctor recommends it, says Donald Hensrud, M.D., editor of *The Mayo Clinic Diet.*

☐ **SLEEP SEVEN TO EIGHT HOURS.** The goal is to get enough sleep that you're able to leap out of bed each morning for work. (Admittedly, leap might be a stretch, but at the very least you should feel reasonably awake.) Seriously, sleep matters. Don't skimp on it.

A FEW TIMES A WEEK

☐ **LIFT WEIGHTS.** When you build muscle, you'll have an easier time carrying home that gallon of laundry detergent. You'll also strengthen your bones and speed up your metabolism, says Jennifer Hoehl, a New York City personal trainer and a spokesperson for the American College of Sports Medicine (ACSM). ACSM recommends working all major muscle groups two to three days a week, whether you use weights, elastic tubing, your own body weight (via push-ups, lunges, and so on), or household items (get your money's worth from that cat litter!). If you can do 12 to 15 reps, you're right on target. Any more and it's time to move to a higher level of resistance.

☐ **SEE YOUR FRIENDS. IN PERSON.** Texting your pals is not as good for your mental and physical well-being as being with them in real life. Head to an art museum, sing karaoke, take a pole-dancing class. Just don't do it solo. Research suggests actual social interaction with friends eases stress and enhances longevity, says Hensrud.

EVERY MONTH

☐ **LOOK AT YOURSELF IN THE MIRROR NAKED.** It's the best way to catch skin cancer early. The American Academy of Dermatology and the National Cancer Institute suggest doing a head-to-toe check in front of a full-length mirror after showering. Look for new skin markings and moles that have changed shape. (If there are marks that you can't see easily—like on your tush—you can ask your significant other to keep tabs, ask a close friend to take a gander now and then, or use a second mirror.) If any are asymmetrical, multicolored, or uneven around the edges, go see a dermatologist.

EVERY SIX MONTHS

☐ **VISIT THE DENTIST.** There's no official recommendation for the frequency, but most dentists suggest this semiannual schedule so that plaque doesn't build up too much. This will also keep you on top of cavities and any signs of trouble.

ONCE A YEAR

☐ **GET INOCULATED AGAINST THE FLU.** And don't tell us the shot always gives you the flu. That's a myth, my friend. There's a lag time of two weeks before it works, so get your vaccination in the fall (October is a good choice) and you'll be protected once the coughing and sneezing around you starts.

☐ **SEE YOUR OB-GYN.** Visit your obstetrician gynecologist every year for reproductive life planning and screenings (breast, pelvic exam) as needed. If you have a family history of breast cancer, she may suggest you be familiar with the feel of your breasts, so you can detect a change in the rare chance that one should occur.

EVERY 3 YEARS

☐ **SCHEDULE A CHECK-UP.** The nice people at the National Institutes of Health say you need only two physical exams in your 20s. But don't skip them, OK? The doctor will check your blood pressure, cholesterol levels, height, and weight to make sure you're on track. Every three years, your primary-care doctor or ob-gyn should also perform a Pap smear and HPV (human papillomavirus) screening, so that cells in your cervix can be screened for cervical cancer.

EVERY 10 YEARS

☐ **ASK FOR A TETANUS BOOSTER SHOT.** It will protect you from the toxic Tetanus bacteria that enter through punctures and cuts. Find out when your last shot was. Chances are, it was probably during your teens, in which case you're due for one right now or at some point before you hit 30.

WAIT—WHEN DID I GET THAT SHOT?

Why, how, and where to keep tabs on your medical contacts and history. Because emergencies happen.

Rocket science, it's not. Keep an accordion file, and whenever you come across anything health-related, toss it in. This old-school method is safer than keeping electronic files, says Sandra Fryhofer, an Atlanta internist and a past president of the American College of Physicians: "Computers crash, smartphones get lost—and with them goes your info."

But if you're more comfortable with the cloud than with a cabinet, choose a software program created by a company you expect to stick around. That could be one offered by your insurance company, HMO, or health network, says Lindsey Turrentine, the editor-in-chief of CNET.com. You can also keep your own e-file: Create a document with contacts, take a picture of relevant documents, then download and save them in a folder. Update and back up frequently. Here's what you should hang on to.

☐ **VACCINATION RECORDS (CHILDHOOD AND ADULT).** Before you book a visit to Botswana (or step on a rusty nail and panic), find out which shots you've had. First, call Mom, who may have this info stashed somewhere. Or try your primary-care doctor or childhood pediatrician. Worst case, you can request a blood test at any general practitioner's office to learn whether you've been vaccinated for certain diseases. However, in most cases, such as with tetanus, there's no harm in getting the

shot again. In the future, jot down each shot on an immunization sheet. (Download one at immunize.org.) "Since you can get shots from different sources—pharmacies, urgent-care clinics, your doctor—you need to keep track yourself," says Fryhofer.

☐ **TEST RESULTS.** Whether it's a blood test at your last physical or special exams done for a particular ailment, always ask for copies of the findings. Keep them forever—your medical history affects how a doctor might treat you for an ailment decades later.

☐ **A LIST OF DRUGS YOU TAKE ON A REGULAR BASIS,** including birth-control pills and supplements (even your green-coffee-bean extract).

☐ **A LIST OF YOUR ALLERGIES**

☐ **A LIST OF YOUR HEALTH-CARE PROVIDERS AND THEIR CONTACT INFORMATION**

☐ **YOUR FAMILY'S HEALTH HISTORY.** If you've never asked Dad about whether his gastro issues are genetic, now is the time.

☐ **AN EMERGENCY CONTACT.** Pick one. Ideally, choose someone who is conscientious, local, and, if possible, a family member, says Fryhofer. After you select this wonderful person, tell her. Then type "ICE" (for In Case of Emergency) in front of her name in your smartphone; paramedics and ER docs will know what this means.

The cure for what ails you

Can't remember how you're supposed to treat the tummy ache, a charley horse, or some other malady that's beached you on the couch? Read on for the best tried-and-true remedies.

THE PROBLEM: Common cold or flu

THE RX

BOLSTER YOUR IMMUNE SYSTEM at the first sign of a tickly throat with zinc and vitamin C supplements, which may reduce the duration of a cold. Hit the water bottle, too. If your pee looks very yellow and concentrated, drink up. Also sip some chicken noodle soup, which has been scientifically proven to ease cold symptoms.

REDUCE FEVER AND HEADACHE with ibuprofen and a cool washcloth.

SOOTHE YOUR THROAT with mint or lemon tea and honey. Reduce swelling by gargling with a teaspoon of salt mixed with a cup of warm water.

LESSEN SINUS AND CHEST CONGESTION with a decongestant, which is designed to open nasal passageways. Carefully read the labels of combination cold products—the kind with a pain reliever *and* a decongestant—so you don't double dose on pain relievers.

CONTROL SNEEZING and runny nose with an antihistamine, which is formulated to dry up excess mucus.

REST. No excuses.

CALL YOUR DOCTOR IF your fever exceeds 101 degrees Fahrenheit or it doesn't break after two days. This could signal a bacterial infection, in which case you'll need a prescription medication, such as an antibiotic.

THE PROBLEM: Gastrointestinal nasties (nausea, indigestion, diarrhea)

THE Rx

ALLEVIATE THE NAUSEA with a ginger herbal tea, or make it yourself by steeping chopped ginger in a cup of just-boiled water. Skip the ginger ale. While it can hydrate, it contains little (if any) of the root.

STAY HYDRATED. When you've got issues keeping things down (or up), you lose a lot of water—not good, because water helps your blood flow to your organs and keep them functioning. So drink plenty of fluids: the gingery concoctions above, plus water, regular tea, and sports drinks, like Gatorade, which help replace lost salts and minerals. Don't gulp the whole drink down at once, which may make you even queasier. Avoid juice, coffee, and other acidic drinks, which exacerbate the issue.

EAT STRATEGICALLY. Crackers, toast, and dry cereal can be digested easily. As you feel better, nibble on some eggs, boiled or scrambled, or plain yogurt. (Yogurt is extra-helpful due to its gut-healthy flora.) Stay away from high-sugar, high-fat foods, which can worsen diarrhea. If you don't have the luxury of being near a bathroom, take Imodium. It will stop the runs temporarily. However, what goes in must come out, so taking it will delay getting the virus to vacate the premises.

CALL YOUR DOCTOR IF your digestive issues grow increasingly worse or last longer than 24 hours, or if you experience severe abdominal pain. Stomach problems could also be a symptom of other types of conditions that require medical treatment.

THE PROBLEM: Cut, scrape, or wound

THE Rx

STOP THE BLEEDING by applying pressure with a towel or a tissue.

CLEAN THE AREA. Rinse away germs and debris with antiseptic or warm, soapy water. Apply a thin layer of antibiotic ointment.

KEEP IT MOIST, so that new skin cells can grow. The ointment will do that, but help it along by covering the wound with a bandage (which will keep you from picking at it, too).

CALL YOUR DOCTOR IF the bleeding won't stop or the cut looks deep (you may need stitches); or if the wound is accompanied by discharge, has red streaks, or feels hot, which suggests that it's infected. If the puncture is from a potentially dirty piece of metal (such as a knife used on raw meat) or from an animal bite and there's a chance you haven't received a tetanus shot in the last five years, get vaccinated immediately. If it's a shallow wound and you've been vaccinated within the last 10 years, you might get away with not getting another shot.

THE PROBLEM: Minor burn

THE Rx

DECREASE YOUR SKIN TEMPERATURE by running cool water on your burn for 15 minutes. Take naproxen or ibuprofen for pain. And don't break the blister.

COVER THE AFFECTED AREA loosely with a gauze bandage. (Ignore the Internet: Butter will not work and can lead to infection. Plus, it smells.)

REPEAT THE ABOVE twice a day until pain abates.

CALL YOUR DOCTOR IF the pain worsens; if you notice swelling, blood, or pus; or if the area isn't improving after a week. You may have a more severe burn, which will require antibiotics, special dressings, or skin grafts.

THE PROBLEM: Pulled or sore muscle

THE Rx

REDUCE SWELLING by applying ice wrapped in a towel, resting the muscle, and keeping it elevated.

REDUCE PAIN by taking ibuprofen and applying a topical analgesic cream, like Tiger Balm.

PREVENT STIFFNESS once the pain has subsided by gently stretching. After three to four days, you can soak in a hot bath. Moist heat enhances circulation and loosens muscles.

CALL YOUR DOCTOR IF your injury prevents you from walking or the soreness hasn't improved in a week. You may have sustained a more severe injury, which requires medical treatment.

3 SYMPTOMS THAT WON'T GO AWAY ON THEIR OWN

DIY medical care has no place here. If you experience any
of these disturbing sensations, call your doctor, stat.

1 | YOU'RE PEEING A LOT MORE THAN USUAL.
In fact, you have to go right now. You could
have a bladder infection, says Brian Stork, a
urologist and a spokesperson for the American
Urological Association. (A common risk factor
is an irritated urethra, which can happen after
sex; that's why you might notice symptoms
about two days after intercourse.) See your
doctor for antibiotics. If you also experience
severe pain in your upper back and abdomen,
nausea, and vomiting, you might have a kidney
stone. If it's a small one (less than four milli-
meters), your doctor may send you home with
painkillers and have you pass it yourself. If it's
larger, they can provide additional treatment.
Worst case, you may require surgery. If a fever
accompanies your symptoms, call your doctor
or go to the ER.

2 | YOUR VAGINA IS...SO...ITCHY. Plus, it really
hurts if you go to the bathroom or have sex.
It may be a yeast infection, which can affect
either your vagina or vulva but is no big deal.
Your gyno can give you meds for your first epi-
sode, then recommend over-the-counter meds
for any future flares. However, if you feel more
of a burn and you see a discharge, it could be
an STD, such as trichomoniasis, chlamydia,
or gonorrhea. This requires speedy treatment
with antibiotics.

3 | YOU GET A SHARP ABDOMINAL PAIN when
you sneeze, cough, or take deep breaths. Is this
pain down and to the right of your bellybutton?
It could be an infected appendix, requiring antibiotics and possibly surgery. If you can't reach
your doctor quickly, head to the ER.

AND NOW FOR A MESSAGE ON SMOKING...

DON'T DO IT. If you've never picked a cigarette up or you quit smoking already, congrats.
You've drastically cut your risks for many
cancers and other awful conditions. Still puff-
ing? You have no greater health priority than
to wean yourself off, *now.* Talk to your doctor about safe, proven methods of quitting,
such as the nicotine patch, counseling, and
hypnosis. What *doesn't* work so well: switching
to e-cigarettes. They have lower levels of toxic
substances than real cigarettes, but much
is still unknown about their long-term effects.
Their vapors contain tobacco-related carcino-
gens and metals. Plus, there have been reports
of e-cigs causing eye irritation, nausea, headaches, sore throats, vomiting, and coughing.

YOUR FIRST-AID ESSENTIALS

Don't fall prey to the next nosy houseguest (not that you have anything to hide, but still). Stock a complete range of health products and the only thing curious visitors will discover is that you're super-organized and prepared for any ailment that might befall you—or them.

☐ **IBUPROFEN,** which does everything aspirin and acetaminophen can do but is also more effective on menstrual cramps. Like aspirin, it can irritate the stomach, but it doesn't damage the liver in high doses, which acetaminophen might.

☐ **DIGITAL THERMOMETER**

☐ **DECONGESTANT,** such as Sudafed. In some states, you'll need to show ID to get it.

☐ **THROAT LOZENGES**

☐ **NONSEDATING ANTIHISTAMINE,** such as Claritin or Zyrtec, which allows you to combat the effects of pollen without zonking out at your desk.

☐ **ZINC AND VITAMIN C,** for a last-ditch effort to fight off that tickle in your throat before it morphs into a bad cold.

☐ **HYDROCORTISONE CREAM,** for persistent itching.

☐ **ANTACID,** such as Zantac or Prilosec.

☐ **BANDAGES, GAUZE, AND MEDICAL TAPE**

☐ **ANTIBIOTIC OINTMENT,** such as Neosporin, to prevent infection.

☐ **ANTISEPTIC,** such as Bactine, to remove microbes and dirt from a wound.

☐ **BROAD-PROTECTION SUNSCREEN** of SPF 30 or more.

☐ **ANTIFUNGAL CREAM,** such as Tinactin.

☐ **ACE BANDAGE**

☐ **COLD-SORE MEDICATION,** if you're prone to breakouts.

☐ **CALCIUM,** to keep bones strong.

☐ **VITAMIN D,** because calcium can't do squat without an assist from vitamin D.

☐ **EMERGENCY CONTRACEPTION,** like Plan B One-Step, which can be purchased at a drugstore without a prescription.

☐ **PEPTO-BISMOL,** for an upset stomach.

☐ **IMODIUM,** for diarrhea.

☐ **TOPICAL ANALGESIC,** like Tiger Balm or ActivOn.

GOOD-BYE TO ALL THAT (ASPIRIN)

Straightening up the fridge is a cakewalk. If you find something fuzzy and green (and it's not a kiwi), it's history. But your medicine cabinet is another story. Here, what to keep and what to toss.

Q. I'VE HEARD I SHOULDN'T KEEP MEDS IN THE MEDICINE CABINET. TRUE?

A. Read the labels. Some meds (like an unopened bottle of insulin, for diabetics) need special handling, like refrigeration. But most health-related items (including ibuprofen, birth-control pills, vitamins, condoms) should be stored in a cool, dry place, away from direct sunlight. So the cabinet in your bathroom, assuming you prefer hot showers, has at least two strikes against it. Translation: You're better off putting all of it in a cabinet, a closet, or a bin in your bedroom.

Q. HOW IMPORTANT ARE EXPIRATION DATES? CAN I TAKE PILLS THAT EXPIRED LAST MONTH? WHAT ABOUT THREE YEARS AGO?

A. According to the U.S. Food and Drug Administration (FDA), expired medicines may undergo a change in chemical composition that makes them less potent. This is even more likely if you keep them in a moist place, like your bathroom. When in doubt, throw it out.

Q. WHAT'S THE RIGHT WAY TO DUMP OLD MEDICATIONS?

A. In most cases, you should follow the directions on that little fine-print insert that came with the drug. Whoops, you threw it out? You can call your pharmacist for advice, or follow this slightly weird protocol recommended by the FDA for disposing of most meds (over the counter or prescription).

1 | Remove the drugs from their packaging.

2 | Mix them with something gross, like cat litter or old coffee grounds, so that pets and dumpster divers won't ingest them by accident.

3 | Seal this unsavory combo in a bag, so it won't leak into the rest of your garbage.

How to find Dr. Right

If you've done tons of recon to decide on a new colorist (two hours on Yelp and counting!), then surely you can do legwork to track down a primary-care doc. Follow these steps and you'll improve your chances of zeroing in on a person you trust and respect.

1 | Ask for recs.

Find out from family and close friends whether they like their own GPs. Ask your derm, ob-gyn, and other health-care providers who they would recommend in your area. They will probably point you to people who practice with a similar philosophy, says Judy Cook, M.D., the author of *To Die or Not to Die: Ten Tricks to Getting Better Medical Care*. With every referral, find out the reason behind the suggestion. Does your aunt like Dr. X because she's super-nice, available via text, or encyclopedic in one particular area? Then ask yourself if those qualities match what you would like to see in your physician.

2 | Do a little detective work.

Log on to ZocDoc.com, where you'll find reviews from people that the site has verified as actual patients. If Dr. X still sounds good, check her bio on the site to make sure that she's board-certified. If it doesn't say, try searching her name at certificationmatters.org, a free site run by the American Board of Medical Specialties. This designation means that, besides having a license in the state in which she practices, she also underwent a rigorous process of additional testing and peer evaluation. And don't you want an overachiever as your doctor? We thought so.

3 | Figure out if you can afford her.

Call the office and see if Dr. X takes your health insurance. If not, find out whether your insurance policy covers out-of-network care. You may be able to swing it if the policy is reasonable and you're willing to do the required administrative tasks—e.g., paying up front and then filling out a form to get reimbursement. (Caution: If you are terrible with paperwork, then move on.) If you're good to go on the financial front, see if her office hours work with your schedule—even the best doctor won't do you any good if the hours are 9 to 5 and you never make it out of work before it's dark outside.

4 | Schedule an informational chat.

This is especially important if you have a specific ongoing medical concern, such as weight-management issues, allergies, digestive problems, or a smoking addiction. If the physician isn't willing to have such a chat, you may want to move on to one who does. Or, if you don't mind, leave the assessment for your first visit. Ask her about her experience in the area of your greatest concern. Find out about her approach. Is she conservative when it comes to prescribing? If you also happen to go to, say, an acupuncturist for back pain, what are her thoughts on complementary medicine? It's also worth asking who would fill in for her when she's away, if she corresponds via e-mail or text, and how to reach her in an emergency. Ask whether she has a good team of specialists she relies on and at what hospital she has admitting privileges, says Anita Varkey, an internist and a clinical associate professor of medicine at Loyola University Health System, in Chicago. Pay attention to how she speaks to you. Can you have a real conversation, or does it feel as if she's talking at you? Do you feel comfortable asking questions? Before you leave, ask the front desk about typical wait times and how quickly you might get an appointment if you're sick.

HEALTH OOPS! No. 1

"I'm crashing at someone else's place for the night and I don't have a toothbrush."

HOW TO FIX: From a health standpoint, it's no big deal if you skip a brushing—it takes about 24 hours for bacterial plaque to build up on teeth. As long as you brush and floss diligently the next day, your teeth won't mind. In the meantime, try to remove particles by eating something crunchy, such as a carrot or apple. You can remove additional particles with a cotton swab or a finger dabbed in your host's toothpaste. Then swish with water or mouthwash.

Why do I always feel like [expletive redacted]?

Everybody has her crappy moments. (Maybe you caught a stomach bug; maybe Mercury is in retrograde.) Sadly, some women cope with symptoms 24/7. Here are the basics on the most common chronic afflictions. Read up, then consult your own doctor for more info.

"I get killer headaches."

IT COULD BE: Chronic migraines.

IF YOU FEEL intense throbbing on one side of the head along with nausea, vomiting, and sensitivity to light and sound, lasting for hours or several days.

YOUR DOCTOR MAY suggest that you keep a journal and make note of the things or habits (certain foods or medications, or lack of sleep) that seem to trigger migraines, says Jason D. Rosenberg, M.D., the director of the Johns Hopkins Headache Center at Bayview, in Baltimore. If adjusting your lifestyle and over-the-counter migraine remedies don't work, your doctor can prescribe stronger medication or alternative treatments.

A GREAT RESOURCE: American Migraine Foundation, americanmigrainefoundation.org.

"I constantly feel sad."

IT COULD BE: Clinical depression.

IF YOU FEEL your state of mind is not allowing you to enjoy things you usually love, every day for most of the day for at least two weeks, and it's tough for you to get through day-to-day life— from doing your job to maintaining relationships.

YOUR DOCTOR MAY refer you to a mental-health specialist who will take a history, discuss your symptoms, and recommend behavioral therapy, antidepressants, or both.

A GREAT RESOURCE: Anxiety and Depression Association of America, adaa.org.

"I am stressed all the time."

IT COULD BE: General anxiety disorder.

IF YOU FEEL worried "extremely frequently and about a variety of things," says Amy Przeworski, an assistant professor of psychology at Case Western Reserve University, in Cleveland—so much so that the anxiety interferes with your home life, work, and relationships. The stress may keep you from sleeping and can give you headaches and gastrointestinal issues.

YOUR DOCTOR MAY prescribe anti-anxiety meds, antidepressants, or beta-blockers (which help ease physical symptoms); depending on the condition, she may also suggest psychotherapy.

A GREAT RESOURCE: Anxiety and Depression Association of America, adaa.org.

"I drink. A lot."

IT COULD BE: Alcohol addiction.

IF YOU FEEL you always crave booze and/or go through withdrawal symptoms when you can't get a cocktail. Or you can't stop drinking once you get started. You may also spend a lot of time thinking about drinking and recovering from bouts of drinking. (Just have a hangover? See page 170 for what makes it better—and what doesn't.)

YOUR DOCTOR MAY talk with you about your relationship to alcohol. If your alcohol abuse has not progressed to a full addiction, she can suggest ways to cut down. (For women, low-risk drinking is no more than three drinks on a single day and no more than seven drinks a week.) If you're already dependent, she may refer you to a detox program or counseling or pursue medication in severe cases.

A GREAT RESOURCE: National Institute on Alcohol Abuse and Alcoholism, niaaa.nih.gov.

"I'm forever having gastro issues."

IT COULD BE: Irritable bowel syndrome.

IF YOU FEEL abdominal discomfort associated with bowel movements, at least three times a month in the last three months, and you have no other medical condition that can explain it. Some people experience IBS as pain and discomfort; others as diarrhea or constipation.

YOUR DOCTOR MAY conduct a physical exam and take a history of your symptoms. She may also do other diagnostic exams, such as a stool or blood test, a colonoscopy, or abdominal ultrasound. She'll also talk to you about dietary changes, stress management, and physical activity, says

Spencer Dorn, the vice chief of gastroenterology at the University of North Carolina, Chapel Hill. She may also prescribe medication, such as fiber supplements, probiotics, laxatives, or antispasmodics, which help control colon muscle spasms.

A GREAT RESOURCE: International Foundation for Functional Gastrointestinal Disorders, iffgd.org.

"I keep losing weight when I'm not even trying."

IT COULD BE: A thyroid disorder.

IF YOU FEEL anxious and weak while noting significant weight loss. These are common symptoms of hyperthyroidism, in which your thyroid gland is making too much thyroid hormone, a substance that plays a central role in the function of nearly all major organs. Conversely, if you're often cold and you have symptoms like weight gain, hair loss, and/or dry skin, you may have hypothyroidism, in which you're producing too little thyroid hormone.

YOUR DOCTOR MAY take your medical history, perform blood tests, and do a physical exam, before prescribing medication that will (in the case of hyperthyroidism) bring thyroid levels to a normal state. In the case of hypothyroidism, she may replace the missing levels of hormones.

A GREAT RESOURCE: American Thyroid Association, thyroid.org.

"I'm terrified of gaining weight."

IT COULD BE: An eating disorder (ED).

IF YOU FEEL like obsessing over how you might avoid food or lose—through purging or over-exercising—the calories you've just consumed. You may also have an ED if your pursuit of thinness causes you to fall 15 percent or more below a healthy-range body weight or suffer unusual side effects, like missing periods.

YOUR DOCTOR MAY treat the conditions caused by the ED, such as anorexia nervosa or bulimia nervosa, and advise counseling, such as cognitive behavioral therapy or family-based therapy.

A GREAT RESOURCE: National Eating Disorders Association, nationaleatingdisorders.org.

THE HEALTH ISSUE YOU SHOULDN'T PROCRASTINATE ABOUT

Don't wait until your 50s to think about osteoporosis. Bone up here.

Those TV commercials may have you thinking that low bone density is only a concern for Women of a Certain Age, but it's something for younger women to be aware of, says Alan Hilibrand, a professor of orthopedic surgery and neurosurgery at Jefferson Medical College, in Philadelphia. That's because your bones reach peak density somewhere between your late teens and mid-20s. After that, you lose as much bone as you build, and that loss accelerates with age, which is why broken hips are such a problem among the older population.

Seize the moment and maximize that bone-building process while you still can: Lift weights, climb stairs, play tennis, just walk. In fact, any aerobic activity in an upright position—elliptical machine, Stair-Master, jogging—helps strengthen bones. And ask your doctor if you should take calcium and vitamin D, both of which are essential to building bone.

CAN YOU MAKE A HANGOVER LESS HORRIBLE?

Aaron Michelfelder, a professor of family medicine at Loyola University in Chicago, offers these tips to ease your pain.

Think before you drink, and pick a clear alcohol instead of a dark one, like bourbon or red wine. Darker drinks contain more congeners—compounds that add flavor and color but also spark a toxic, inflammatory response that can bring on a hangover. You can also pop Hangover Prevention Formula, an herbal supplement that can prevent some symptoms, two hours before you start drinking. Take a painkiller the night of and once the dreaded morning arrives. (Anything but acetaminophen, a.k.a. Tylenol, since it is processed through the liver—and your liver is already working overtime.) Eat something easy to digest, like a banana or toast, without butter. Contrary to popular belief, greasy foods don't help. In fact, they can aggravate an upset stomach. And get out of bed if you can. Exercise—a walk, not a spin class—will increase circulation by up to three times its normal rate and get your lungs going. Hangover-inducing toxins are filtered through the liver, kidneys, and lungs. A little exercise can speed up the process.

Browbeaten no more

*I hated my "hideous defect," and no one—not my mom, not Frida Kahlo—could change my mind. How I transformed my body image. By **Jessica Soffer***

IRAQI JEWS CONSIDER BODY HAIR on females to be a sign of beauty. And because my father was an Iraqi Jew, I operated on that assumption—feeling just pride in my fuzzy arms and legs and unibrow—until a little punk in my second-grade class said I looked like a chimp.

I started begging for hair removal that evening, but it wasn't until fourth grade that my mother gave in, letting me Nair my legs. However, she insisted that the unibrow remain. "It's on your face," she said. "And it's who you are." My father had one too, so maybe she felt like it would be an insult to him and his culture, or maybe she just wanted me to love myself. It didn't work. I felt beastly. Sometimes I'd scratch at the area, hoping the hairs would fall out; and if one did, I'd wish on it (as if it were an eyelash) that the rest would follow. In the meantime, I wore glasses with no prescription to cover the bridge of my nose and avoided my reflection. I was certain I was the opposite of kempt, the opposite of pretty.

My mother promised me, finally, I could get my brows waxed when I was 12. On my birthday, on the way to the waxer, my mother invoked the famously unibrowed Frida Kahlo, mentioning her artistic brilliance and independence. Sorry, Frida: Within minutes of arriving at the aesthetician's office, my own unibrow was gone.

For the next decade-plus, I waxed diligently, and between appointments I used a magnifying mirror to scavenge for hairs and tweeze them out.

But last year something shifted: I grew tired of all the upkeep, which didn't feel like me. I met with a "brow expert," who convinced me to let my unibrow grow back in so, as she put it, "we can see what you really have."

In the weeks that followed, I didn't touch a tweezer. At first, I wore sunglasses to hide my face. But eventually I abandoned them. I sort of forgot about my unibrow. Once I stopped thinking about fixing my brows, I had stopped thinking about them entirely.

Soon enough, the brows I hadn't seen in 16 years were back. When I went to my follow-up appointment, the stylist was thrilled. "They're amazing," she said, the first time anyone had ever complimented them. She shaped them ever so slightly. "How do they feel?" she asked.

As I looked in the mirror, two things popped into my head: that once again I looked like my father; and that I wasn't an insecure, body-hating 12-year-old anymore.

"They feel like me," I said. The stylist put down her tweezer. We were done.

JESSICA SOFFER IS THE AUTHOR OF THE NOVEL *TOMORROW THERE WILL BE APRICOTS.*

YOU DON'T KNOW YOU'RE BEAUTIFUL

And you're not alone. In one survey, nearly four out of five adult women said they had complained to someone about their looks at least once in the last month. How can you feel more confident in your body? Jes Baker, a blogger and the founder of the Annual Body Love Conference, gives her best suggestions.

RECOGNIZE THAT BODY HATE IS LEARNED. All of us started out as small children who reveled in our bodies. We thought they were miraculous things with fingers and toes that you could put in your mouth and a belly you could squish. And somehow, since then, we've changed into adults that feel like our bodies are broken, inferior, and ugly. But you know the neat thing about all this jazz being learned? We can unlearn it.

REMEMBER THAT HAPPINESS IS NOT A SIZE. I used to look at old pictures of myself and spiral into a place of shame. I was so much skinnier back then, I would think. Which meant I was more beautiful. And which meant I was happier. But these days I'm fatter than I have ever been and somehow happier, too. I have a career and mission in life. I have fulfilling relationships. I am solid in my beliefs. I have people who love me, lovers who want me, and goals that I'm achieving.

This simply proves that happiness is not a size. Happiness is about finding what you love about yourself and sharing it. Happiness is about taking what you hate about yourself and learning to love it. Happiness is an internal sanctuary where you are enough just as you are.

WEAR WHAT SCARES YOU. I remember the first time I wore a crop top. Feeling the breeze on my stomach felt so vulnerable and, well, unnatural. You don't need to wear a crop top, but you do need to break free of conventional rules and wear something you've always wanted to but never had the guts to try. You'll be surprised by how good you'll feel later.

ALLOW YOURSELF TO HAVE BAD DAYS. We have to allow ourselves to fall down. The goal isn't to only have good days; the goal is to learn how to let the good days outweigh the bad. Allow yourself to have "weak" days. Cry, mourn, sob, yell, throw things. Then get up, brush yourself off, and move forward.

"Commit to a trifecta of wellness: good sleep, excellent nutrition, and daily fitness. The 20s is the decade where what you did in college will no longer pass for acceptable, and where if you do things right, you will literally set yourself up for a lifetime of excellent health. This means regular sleep of seven to nine hours a night, eating foods that provide clean fuel for your body, and finding a workout routine that becomes a daily habit."

JENNIFER ASHTON is a board-certified ob-gyn. You've probably seen her as one of the hosts on *The Doctors*.

HEALTH OOPS! No. 2

"I had to shower at the gym without my flip-flops."

HOW TO FIX: Unappealing, yes, but not the end of the world. You can reduce your chances of getting athlete's foot or some other fungal infection by drying your feet really well with a towel. We mean it: Get the towel between your toes, then sit down and swing your feet to air-dry. When you get home, wash well with soap and water. Apply antibiotics to any exposed cuts. And if you're prone to fungal infections, spray or rub your feet with an antifungal, which can be used to prevent as well as treat a flare-up, says Stephen P. Stone, the director of clinical research in dermatology at the Southern Illinois University School of Medicine, in Springfield.

Diet or exercise?

Obviously, they both matter to your well-being and your waistline. But what if you want to achieve something specific—to drop a dress size or to pump up energy (without mainlining Monster)? In certain cases, focusing on one over the other will give you better, faster results.

IF YOU WANT TO...**lose weight**

FOCUS ON: DIET

"You need to restrict calories in your diet to lose weight—and exercise to keep it off," says Tim Church, a professor of preventive medicine at Pennington Biomedical Research Center at Louisiana State University, in Baton Rouge. "Most people who exercise to lose weight and don't restrict calories shed only 2 to 3 percent of their weight over 6 to 12 months." Here's why: It's much easier to deny yourself 500 calories a day—the amount you typically need to cut to lose a pound a week—than to burn that much through exercise. For example, to work off almost 500 calories, a 155-pound woman would have to spend an hour pedaling a stationary bike at moderate intensity. Compare that with swapping a Starbucks Grande Caffé Mocha with 2 percent milk (200 calories without whipped cream) for a plain brewed coffee (5 calories). No contest.

HOW TO TAKE ACTION: Eating fewer calories always sounds like a nightmare. But it's pretty simple when you follow three guiding principles. First, stick with a primarily plant-based diet (fruits, vegetables, whole grains, beans, nuts, and heart-healthy fats, like olive oil). Second, avoid processed foods, such as frozen meals, deli meats, and refined carbohydrates, including pastries and white bread, which contain lots of empty calories.

If you follow these two rules, you'll automatically be doing a third thing linked to reduced calorie intake: eating more low-calorie–dense foods. High-calorie–dense foods (like full-fat cheese and red meat) pack more calories ounce for ounce than low-calorie–dense ones (like vegetables and fresh fruits). According to one study, eating a low-calorie–dense diet (by decreasing fat, eating more produce, or adding water to recipes) helped people consume 230 to 396 fewer calories a day. With these strategies, you'll also eat foods that are higher in fiber, so you'll stay satisfied.

IF YOU WANT TO...increase energy

FOCUS ON: DIET

Yes, exercise can give you a surge of energy, but smart eating throughout the day will provide a steadier supply. "With proper nutrition and well-timed meals, you'll keep your blood sugar balanced. This is important, since blood-sugar spikes and drops are a leading cause of energy fluctuations," says Shawn M. Talbott, Ph.D., a nutritional biochemist and the author of *The Secret of Vigor.* You'll also help to balance your brain's neurotransmitters, which are chemical substances—including the important trio of serotonin, dopamine, and norepinephrine—that keep your mood up and your energy in gear.

HOW TO TAKE ACTION: To maintain an even blood-sugar level, eat five to six times a day, or about once every three hours. In addition to your main meals, fit in two to three 200-calorie snacks. Ideal snacks contain lean protein, healthy fats, and complex carbohydrates—say, yogurt with granola or peanut butter on crackers with a banana. Frequent eating can also help reduce feelings of anxiety and depression (both of which can influence energy), since low blood sugar can raise your level of the stress hormone cortisol.

Another way to keep from falling asleep at your desk: Load up on foods rich in flavonoids, like blueberries, blackberries, and açaí juice. "Our research shows that flavonoids interact with receptors in the brain that lessen the perception of tiredness. So while they're not necessarily energy-boosting, they are fatigue-reducing," says Talbott. A half cup of blueberries will do the trick. Also, drink water throughout the day. The feeling of exhaustion you get around 4 P.M. is often your body telling you it's low in fluid, says Talbott. The best gauge of hydration is the color of your urine, which should be almost clear. Keep a bottle of water nearby and sip it all day, and drink a large glass with every meal or snack.

IF YOU WANT TO...reduce your risk of heart disease

FOCUS ON: EXERCISE

One major study found that the most physically fit women were the least likely to die from any cause, including cardiovascular disease, the number one killer of U.S. females. Besides helping you stay trim, exercise alleviates stress, lowers cholesterol, and increases blood flow.

HOW TO TAKE ACTION: Aim to do cardio exercise for at least 150 minutes a week. The intensity should vary from moderate to vigorous, so that you increase your cardiac capacity without overtaxing yourself. Two times a week, also do a 20-minute session of resistance training, such as weight lifting. Both types of exercise make your heart pump more blood, which strengthens it.

Also, sit less. A study from the University of Leicester, in England, revealed that the more sedentary you are, the more you increase your risk of heart disease (and diabetes). "When we sit for long periods, enzymes in the postural muscles change. This affects how the body metabolizes glucose and lipids, which leads to higher levels of bad cholesterol and glucose, among other things," says Emma Wilmot, Ph.D., the study's lead researcher. To cut down on sitting time, stand during coffee breaks, or set a timer to go off every hour, then get up and move around.

IF YOU WANT TO...be hornier

FOCUS ON: EXERCISE

"Exercise is one of the best ways to improve body image, which affects libido," says Heather Hausenblas, an associate professor of health sciences at Jacksonville University, in Florida. Your sex drive is also affected by mood and self-esteem, and exercise can improve both.

HOW TO TAKE ACTION: Yoga is one of the best exercises for women with low libido, says Lori Brotto, Ph.D, an associate professor in the department of obstetrics and gynecology at the University of British Columbia, in Vancouver. Brotto says that studies have found that yoga can decrease stress and anxiety, bring on a state of relaxation, and help women focus—all of which can improve sexual health. Downloading images of Ian Somerhalder wouldn't hurt either.

CHOOSE THE RIGHT WORKOUT

Nothing is worse than making a commitment you're not certain about. So before you sign that 24-month gym contract, spend a little quality time with our handy flow chart.

START HERE:

HOW WELL DO YOU WORK OUT WITH OTHERS?

I NEED MY SPACE.

HOW MOTIVATED ARE YOU?

Pumped!

WOULDN'T HAVE IT ANY OTHER WAY.

WOULD YOU EXERCISE OUTSIDE YOUR HOUSE?

Meh. I'm OK either way.

IS MUSIC ESSENTIAL?

NO! YES.

NO WAY. HELL, YES.

HOW DO YOU FEEL ABOUT HEALTHY COMPETITION?

CHOOSE A LIVE ONLINE STREAMING WORKOUT, LIKE DAILYBURN OR EMG LIVE FITNESS.

Bring it!

HOW DO YOU FEEL ABOUT INSTRUCTORS WHO GET A LITTLE SPIRITUAL?

Love it!

WHEN DID YOU LAST PICK UP A BALL?

Ewww.

SO YOU THINK YOU CAN DANCE?

Five minutes ago.

Third grade.

JOIN A LOCAL SOCCER / BASKETBALL / SOFTBALL LEAGUE.

CAN YOU DEAL WITH TOUGH LOVE?

GET A DAILY-ACTIVITY TRACKER, LIKE FITBIT, AND MOVE ENOUGH TO HIT A SET GOAL.

I told you: No. Disposable. Income.

DO YOU OWN AN XBOX?

I do!

USE A VIRTUAL TRAINER, LIKE XBOX 360'S NIKE + KINECT TRAINING.

What's disposable income?

My couch is really comfortable.

DO YOU HAVE A LOT OF DISPOSABLE INCOME?

YES.

HIRE A PERSONAL TRAINER.

I'm an indoors person.

DIY WORKOUT AT THE GYM.

SIGN UP FOR POWER YOGA.

LIKE THE GREAT OUTDOORS?

I'm all about nature.

RUN OR WALK.

HOW'S YOUR FLEXIBILITY AND BALANCE?

Want to see my splits?

Not so much.

TRY SPIN CLASS.

NUH-UH.

CONSIDER CARDIO BOXING.

YEP.

SHAKE IT AT A ZUMBA CLASS.

JOIN YOUR LOCAL CHAPTER OF THE ROAD RUNNERS CLUB OF AMERICA.

Dish it out, baby.

TRY CROSSFIT, A TOUGH CORE-STRENGTH AND CONDITIONING PROGRAM.

I have enough stress, thanks.

It's that time
of the month again

Just in case you forgot everything you learned in sixth-grade sex ed, here's a quick refresher course.

Days 1 to 7

Both estrogen and progesterone levels are at their lowest point of the month, which usually means one thing: Aunt Flo is in town! Adding to the messiness of the blood and tissue being flushed out from the lining of your uterus, you have high amounts of prostaglandins coursing through your bloodstream, which causes your uterus to contract (*ow*) and blood vessels to constrict (headaches, dizziness, diarrhea, oh my). Meanwhile, an egg starts maturing in one of the tiny sacs, called follicles, within your ovaries.

HOW TO DEAL: Thank goodness for ibuprofen. Pop one or two, lie down for a few minutes, and the pain miraculously dissipates, at least for a little while. Keep the water coming, too. It will help the blood and tissue flow more easily. Heat packs or hot water bottles might help as well, says Luu Ireland, an obstetrician gynecologist at the University of California in Los Angeles Medical Center.

Days 7 to 13

(THOUGH THIS CAN START AS EARLY AS DAY 4 FOR SOME FORTUNATE WOMEN)

Tampons, back in the drawer! Estrogen is on the rise as your uterus starts building its lining again, says Hal Lawrence, the president of the American College of Obstetricians and Gynecologists. Progesterone levels wane. The egg continues to mature in its follicle. Your body should feel pretty awesome for the next few days.

Days 14 to 20

Around day 14, when estrogen levels are at their highest, the egg springs forth from the follicle and into the fallopian tube, causing some mild cramping: It's ovulation time. As the egg moves down the tube, the lining of your uterus keeps building up, on the off chance that a sperm appears on the premises, fuses with the egg, and creates an embryo in need of a thick surface to attach to. Progesterone levels creep up, kicking off a slew of biochemical reactions, including stimulating sebum and closing up skin pores—which (oh great, just what you need) zits love. You start feeling bloated and moody. PMS sucks. Life is the worst.

HOW TO DEAL: Go light on the pretzels; more salt = more bloat. Be extra good about exercise too. The endorphins will help keep you from going into a BLIND RAGE.

Days 21 to 25

If no sperm unites with your egg, then your hormone levels will start to fall. This can make you feel tired, hungry, bloated, and distracted for the next few days. If an embryo does form, it attaches to the lining and will start developing into a fetus—meaning you're pregnant.

HOW TO DEAL: Some studies suggest that calcium alleviates grouchy symptoms, so make sure you're getting your recommended daily amount.

Days 25 to 30

Somewhere in this time frame, your hormone levels reach their lowest point. You may feel tired and bloated as you close in on the end of your cycle. Finally, the lining sheds, and it's time to take out the tampons again.

HOW TO DEAL: Monster cramps? Reach for the ibuprofen a couple of days before your period. "It's easier to prevent cramps than to relieve them," says Ireland.

HEALTH OOPS! No. 3

"I slept in my contact lenses."

HOW TO FIX: Once you realize this, take them out ASAP. Contact lenses not only limit the oxygen your corneas get (and as a result slightly alter their physiology) but also act like a magnet for irritants and germs, says Thomas Steinemann, M.D., a clinical spokesperson for the American Academy of Ophthalmology. Most contact lenses should be worn during waking hours only, for about 12 to 15 hours. Even those designed to be slept in are best removed at night. When you take them out, clean them (rubbing and rinsing them with a multipurpose solution) as usual and put them in a clean case with fresh solution. Wear glasses for the remainder of the day so your eyes can recuperate.

Problem periods

Predictable and boring: bad words to describe your last date, good words to describe your monthly visitor. Because, really, a surprise is the last thing you want from your menstrual cycle. If one sneaks up on you anyway, here's how to cope.

UH-OH: You missed your period this month—but you're absolutely, definitely not pregnant.

Are you inexplicably gaining weight? Losing the hair on top of your head but finding more on your body? And to cap it all off, are you feeling down? You may have a hormone imbalance. This must be treated with low-dose birth-control pills or some other prescription medication from your doctor.

Otherwise a missed period may mean you've lost too much weight or are exercising too much, both of which interfere with estrogen levels. Ease up. Focus on eating healthy foods, make sure you get enough calories each day (roughly 1,500 to 2,000 calories for most average-size women), and take your workout down to half an hour of moderate-intensity activity three times a week.

If, however, your weight and exercise regimen have remained steady, then stress might be the culprit. Stress interferes with the brain's hypothalamus—the region that's also responsible for telling your body to secrete the hormones involved with your period. So zero in on what's stressing you out. Try to control it and carve out time to do something you love. We know, easier said than done—but at least try. If this continues for two or more months, call your doctor.

UH-OH: You're spotting, including after intercourse.

If you're not getting your period but are spotting, the first thing to do is take a pregnancy test. If you're not pregnant, there are a number of things that can lead to spotting, and most of the time the causes are harmless. Spotting may signal a polyp or a fibroid, both of which are growths in the cervix and usually benign. It could be a side effect of your birth-control method. Less commonly, it could be a sign of precancer or cancer of the cervix or uterus. Bottom line: Call your ob-gyn.

UH-OH: The crimson wave this month is more like a tsunami.

Meaning you're changing tampons or maxi-pads every two to three hours, or you're having to double up. This may mean nothing, especially if this has been your typical flow pattern since eighth grade. But it could be problematic if your period suddenly became heavy or got increasingly heavy within a particular month. Possible causes are cysts, fibroids, or a thyroid disorder. Once again, see the doctor about any ongoing concerns.

UH-OH: Your cramps are killer.

If your cramps are really, truly awful (like can't-go-to-work bad), try taking ibuprofen three times a day beginning the day before your period is expected. Continue taking it throughout your period. If you're still having pain, head to an M.D. Some women have very painful periods, a condition known as dysmenorrhea. There are many treatments, including hormonal contraceptives, that can relieve monthly pain. Certain things can cause painful periods: Fibroids or endometriosis, a condition in which uterine cells grow outside the uterus, could be an underlying cause. Less commonly, pain can be caused by a pelvic infection. Sometimes a recently inserted intrauterine device (IUD) could cause cramping; the cramps are usually relieved by ibuprofen and go away after three to six months. You know the drill—make an appointment with your doctor.

IF YOU DO ONLY ONE THING...

"Create a sustainable 'health style' that makes your healthy behaviors the default for your everyday routines—like walking or biking anywhere you can, taking the stairs instead of the elevator, and scheduling time for one activity a week that you love so much, it doesn't even feel like exercise."

JULIE GERBERDING is an executive vice president of Merck Vaccines and a former director of the Centers for Disease Control and Prevention.

HEALTH OOPS! No. 4

"I forgot to take my birth-control pill yesterday."

HOW TO FIX: As soon as you remember, take the missed pill, even if that means taking two in the same day. Then take the rest of the pack as usual. As long as you have been taking them consistently and correctly the rest of the month, you will be protected. Just know that you might experience some spotting or a little nausea. If you missed two or more pills, then for one week use a backup method of birth control (such as a condom) if you have sex.

Birth control 101

Unless you are in a monogamous relationship (and your partner is, too), you should probably use condoms. This full-coverage barrier method is the only one that protects you from sexually transmitted diseases and HIV infection as well as pregnancy. Consider using condoms in combination with another method. We enlisted Sheila Mody, an assistant professor of obstetrics and gynecology at the University of California, San Diego, to match your top priority with the best birth-control option.

YOUR CONCERN: "I don't want to plan ahead for sex."

YOUR BEST BETS: Easy-to-put-on-and-take-off barrier methods.

CONDOM: You know how it works: It collects pre-ejaculatory fluid and semen from entering the vagina (and anus and mouth, too).

SUCCESS RATE: 98 percent, provided you use them correctly every time you have sex.

PROS: Easy to find in drugstores; inexpensive; you don't need a prescription; prevents the spread of STDs and HIV.

CONS: The latex can cause an allergic reaction in 6 percent of users; your ex says it dulled sensation, but really, it didn't seem to bother him all that much at the time.

FEMALE CONDOM: It's a pouch with rings on both ends—the closed end is inserted deep into the vagina; the open end remains exposed.

SUCCESS RATE: 95 percent, if used correctly every time.

PROS: Available in drugstores without a prescription; can be used by those with a latex allergy; allows you to take control of STD and HIV prevention.

CONS: May cause irritation, and for some it dulls sensation.

DIAPHRAGM: Used with spermicide, this shallow cup covers the cervix, which blocks the sperm from moving up to the uterus; leave it in at least six hours after vaginal intercourse for it to be effective.

SUCCESS RATE: 94 percent, if used correctly every time.

PROS: It's portable and ready to go when you need it. It works for as many times as you have sex, as long as it all happens within 24 hours of inserting the device.

CONS: It can be difficult to insert, and it can shift depending on penis size, thrusting, and sexual position. There's some maintenance involved (warm soap and water, plus air-drying after each use). The spermicide that you need to use with it could cause some irritation.

YOUR CONCERN: "I want to get it and forget it."

YOUR BEST BETS: Surgically implanted devices. While the initial procedure may be a hassle, they remain effective for a long time; for some, that trade-off is well worth it. The two below allow for spontaneity and very low risk for user error (like we said, they're implanted).

ARM IMPLANT (IMPLANON, NEXPLANON): This matchstick-size rod, inserted into your arm (it takes a few minutes in the doctor's office), releases the hormone progestin into your body for three years or until you remove it.

SUCCESS RATE: More than 99 percent.

PROS: Stays in place; little if any discomfort upon insertion.

CONS: Possible irregular bleeding; replacement needed sooner than the IUD; you can't see it, but you can feel it under the skin, which can be a little weird at first.

IUD (INTRAUTERINE DEVICE): A soft plastic T-shape device is placed into your uterus (it takes a few minutes in your doctor's office) and prevents pregnancy, either with copper (the Paragard IUD), which lasts for up to 10 years; or with progestin (Mirena or Skyla), effective for up to five and three years, respectively.

SUCCESS RATE: More than 99 percent.

PRO: It's the most long-lasting form of birth control. Completely reversible. Progestin IUDs may make your periods lighter.

CONS: Possible cramping when the device is first inserted.

YOUR CONCERN: "I'm creeped out by the idea of something implanted in my you-know-where."

YOUR BEST BETS: Hormonal birth control. These highly effective methods also allow for sexual spontaneity, though there's a much larger chance for user error compared with implants. The hormones may also offer the fringe benefit of reducing menstrual flow, cramping, and acne. Certain drugs (like antiseizure medications) and supplements (such as St. John's wort) can decrease efficacy, so discuss any other medications or supplements you are on with your doctor when you obtain the prescription. Except in the case of the shot, your cycle will return (and you can get pregnant) within a few months of stopping these methods.

THE PILL: Different brands use various levels and forms of estrogen and progestin to prevent the egg from leaving the ovaries, and to thicken the cervical mucus (so it's harder for the sperm to swim up).

SUCCESS RATE: More than 99 percent.

PROS: Few things are easier and quicker than popping a pill; allows for spontaneity.

CONS: You have to remember to take it every day.

THE PATCH (ORTHO EVRA): Hormones are absorbed into the skin via a thin plastic two-inch-diameter patch placed on your rear end, stomach, upper outer arm, or upper back. You replace it once a week for three weeks, followed by a patch-free week. Then you start the cycle over again.

SUCCESS RATE: More than 99 percent.

PRO: You don't have to remember taking a pill.

CONS: You do have to remember to switch it out; it's also visible to others, depending on where you wear it.

THE SHOT (DEPO-PROVERA): Your health-care provider administers the hormones with an injection in the arm once every three months.

SUCCESS RATE: More than 99 percent.

PROS: There's no pill popping or patch changing—just remember to show up for the shot every three months.

CONS: Well, some women forget to show up; also, it may take 6 to 10 months for your regular cycle to return, so this isn't ideal if you're planning to get pregnant within that time frame.

THE VAGINAL RING (NUVARING): This ring, slipped into your vagina once a month, releases estrogen and progestin for three weeks, after which you go ring-free for a week. Then you start another cycle with a new ring.

SUCCESS RATE: More than 99 percent.

PRO: You have to deal with it only once a month.

CONS: You may forget to replace it; it may cause vaginal irritation or slip out.

Note: Costs for some methods may be waived or reduced, depending on your insurance coverage and health-care provider. Efficacy percentages are for ideal use—meaning you are using the birth-control method correctly every single time. All success-rate figures are for correct usage according to the Planned Parenthood Federation of America.

YIKES—THE CONDOM BROKE!

When your birth control fails you, keep calm—and carry emergency contraception. Doctors recommend that you have a stash at-the-ready. Do not, however, use it as a regular form of birth control, since other forms of contraceptives are much more effective and much cheaper. The options below delay the release of the egg from the ovaries and prevent sperm from fertilizing it, so they are not abortion pills. You should use emergency contraception within 120 hours (or five days) of unprotected sex.

▶ Your over-the-counter choices include Plan B One-Step and the generic Next Choice One Dose. They are 89 percent effective. They work better the sooner you take them after unprotected sex. However, you can take it up to 120 hours (five days) after unprotected sex.

▶ Another option is Ella, which is more effective than over-the-counter pills, especially for overweight women. It should also be taken within 120 hours of unprotected sex. You'll need a prescription for it, however.

But I don't want to be pregnant...

You got some unwanted news, courtesy of the pee stick. Don't panic. Just take the following steps.

MAKE AN APPOINTMENT WITH YOUR GYNECOLOGIST or your local Planned Parenthood center (see plannedparenthood.org for locations). The goal here is to confirm your pregnancy and discuss all of your options with a knowledgeable, supportive, impartial professional, says Deborah Nucatola, M.D., the senior director for medical services at Planned Parenthood in New York City.

BEWARE OF SO-CALLED CRISIS PREGNANCY CENTERS, which claim to be legitimate clinics but are typically run by anti-abortion groups who will not inform you of all your options. Call the clinic first to find out the name(s) of the medical doctor(s) on staff, then Google her (or them) to check credentials. Ask about the services offered. If the response is evasive, find another clinic.

WEIGH YOUR CHOICES. List the advantages and the disadvantages for abortion, adoption, and proceeding on with the pregnancy. Then rate each pro and con based on what's more or less important to you. For a helpful guide in exploring each scenario, log onto plannedparenthood.org and search "Pregnancy Options."

TALK THE ISSUES through with your significant other, a trusted, supportive friend, or a family member. You don't have to tell anyone, of course, but many women feel better when they have a loved one helping them.

MAKE A DECISION. This may be one of the most important choices you'll ever make. Don't rush it. At the same time, realize that if you choose to end the pregnancy, the earlier you do so, the easier it will be to obtain an abortion. And if you choose to continue with the pregnancy, the sooner you start prenatal care, the smoother the next nine months will be.

CHAPTER 8

DECORATING AND CLUTTER-BUSTING

The world of interiors has never been so diverse and creative and exciting—nor so exhaustively documented in freakishly well-staged design blogs. Not a prop stylist? No worries.

In this chapter, we'll provide decorator-endorsed tips for finding your design niche, making the most of small spaces, and fostering harmonious furniture arrangements—and equally harmonious negotiations with aesthetically challenged roommates.

Quiz: What's your decorating style?

Nobody makes a direct leap from dorm room to dream home. But you're bound to get there faster if you have a clear road map in mind, so you don't end up detouring into every flash-in-the-pan trend that crosses your path. (Wait—did chevron peak already?)

Clues to your decorating style are all around you—in your closet, in your cupboards, and even in your DVD collection, not to mention your InstaTumblPin feeds. With advice from design expert Carrie McCarthy, a coauthor of *Style Statement: Live by Your Own Design,* we've created a plan to help you nail a cohesive interior look by teasing out opinions you didn't even know you had, so you can build a home that will make you blissfully happy for years to come. (Or until you're ready to start all over again.)

Step 1: Survey your domain. Judge everything.

With a notepad or a smartphone in hand, walk from room to room examining your belongings and make two lists: "Love It" and "Ugh." Catalog everything you can. Listen to your gut, and be brutally honest. You don't have to like a framed photo just because you like the person who gave it to you. "It's all based on how things make you feel," says McCarthy, not how you think they *should* make you feel.

Step 2: Pull together small items you love, including clothes.

Check the top of your dresser, your bookshelves, your jewelry box, your shoe rack, your stockpile of nail polish. Sift through collections and mementos. Gather the favorites on your bed. Then pull special clothes from your closet. "Focus on the items that make you feel beautiful and joyful, the ones that inspire you to stand tall," says McCarthy. These will be your visual cornerstones.

Step 3: Go to your happy place.

Close your eyes and think about the places you love to be and why—from a local café to a faraway beach. Recall paintings, movies, and books that have stuck with you. Then go into fantasy mode. "Imagine that real-world constraints don't apply," says McCarthy. "Picture your dream home. If you could live anywhere, would you choose a loft in New York? An English manor? A tree house in the tropics?" Then think outside of home: "If you were invited to the Oscars, what would you wear? Include jewelry and shoes." This is not about your actual life and budget—but it all ties in, we promise. Don't forget to jot down your answers.

Now for the hard part

Look for common threads—design, colors, shapes, materials, themes—among the things you love. Choose which style best jibes with the items you've chosen.

If you're drawn to timeless pieces and luxe materials, you'll probably like the style **SOPHISTICATED CLASSIC.**

If you're into color, contrast, and clean lines, you'll probably like the style **MODERN GRAPHIC.**

If you're about comfort and warmth, you'll probably like the style **COZY CASUAL.**

If you go for history, quirks, and curves, you'll probably like the style **VINTAGE ECLECTIC.**

About these styles
SOPHISTICATED CLASSIC

All gloss, no grit. It's the LBD of decorating styles—an elegant blend of refined traditional furniture, jewelry-like accessories, dark woods, and pale everything else. A good pick for the girl who doesn't leave home without a perfect blowout and a statement bag. Instantly grown-up and trend-agnostic; safe for splurges, since everything will stand the test of time.

LOOK FOR:
• Delicate furniture pieces with feminine lines and tapered legs.

• A palette of neutrals and soft colors.

• Luxurious fabrics, like silk and velvet.

• Rich dark woods with polished veneers.

• Fancy accent materials, including metal, marble, and glass.

WHERE TO SHOP YOUR STYLE: Estate sales, Z Gallerie, Serena & Lily, Zara Home, Canvas Home, WilliamsSonoma Home, Aero, Ballard Designs, Restoration Hardware, Burke Decor, H&M Home.

MODERN GRAPHIC

A fresh, fun, contemporary look that combines urban styling (imagine an art director's downtown loft) with edgy, colorful elements and midcentury design. Simple furniture forms balance out bold accents and patterns. Think the Museum of Modern Art, Frank Lloyd Wright, a Rubik's Cube. Turn here if you love Italian motorbikes, skinny leather jackets, and art-house films.

LOOK FOR:
• Furniture with clean lines and no extra adornment.

• Blocks of saturated color.

• Boxy upholstery with plain legs or skirtless bases.

• Lacquered finishes and a mix of woods, both light (birch, oak) and dark (walnut, mahogany).

• Geometric or abstract patterns and Pop Art–inspired accessories.

WHERE TO SHOP YOUR STYLE: CB2, Ikea, Jonathan Adler, West Elm, AllModern, HD Buttercup, Chairish, Apartment Therapy classifieds, Urban Outfitters.

COZY CASUAL

A warm, traditional look made for next-level relaxing (the kind of place in which the cabinets are always stocked with tea and snacks). Draws on English and Early American furniture designs, as well as laid-back country, cottage, beach, and farmhouse styles. Weathered, low-maintenance furnishings are easy, inviting, and built for daily life. The overall look is nearly impossible to screw up. Bring on the fisherman's sweater!

- Plush upholstery, often slipcovered, with roll or square arms and skirts or ball feet.
- Indestructible tables with turned legs, trestles, or substantial pedestal bases.
- Warm wood tones with rustic or distressed finishes.
- Natural fabrics, like cotton and wool.
- Solid textiles, simple stripes, and unfussy florals in muted colors.

WHERE TO SHOP YOUR STYLE: Crate & Barrel, Pine Cone Hill, Pottery Barn, Hayneedle, L.L. Bean, Home Decorators Collection, Dash & Albert, Target, Wayfair, Schoolhouse Electric & Supply Co.

VINTAGE ECLECTIC

A rich, layered look combining flea-market finds, furniture designs from various time periods (including Victorian pieces and 18th-century French styles), and a diverse collection of accessories and artwork. Dusty colors, timeworn or handmade textiles, and collected objects suggest a passport full of stamps (and the travel stories to match). Perhaps the most forgiving option, since frayed edges, chipped paint, and faded rugs all add to the charm. It's also magic for making a rundown older building seem romantic or a bland white-box apartment feel more soulful.

LOOK FOR:
- Furniture with shapely, feminine silhouettes, intricate detailing, and weathered finishes.
- Jewel tones mixed with washed-out, chalky shades.
- Antique and vintage elements interspersed with newer, offbeat items.
- A varied mix of fabrics (on pillows, upholstery, and window treatments), including jacquards, paisleys, ethnic tapestries, folk motifs, botanicals, and florals.
- Embellished lamps.
- Decorative accents on walls and surfaces.

WHERE TO SHOP YOUR STYLE: Vintage stores, Anthropologie, Cost Plus World Market, Pier 1 Imports, One Kings Lane, Society Social.

IF YOU DO ONLY ONE THING...

"Allow yourself to evolve. I used to be a preppy girl. I had a gingham futon and a denim love seat. I thought they looked amazing. But one day I woke up and was like 'How do I get these things out of my apartment?' My eye was developing. I got a navy blue velvet sofa, which was great for that time in my life."

ELIZABETH BAUER is an interior decorator who owns her own design firm in New York City.

10 rules for small-space living

Chances are, your first apartment is going to be smaller than the house you grew up in. (It may even be smaller than—gulp—your dorm room.) Here, a few universal guidelines to apply for making bitty spaces feel just right.

1 | Leave the *Tiny Furniture* to Lena Dunham.

You have a small space, sure. But that doesn't mean everything has to be Lilliputian (tuffetlike chairs, spindly side tables). Your space will appear bigger, more grown-up, and more glamorous with regular-size furniture. The key is to bring in fewer pieces of it.

2 | Multitask, multitask, multitask.

Rule number one works best when you choose furniture that does more than one thing, rather than über-specific, single-purpose items. "Instead of buying a desk, get a great dining table that you can stack with coffee-table books and plants. It goes from library table to desk to dinner-party table or sideboard. And it has that cabinet-of-curiosities effect—you're curating the table. If the heights match up, you can even move your sofa along one edge to use for dining," say John Loecke and Jason Oliver Nixon of design duo Madcap Cottage.

3 | Make every room a living room.

There are a great many things you can do in your living room, right? So don't relegate all the other areas in your place (foyer, bedroom) to lowly single-function status. Be creative: For example, imagine a craft desk within an office nook within your open-plan kitchen. Architectural details, like large door frames or columns, can be used to your room-dividing advantage, as can low-cost, no-commitment elements, like area rugs, different lighting schemes, curtains, and screens. Tip: To avoid creating too much of a decorative crazy-train effect, keep a similar color palette going throughout all the room's zones.

4 | Embrace your center.

People in small spaces often try to make a room feel bigger by moving stuff to the edges," says Maxwell Ryan, the author of *Apartment Therapy's Big Book of Small, Cool Spaces.* "But doing that kills warmth." Imagine the difference between your sofa and chairs all coming in for a perpetual group hug, rather than slouching against the walls with their imaginary arms folded across their imaginary chests. Which arrangement do you think will feel nicer?

5 | Accept that your storage will be seen.

It could be years before you have a home with all the closets that your heart desires (if such a utopia even exists). In the meantime, some crap is going to have to live out in the open. Furniture pieces with storage built in—a handy hollow ottoman, a trunk that works as a coffee table— are the small-space inhabitant's best friend. Your next-best friends? Storage devices that pass as decorative objects, like oversize baskets and nice lacquered boxes.

6 | Acknowledge your needs.

Arrange your space based on your personal habits. If you never eat in the kitchen, ditch the table to make a spot for more useful items—like a bar cart with storage for party supplies and a slim free-standing cabinet to hold cleaning materials in lieu of a utility closet.

7 | Kill the accent wall.

Conventional wisdom says that white walls are the way to go in small spaces, and they're certainly a no-risk proposition. But if you're going to do color, don't try to pussyfoot around with an accent wall, which is like hanging a neon sign that says you're too scared to paint them all. Experts say that if you're going to do wallpaper, commit to it. Navy paint? Forward, march. "One of our favorite small-space design tricks is using bold color and pattern in a small bathroom," say Anne Maxwell Foster and Suysel dePedro Cunningham of the New York design firm Tilton Fenwick.

"We always opt for a large- or medium-scale patterned wallpaper in vibrant colors, and we often pair it with painted moldings and ceilings. It ends up feeling like a gorgeous jewel box."

8 | Create design "moments."

A space doesn't have to be a traditional "room" to play an important role in your home. "Doing something interesting in a hallway or a pass-through space—like a tightly packed floor-to-ceiling salon grouping of paintings and photographs—makes people stop and linger, and that creates a feeling of a new space," says Loecke. "Even if it doesn't make that specific hallway feel larger, it heightens the experiential quality of the home as a whole and makes it seem like there's more to it."

9 | Shop the past.

"We're huge fans of using vintage furniture because it's so well proportioned, not supersized," says Nixon. "Plus, it's eco-friendly. And having vintage pieces in your home gives it dimension and depth." Focus on sofas and chairs—the items that tend to be the hugest in their modern iterations. The ideal find will have exposed legs (which also help a room feel more spacious) and a wood frame that can easily be reupholstered (and reupholstered and reupholstered).

10 | Preserve some negative space.

"Not every square foot needs to be covered," says San Francisco–based interior designer and prop stylist Lauren Nelson. "Negative space can be a good thing for walls. Choose one large piece of art or several smaller pieces and group them together over a piece of furniture. Off-center groupings are a nice surprise, too."

BUT WAIT—THERE'S MORE!

Try these low-effort, high-impact tweaks.

FAKE A BIGGER WINDOW. When curtain rods extend past the window frames, more light is allowed in and the eye is drawn outward. "Windows are the eyes of the room," says author Maxwell Ryan. "When you cover them up, you make your place smaller." Hanging curtains in the same shade as or slightly lighter than the wall color takes the trick to the next level, since contrasting colors interrupt the eye's movement and break everything up into segments (to space-shrinking effect). If all else fails, go for something lightweight and sheer.

CHART A PATH THROUGH THE KITCHEN. If you can move unencumbered among the three key work areas—sink, stove, and refrigerator—it's smooth sailing. It's far more important to have an efficient, easy-to-navigate cooking space than a huge one.

TURN A STACK OF BOOKS INTO A SIDE TABLE. "It's a smart way to have all your beautiful coffee-table books out on display at once," says designer John Loecke, and it also saves you the expense of buying one more piece of living-room furniture. (Remember to cover the top with coasters or a tray if you want the covers to stay in presentable shape.) Other clutter-into-charm conversions? Stash skeins of yarn, colorful silk scarves (rolled or tied in loose balls), or any other bright and relatively compact item inside a large glass jar or urn, rather than strewing them over a dresser top or shoving them in a closet. Display the urn and call it conceptual art.

TAKE A CUE FROM TOM CRUISE AND GO CLEAR. Transparent tables, glass-front cabinets, and open shelving give rooms an airy, uncluttered feel. But do limit yourself to only a few see-through pieces so the apartment doesn't take on a sci-fi–meets–South Beach bordello look.

QUEEN BEDS RULE. You're an adult now, and adults don't sleep in single beds. Make room for it by forgoing a second nightstand (if you're single, you don't need it) and shoving the bed against the wall. Then build around it with artwork and drapes to carve out a corner space, and mount wall sconces instead of table lamps. Or free up real estate elsewhere by buying a pair of small chests of drawers to use as nightstands, instead of having a separate bureau and night tables. And if square footage won't allow for a queen bed (we, too, have inhabited touch-both-walls-with-your-fingertips cubbies), at least go for a full.

GO SCOUTING DOWN UNDER. Whatever size bed you end up with, "take advantage of under-the-bed storage," says stylist Lauren Nelson. "You can fit a lot under there!" Bonus: Less space for dust bunnies to congregate and multiply!

Get high on vertical space

When you hear people yammering about maximizing vertical space, all it means is making the walls so interesting and useful that no one notices the room is the size of a shoebox. These six examples are only the start. The sky—not even the ceiling!—is the limit.

THE STRATEGY: Pick up a paintbrush.

WHY IT WORKS: Painting the ceiling the same color as the walls creates the illusion of more space by letting the eye travel in one continual unbroken line across every surface. (It's the decorating equivalent of the "wear nude-colored shoes to make your legs look longer" trick.)

THE STRATEGY: Employ archi-texture.

WHY IT WORKS: Adding decorative moldings, bead-board panels, textured wallpaper or panels, or other architectural details—even the 100 percent faux ones—gives a room depth, dimension, and character. (The plain-white-box dwellers in your apartment building will be wondering why your unit is so special.)

THE STRATEGY: Consider bold lighting.

WHY IT WORKS: If your ceilings are high, swap out a few of your apartment's more boring lighting fixtures for statement-making pendant lamps or modern chandeliers. (The statement's being "Look how friggin' high my ceilings are! Never mind about the square footage!")

THE STRATEGY: Play with fabrics.

WHY IT WORKS: Hanging super-long curtains exaggerates the height of your ceiling and thus the size of the room—especially if you use hits of color near the top and the bottom to attract the eye to both extremes. Try adding a contrasting stripe to the curtain hems using fabric paint or a wide ribbon and hot glue, or paint a wooden curtain rod bright red or yellow—a DIY project you can finish in half an hour. Regardless, do get a real rod and rings and full-length curtains. Worried that they look inexpensive? Take the hems down a bit (cheap), or have the curtains lined at the dry cleaner's (pricier).

THE STRATEGY: **Add some mirrors.**

WHY IT WORKS: "Mirrors are a tried-and-true way to open up space," says Susan Zises Green, a New York interior designer. "They almost always help a small room." Plus, they subtly amplify light where there isn't much—which is useful if, say, your home office has a window facing an air shaft or is located inside the hall closet.

THE STRATEGY: **Elevate your artwork.**

WHY IT WORKS: Is your ceiling so low you can practically touch it? It will seem loftier if you hang a larger picture (or a large group of them) that reaches up to within a foot or so of the ceiling. (The center point of the artwork should still be at eye level, though.) "The most important thing is to draw the eye up and not down," says Matthew Dennison, a coauthor of *At Home With Color*. Just don't place a single small item up very high—it will look like a sad, little lost balloon floating off from a kid's birthday party. Instead, go for a massive flag, a vintage poster, or even macramé. Yes, the experts swear, it's coming back.

WAIT—DON'T THROW THAT OUT!

Genius organizing and decorating solutions can be found in the unlikeliest of places—like a closet, a cabinet, or the junk drawer. Give these repurposing ideas a try.

Fill a **MASON JAR** with battery-powered lights to add flair to a nightstand.

Loop **RIBBONS** through each hole of a shower curtain to tie the curtain to the rod with panache.

Slice old **UGG BOOTS** into squares to make nifty pot holders.

Discarded **HAIR ELASTICS** can corral tights and keep socks together.

Slip bracelets and bangles over a **CANDLE-STICK** and let them accessorize a dresser.

Air-dry a soggy sponge by propping it up in a **BINDER CLIP** next to the sink.

Give dresser-drawer knobs a cheerful upgrade by attaching a few pretty **BUTTONS** with superglue.

Fill a vase with old **COFFEE BEANS,** then add a pillar candle. The beans will keep the candle steady and catch the wax.

Turn a clean **JAM JAR** into a mini terrarium; fill it with small ferns and moss.

Scrimp or splurge?

Sofa = Splurge
"The goal is to get something that feels good and will last, not something that just feels good and looks good this year," says Burnham, who also founded Instant/Space, an à la carte room-design service. This is especially important, since even the cheapest of the cheap costs a few hundred bucks, and secondhand sofas may harbor bedbugs or other horrifying internal issues that you won't know about until it's too late. Take the time to shop around. And do it in person, so you can ask the salesperson about the sofa's construction and materials (down-wrapped foam cushions and a durable fabric, like corduroy, are ideal) and any life-span guarantees. Conduct your own examination, too. Look for straight seams, cushions that bounce back up after you sit on them (a.k.a. the butt test), and comfortable dimensions—nothing too shallow or low to the ground. And if you have your heart set on an all-white model, make sure it's slipcovered, so you can clean it.

You're ready to upgrade from that futon bed and wire-crate-cubby system, but you don't want to live in a replica of an Ikea showroom. Fair enough. Let Los Angeles–based interior designer Betsy Burnham be your smart-shopping guide.

Coffee tables and side tables = Scrimp
"There are so many inexpensive options out there," says Burnham, "and swapping them out is an easy way to update a room." Look for a sturdy coffee table that's at least 24 by 48 inches, if your room can handle it. "Anything smaller or too fragile never feels as homey as a more generous piece," she says. Also, you don't want it to collapse when you put your feet up at the end of a long day—or topple under the weight of unevenly spaced glasses of wine.

Lighting = Scrimp
"My favorite trick with lighting is to go vintage. It takes a little more time and shopping, but it can give your room a personalized twist without costing a lot of money," says Burnham. (How likely is it that you'll spot the same amethyst-colored geode slab lamp on a friend's side table?)

"Also, I'm a big believer in bringing in multiple sources of light that you can adjust for different moods and settings," says Burnham. "You probably already have built-in overhead lighting, but I would still add a table light and a standing lamp—a combo of new pieces and vintage."

Rugs = Scrimp

Unless you've inherited a hand-knotted Tibetan heirloom, you'll be cheaping it up in this area for a while. Wool is the most durable choice. "A little cotton rug is going to behave more like a bath mat. You're going to trip over it, it's going to wad up, and it's going to stain easily," says Burnham. "But one of my favorite pieces in the last few years was a wool Ikea rug with a crooked stripe—I've used it in both high-end houses and apartments with smaller budgets."

Storage = Depends

This one is all about moving parts. For a basic bookshelf, there's no reason to break the bank. Great-looking modern models abound at CB2 and Ikea. ("We use Ikea's white lacquer ones in our office," says Burnham.) Dressers are a different story. "Anything with a drawer, you want it to function well, and you don't want it to feel like cardboard. Get something sturdy and made of wood." It should be something you don't need to put together yourself. No more Allen wrenches!

Accessories = Scrimp

Home accessories are what flea markets were invented for. Go once a month and pick up a few cheap, quirky things at a time. Mix them in with a great tray and some beautiful coffee-table books.

Bed = Depends

You can't put a price on beauty sleep (only on the cosmetics you use to make up for the lack of it). That's one reason you shouldn't be stingy about your bed. Start with a good mattress—basically anything from the big, old-time brands you've heard of, like Sealy and Simmons. Their mattresses are proven to last, and you can often find

them marked down during seasonal sales. "Then buy the best bedding that you can afford," says Burnham. Avoid poly blends and bed-in-a-bag sets (a first-apartment dead giveaway), and find all-cotton sheets in the 250- to 400-thread-count range, which get better with time if you take care of them. The one place you can be a total tight-wad? The bed frame. Four-poster, platform, sleigh—whatever style you prefer, you're mostly paying for the design, and there are affordable versions of all of them.

Dining set = Scrimp

"If you're trying to get a nice matched set, you're going to spend a chunk of money on it—there's no way around it," says Burnham. "You would be astonished by how much six or eight dining chairs cost." Instead, get a midpriced table, since cheap ones can wobble or develop cracks in the veneer. Then top it with a great tablecloth or runner and plates that you love. As for the chairs, mismatched ones can be fun, and secondhand seating is easy and cheap to re-cover.

Home-office furniture = Depends

Save on the desk; splurge on the seat. You're buying your comfort (and freedom from future back pain). Still, you don't have to get a traditional chair from an office store. "It doesn't have to be on wheels or move up and down unless you want it to, and you're going to spend a lot of time in it," says Burnham. "It can be a comfortable dining chair. And if you're going to be in it only for an hour on the weekend, just get something affordable and cute." The desk can be a multitasking table (business by day, craft station or café setup by night) or a section of a bar counter in the kitchen. If it's good enough for the hipster coffee shop, it's good enough for you.

The object of my affection

Some people pine for cars or jewelry. Personally, I pine for tables made of mahogany and, well, pine. *How my fondest furniture dream came true.*
By **Edan Lepucki**

I WAS PROBABLY ONLY 12 when I began fantasizing about owning a dining-room table. My future glimmered somewhere on the other side of 21: I'd have a successful writing career, a lovely and smart man to talk to and kiss all night long, fresh baguettes with dinner (Where did I live in this future? Paris?), and a farm table with fabulous wood grain to call my own. At this table, I'd preside over dinner parties, of course: big, candlelit ones with good wine and better conversation.

I spent the decade after college yearning for such a thing. When we first moved in together, my husband and I ate meals on my grandmother's ancient card table. When I attended graduate school, we purchased an adorable 1950s Formica table, chromed like an old convertible—but it only sat four, and our plastic patio chairs didn't quite complete the look. We still had people over, but mostly to drink bad wine.

Eventually my husband and I got pink vinyl chairs to match the Formica table, but it still didn't seem quite right. The table was starting to rust, and the nails beneath would scratch your thighs if you didn't sit down carefully. The chairs were unbearably sticky in the summer, and they squeaked with every move. Besides, it was a kitchen table, not right for a big dinner party. Adulthood— where was it?

When I was 31, a decade into adulthood as I'd conceived it, I sold my first novel. *Now,* I thought, *where is that table?* There was space in the house my husband and I were renting, and I could finally afford such a large purchase.

I researched (read: shopped) for a month or two, and when I got the first check from my publisher, I bought a rectangular table made of a deep brown mahogany. It seats six. The legs are heavy but thin and made of iron. The chairs are metal: four are silver, and the two red ones go at each end. It's a beautiful table. The day the delivery people placed it in the dining room, I felt so unlike myself—as if I were speaking with a British accent or wearing a headdress of peacock

> The day the delivery people placed it in the dining room, I felt so unlike myself—as if I were speaking with a British accent or wearing a headdress of peacock feathers. I was an adult! Finally!

feathers. I was an adult! Finally! Those first few days after it arrived, I remember running my hands across its surface. I felt proud, like I'd finally stepped into my own glimmering future.

The thing is, adulthood looks and feels a lot like pre-adulthood. It's true that I now own an impressive and cool table, and it makes our small two-bedroom house feel more like a home. I am happy to eat breakfast on it every morning with my husband and son. And it's true that I've thrown numerous terrific dinner parties. We've cooked carnitas tacos, braised short ribs, jerk chicken, and various bad-for-you pastas that make everyone groan with pleasure. More than once, I've looked across the table's expanse at my husband and my son and my friends, overcome with affection.

But, you know, it's just a table. I throw the mail on this table, and every week I lament how cluttered it looks. Its surface is always dusty or sticky, no matter how often I wipe it down. It turns out, a dining-room table isn't adulthood itself but an accoutrement of adulthood—one that requires attention and a special cleaning spray.

I now have all the things I dreamed of when I was 12: the career, the partner, even a child. I also, you should know, have the baguettes. When they get stale, my son pretends they're swords and thwacks me in the shins with them. In those moments, I laugh and gripe, and I'm relieved to have my dining-room table to lean against. That particular use wasn't in my fantasy, but I'm happy it's part of real life.

EDAN LEPUCKI IS THE AUTHOR OF THE NOVEL *CALIFORNIA*.

How to rescue a blank wall

Nothing says "I just moved in" like bare white walls. But nothing says "I'm broke" like your post-security-deposit checking-account balance. Here are four DIY strategies for filling the void, fast.

1 | The Centerpiece

Tackling the vast area behind the sofa is no small project. Try this easy-to-adapt strategy, which you can fine-tune over time: Buy a bunch of similar frames with precut mats (Target and West Elm usually have workable options), then print out favorite images to fill them at whatever size you need. No matter what you put inside, it will feel cohesive. Before you hang anything, though, play around with arrangements on the floor. Start with a low centerpiece, then place the largest works on the ends to provide boundaries and visual weight. If you have pairs of images, keep them close to one another for unity. Line up the bottom edges of the display, and align the sides of the art to create crisp vertical columns of white space between the pieces.

2 | The Skyline

Gather up photos, paintings, and silhouettes in plain frames. Begin with a large item centered above a desk or a table (or simply in the middle of a wall) and at eye level. Add a piece to each side, hanging the frames close enough to touch but intentionally creating an uneven line on the top and the bottom. Continue, one on the right and one on the left, building out from the center. You can fill the width of the wall or not. Vary the subject, the medium, and the orientation (vertical or horizontal) for a playful feel.

3 | The Textile Fill

Mounted flea-market handkerchiefs or silk scarves make cheery, inexpensive multiples that you won't see (at least not exactly the same way) on anyone else's bedroom walls. For the backdrops, cut heavy construction paper to fit the frames (use the cardboard inside the frame as a template). Iron the fabric, then attach it to the paper with one piece of double-stick tape near the top. Smooth it with your fingers and place it in the frame. Hang a series in a tall row or a square formation, depending on your space, measuring an inch or so between frames.

4 | The Stop-and-Stairwell

If you live in a multilevel house (and your roommates don't mind your playing decorator), you can do a floor-to-ceiling stairwell scheme with any theme you want (antique maps or mug shots, flea market paint-by-numbers, photos of clouds that look like animals). Start by hanging a favorite piece at approximately eye level. Stagger the frames as you add them, placing the next one an inch or two to the right and another to the left (don't measure—keep it loose), then above and below. Now step away and look at the wall as a puzzle, filling in any major gaps.

IF YOU DO ONLY ONE THING...

"Be curious. Design is all about discovery, so travel! If you don't have the means, at least take a road trip."

KELLY WEARSTLER is a renowned decorator with her own line of home-decor items, furniture, jewelry, and more.

WHAT TO KNOW BEFORE HANGING ARTWORK

So you don't fill your wall with unnecessary holes.

AVOID EXCESSIVE SUNLIGHT AND HEAT. If it's bad for your skin and hair, it's probably bad for your beloved dog portrait, too. Too much light and heat can damage art, so when you have nicer pieces framed, ask for UV-coated glass. And be strategic about where you hang the frames relative to windows and radiators.

TIGHTEN SLACK WIRES on the backs of frames, especially if your goal is precision hanging (lining up art in a grid, say). A loose wire makes it hard to control the height of a piece, and you'll end up hammering six different "oops" holes in the wall before you get it right.

TO PROTECT WALLS, use peel-and-stick clear rubber bumpers on the back corners of frames. (You'll be glad you did come move-out time.)

CHOOSE THE RIGHT HOOKS for the weight of the artwork so you don't make massive holes for ephemeral items or risk a heart attack–inducing crash when an insufficiently supported larger piece performs a sudden dismount.

FIX MISTAKES on a white wall with Spackle and a fingertip. Apply a tiny dot over a hole, then smooth with a damp paper towel. (Or use white toothpaste in a pinch.)

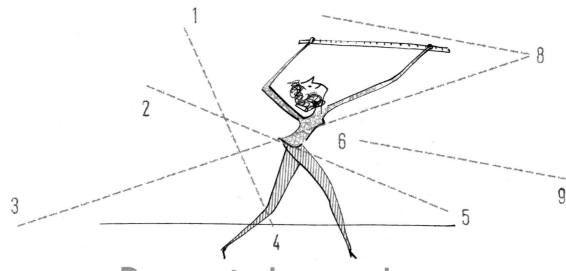

Decorate by numbers

Some people can waltz into an empty room and wing it. For the rest of us, there's this no-creativity-required guide, which will make you look like a design genius (even if you don't know why these rules work). All you need now is a tape measure.

RULES FOR THE LIVING ROOM

This is the room you most want to get right, since it's the one all your friends are guaranteed to see. Here, decorator Brad Ford delivers his formula for a well-balanced space that's as good for welcoming guests as it is for the post-workday wind-down.

THE RUG: A rug is not a coaster for the coffee table, so if that's the only piece of furniture touching your rug, it's too small. You want a rug that spans close to 60 percent of the room, leaving at least 12 inches of floor space all around. And don't forget to factor in furniture. If your sofa has a skirt or sits very low to the ground, keep all four legs on or off the rug.

ART ABOVE THE SOFA: Rookie mistake—hanging art behind the sofa that's exactly the same width as the sofa. (It pretty much tears a hole in the fabric of the universe that all your belongings will go whooshing through after your brain explodes.) Try this instead: Choose a painting or a print that's two-thirds as wide as the couch, and position it so that its midpoint is about 60 inches from the floor and centered. The bottom edge should be 8 to 10 inches above the sofa back. Everyone will be safe and happy and aesthetically pleased.

THE COFFEE TABLE: Shoot for a coffee table that's about the same width as the artwork behind the sofa and you'll create a satisfying symmetry. You should also check the height of your couch cushions when selecting a table. It should be a couple of inches lower than the seats (which are typically 14 to 16 inches off the floor). Then, ideally, leave about a foot and a half between the table and the seats so that people can walk by but still reach their drinks, says Ford. If you're also working side tables into your scheme, go for ones that are the same height or a few inches shorter than the sofa arms.

THROW PILLOWS: Want an easy way to calculate how many pillows to get for the couch? There should be one pillow for every butt that can comfortably be seated, not the total number that can be squeezed in during movie night (that would be *waaay* too many pillows). So, for a standard three-seat sofa (or a long two-seater, around seven feet), you'll need three 20-inch square pillows. Put two on one side and one on the other; an odd number is best so the look isn't too perfect. Try a different pattern for each, or pair a matched set (in a bold motif) with one that contrasts (in a subtle print).

LAMPS: For table lamps near sofas and chairs, make sure that the bottom of each shade is at eye level when you're sitting; otherwise you and your guests will be squinting from the glare of bare bulbs. In most cases, aiming to have the middle of the shade hit at 36 to 42 inches from the ground will solve the problem.

FLOOR LAMPS: Sixty-eight inches is the ideal floor-lamp height, since it conceals the bulb whether you're seated or standing. Ford's tip: Try a floor lamp on one side of the sofa and a table lamp on the other. That will also allow you to update the look of your room by changing just one of them out at a time.

RULES FOR THE DINING ROOM

Whether you have a full dining room or a corner of the kitchen carved out for mealtimes, these tips from interior designer Amanda Nisbet will help you cook up an appealing arrangement.

THE DINING TABLE: Elbowroom is essential. Unless you routinely invite friends over for communal juice cleanses (and, may we suggest, please don't), your table should be large enough for each person to claim a 24-inch-wide utensil-wielding territory. If you have a whole room for your dining setup, center the table within it. If not, put the table wherever it will fit in the least awkward way.

CHAIRS: "Wherever it will fit" has one caveat: Allow for at least a two-foot passageway between the wall and the backs of the pulled-out chairs. Crawling under the table to reach the far-middle seat is not OK, even for the host.

RUGS: Besides helping to delineate a dining area that sits within a larger, multipurpose space, an area rug buffers sound so you can better hear your friends' gossip—er, dinner conversation. Go big with the rug so that it encompasses almost the whole dining area. If that area is a proper separate room, leave just a five-to six-inch perimeter between the carpet edge and the wall, says Nisbet.

CURTAINS: Having a separate dining room is already pretty damned grown-up, but the space will seem even more impressive if you add window treatments. "Curtains should skim the floor or have a half-inch break," says Nisbet. "Or add two to three inches if you want them to puddle and have some volume."

TABLECLOTH: A great tablecloth is essential when your dining surface is subpar. It works best with a generous drape: Allow 15 inches or more of overhang on each side. But don't go too long; the cloth can touch the floor but shouldn't pool. (Unless you want guests to trip over it or step on the edge, pulling dishes and glassware into their laps, like something out of the Three Stooges.)

RULES FOR THE BEDROOM

The bedroom needs love, too—even if you're mostly in there with the lights out. Here, designer Elaine Griffin gives advice on keeping this space dreamy but defined.

ART: "After the bed itself, the wall above the bed is the most visible real estate in the room, so don't leave it empty," says Griffin. "Fill it with something that makes you smile." (As long as that's not an Imagine Dragons poster.) The art should take up at least two-thirds of the area above the headboard but not extend beyond its edges.

THE HEADBOARD: "I like a headboard to be four feet tall, so you can see it when the pillows are standing up but it doesn't overwhelm the other furniture," says Griffin. Anything much larger will only make a low ceiling feel more bunkerlike. A higher ceiling can handle a grand headboard, but scale up other pieces to keep the room balanced—bearing in mind that going full-on Versailles might send a princessy message to potential suitors.

BEDSIDE TABLES: These look best when they're a couple of inches lower than the top of the made bed—typically 24 to 27 inches high. They don't have to be identical, but their heights should come within two inches of each other.

LAMPS: Like the tables they will top, bedside lamps should stand between 24 and 27 inches tall. "You don't want a tiny lamp on a big table or a small table with a towering lamp," says Griffin. If you have two of them, the lamps don't have to match, but the look is more pulled-together if they do, especially when you're not using uniform tables beneath them. Either way, the tops of the lamps should be the same height, which you can fudge by stacking pretty books under the base of the shorter one. And if you don't have a lot of table depth to play with, use an oval or rectangular shade rather than a round one.

PILLOWS: Start with at least four pillows, arranging them in descending order, with the largest in back, says Griffin. (Think stadium seating.) "No matter how many pillows you have, the secret is to vary the sizes but stick to this order," says Griffin. If you have only a matched, standard sleeper set so far, pick up a pair of oversize square ones in the same colors as the bedding (but perhaps a different pattern) to prop behind them. Then you can put small, decorative pillows in front if you wish. Instant hotel-bed polish.

THE RUG: With bedroom rugs, size is more important than position. (Go ahead—snicker away.) The rug should be significantly larger than the bed—at least a foot larger on each side—but you don't have to center the bed right in the middle. "It's OK to turn the rug sideways if that suits the room," says Griffin. If you prefer a pair of small rugs on either side of the bed—or one small rug on one side, if the bed is pushed into a corner—seek out a style that covers 75 percent of the space from the end of the nightstand to the foot of the bed.

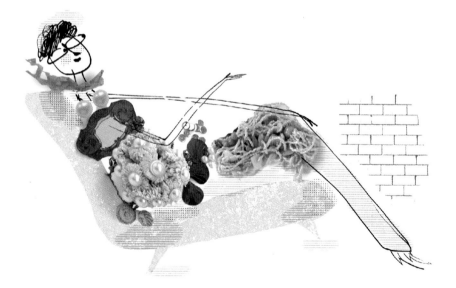

Declutter your problem spaces

Everything looks great when you first move in. But the daily accumulation of junk mail and other deal-with-it-later detritus can mar even the sparest of spaces. Here's how to regain control of the four most crap-clogged areas.

ORGANIZING THE KITCHEN

A neat kitchen allows you to cook more efficiently, clean up quickly, and never lose five minutes hunting for the corkscrew/spatula/takeout menus again.

☐ **TAKE INVENTORY.** Pull everything out of the cupboards (yes, every single thing) and place it all on a large table or carefully on the floor. Sort items into groups, creating a loose hierarchy based on how often you use each thing. And cut the b.s.: You don't get extra points for pretending that you use that manual juicer if Minute Maid is your morning staple.

☐ **DONATE OR TOSS.** Evaluate each item. If you have three identical frying pans, donate one. Discard anything that is broken and can't be repaired or is missing key parts, like a pot without a handle, which is possibly the most useless object on the face of the earth.

☐ **PUT STUFF AWAY IN SENSIBLE PLACES.** When it's time to put everything back, choose what should go where. Keep frequently used cookware and appliances immediately on hand. Stow things you use only now and then, like muffin tins and cookie sheets, in a less accessible cabinet. Move items you use once a year, like a roasting pan for turkey, out of the kitchen altogether—that is, if you have storage space elsewhere.

☐ **ORGANIZE CUPBOARDS WITH ACCESS IN MIND.**
Position heavy stuff below the counters, lighter stuff above them. An avalanche of empty Tupperware landing on your head is one thing—the same scenario with heavy glass bowls is quite another.

☐ **ORGANIZE ITEMS BY TYPE.** Pots and pans should be grouped by kind and placed one inside the other, from smallest to largest, like matryoshka dolls. If you have room, it's best to keep lids on their pots; otherwise arrange lids from smallest to largest and keep their partners close by.

☐ **ASSEMBLE YOUR A-TEAM.** Designate a place around the stove and the sink for the essentials—oil, vinegar, knives, cutting board, Maldon salt—whatever you reach for on a daily basis. If you cook frequently, keep ingredients where you will be using them: the basket of potatoes near the cutting board; sugar and flour near the standing mixer.

☐ **PUT WALLS TO WORK.** Hang racks or pegs to keep favorite utensils, pot holders, and dish towels in plain sight, especially if cupboard space is scarce.

☐ **MAKE RECYCLING EFFICIENT.** Having a bin for bottles and cans right next to the one for regular trash instead of by the back door streamlines cleanup.

☐ **ORGANIZE UNDER THE SINK.** Start by throwing out anything rusted, crusted, congealed, or of unknown origin. If it's a rat's nest down there (a metaphorical one; see page 223 for living, breathing rodent advice), consider installing a pull-out trash can on gliders and door attachments to hold sponges, brushes, plastic wrap, and aluminum foil. It makes an almost miraculous difference. At the very least, corral cleaning products and supplies on one side of the cabinet in a plastic caddy.

☐ **ARRANGE FLATWARE FOR EFFICIENCY.** Use drawer dividers and utensil trays (large enough to accommodate oversize pieces) to keep your kitchen accoutrements in order.

☐ **REARRANGE THE FRIDGE.** Believe it or not, it matters where you put things. Perishable foods should go at the bottom and toward the back, not on the door. The lower shelf, which is coldest, is best for dairy products. Produce stays fresher in a crisper drawer. Use the shelves on the door to store bottled food and condiments.

☐ **ORGANIZE THE FREEZER.** Consider making designated sections for frozen foods (entrées, veggies and sides, desserts), and use dividers, baskets, or multilayer ice caddies to keep everything neat and accessible. Be sure to label any reusable containers so that you don't mistakenly thaw out leftover turkey chili thinking it's apple cobbler.

ORGANIZING THE BEDROOM

Your bedroom should be an oasis of calm, not a *Hoarders*-style junkfest. Keep it cool and collected with a few simple tricks.

☐ **USE UNDER-THE-BED SPACE.** Store out-of-season clothing and other items in containers made of plastic, canvas, or wood. Keep cold-weather blankets in large plastic containers for extra protection. If you would rather go with wooden boxes, choose cedar, which helps deter moths, and line the boxes with plain unbleached muslin to counter the wood's acidity. (This sounds like a lot of effort, but it's really not.) Use canvas for delicate items, such as cashmere sweaters, which require circulating air to stay in good shape. Most important, make sure all clothing and blankets are cleaned before storing, since there may be stains or oils that you can't see that will set over time and attract stain- and oil-eating insects.

☐ **STOCK THE NIGHTSTAND DRAWER.** Stow away the unglamorous stuff that you would rather not advertise (eye mask, earplugs, prescription-strength foot cream).

☐ **ARRANGE THE NIGHTSTAND TOP.** Things you can get away with displaying: an alarm clock or an iPhone dock, a water carafe and glass, a candle, a small vase, a book (or a few), and small framed photographs. Gauge the space, though: You don't want it to feel crowded, and you don't want to topple things in the dark.

☐ **RECONFIGURE THE DRESSER.** Bureaus often have smaller drawers at the top and larger ones at the bottom. Underwear belongs in the top drawers. (The limited space should serve as a reminder to weed out raggedy bras and undergarments.) Bulkier, heavier clothing goes in the bottom ones. Make sure everything is in the right spot, and refold anything that's gotten rumpled over time.

☐ **INSTALL DRAWER DIVIDERS.** Plastic ones are especially helpful for organizing small items, like underwear, bras, socks, and tights. (Note: Wood dividers can snag clothing or, worse, shed splinters into your skivvies, leading to a midday discovery every bit as painful as it sounds.)

ORGANIZING THE BATHROOM

When the shampoo and exfoliators and body sorbet threaten to take over your bathroom, it's time to fight back. Follow these steps and you'll have a vanity to be proud of.

☐ **DO A DATE CHECK.** Many products have a "period after opening" label, a number followed by the letter M, which indicates how many months the item is effective for after it's opened. In general, eye makeup is good for six months; foundation, a year; and lipstick, two years. Pay special attention to preservative-free products, which may degrade more quickly than others. Toss any items past their prime.

☐ **DO A SNIFF TEST, TOO.** Throw out anything that smells or looks funny or that you know you've had in your makeup kit since junior year of high school.

☐ **CREATE A DAILY-USE TRAY.** A makeup bag is fine for your purse, but your mornings will be more efficient if you keep your daily makeup arranged on a small tray on the counter rather than in a pouch you have to rummage through.

☐ **DIVIDE EXTRA COSMETICS BY TYPE.** Pack a drawer with shallow boxes, trays, or tins and gather extra cosmetics in them, sorted by category (lip colors, shadows, blushes, etc.). If the drawer is deep enough, place the daily-use tray on top and close it all up after each day's routine.

☐ **CORRAL BRUSHES IN A JAR.** Keeping makeup brushes upright and accessible in a tumbler is a space-saving (and powder residue–catching) move.

☐ **SET UP A T.P.-REFILLING STATION.** Buy a bin or a basket that can hold several rolls. Keep it fully stocked and (ideally) within arm's reach of the toilet—for your own sake as well as your guests'.

☐ **STASH THE SEASONAL STUFF.** Separate daily skin-care essentials from the products you use on an as-needed basis—summer sunblock, winter lip salve, fancy soaps for visitors. Store the former in the medicine cabinet for easy access; move the rest to a closet or a closed cabinet.

☐ **RECYCLE THE DREGS.** Transfer the contents of almost-empty bottles of shampoo, conditioner, and lotion into refillable travel-size containers. Store them in a plastic bag inside your suitcase. Toss the empties.

☐ **CREATE A HAIR-SUPPLY CADDY.** Use a tote bag with compartments to store your hair dryer, curling iron, brushes, and styling products all in one place. (Wrap the cords of the appliances loosely, like lassos, to maintain their life.) Hang the bag handle over a doorknob when you're doing your hair, then store the whole thing under the sink or in a closet when you're done.

☐ **JUDGE YOUR TOWELS.** After washing towels and washcloths, sort them and remove any incomplete sets or stained, torn, or worn ones. These can become rags for grubby jobs.

ORGANIZING THE LIVING ROOM

Unless you live alone, keeping this area in order will require a joint effort. If you tackle the first round of organizing with your roommate, you'll be on the same page (or closer to it) for future tidying.

☐ **DO A MAIL PURGE.** Gather all junk mail, bills, magazines, and catalogs. Trash or shred what you can, and address or file the rest.

☐ **ESTABLISH A REMOTE LOCATION.** Pick out a tray, a basket, or a wide-mouth vase to become the clicker's permanent resting place.

□ **DECLUTTER TABLETOPS.** Equip the coffee table (and other surfaces that tend to get piled up) with a few nice-looking trays, bins, or bowls. Use them to corral odds and ends.

□ **MOUNT A WAY STATION.** A small shelf with a row of hooks, installed near the front door, will help catch some of the potential incoming clutter (mail, keys, dog leash) before it wanders into the living room and settles elsewhere.

□ **DITCH THE DVD DISPLAY.** Get rid of DVDs you know you'll never watch again. (Even *Magic Mike* gets old eventually.) Transfer the rest to fabric-covered boxes for a more streamlined look.

□ **EDIT BOOKSHELVES.** Take those old college textbooks to a reseller. (Trust us—it's highly unlikely that you'll crack open *Introduction to Biology* anytime soon.) Donate other onetime reads to a library or a women's shelter.

□ **SHED SOME LAYERS.** You need only one neatly displayed throw or blanket out at a time. Fold the rest and stash them in a closet or a big basket next to the sofa.

□ **UNTANGLE CORDS AND CABLES.** Use twist ties, binder clips, and other grabby devices to tame the cord chaos behind the TV.

□ **MAKE AN OUT-BOX (OR TWO).** For all the stuff you find on the floor that it's not your job to put away but you keep tripping over—or for the stuff that you fully intend to put away but never get around to. A designated tote bag or basket for each housemate works nicely.

ORGANIZING MANTRAS TO LIVE BY

1.
ONE IN, ONE OUT.
WHENEVER SOMETHING ENTERS YOUR HOME, GIVE ANOTHER ITEM THE BOOT.

2.
THOU SHALT NOT TRANSFER CLUTTER.
DON'T BURY THE DRESSER TOP TO SAVE THE COFFEE TABLE.

3.
DOUBLES ARE TROUBLE.
YOU DON'T NEED TWO CAN OPENERS OR FIVE TWEEZERS. TOSS DUPLICATES.

4.
KEEP IT WHERE YOU USE IT.
STASH TONER WITH THE PRINTER AND THE T.P. UNDER THE BATHROOM SINK.

5.
MAKE LABELS, NOT WAR.
MARK SHELVES, BINS, AND BOXES SO ROOMMATES (AND HOUSEGUESTS) KNOW WHERE EVERYTHING GOES.

6.
HAVE A PLACE FOR NOTHING.
AIM TO CREATE ONE EMPTY CABINET, SHELF, OR DRAWER IN EACH ROOM. THIS IS YOUR BACKUP SPOT WHEN THE BALANCE TIPS. (AND IT WILL TIP.)

7.
A TO Z (NOT A.D.D.).
FIX ONE SPOT START TO FINISH, RATHER THAN JUMPING AROUND FROM MESS TO MESS.

8.
PICK YOURSELF UP, DUST YOURSELF OFF, AND START ALL OVER AGAIN.
ORGANIZING IS A CIRCLE, NOT A STRAIGHT LINE.

Here, the novice's guide to cultivating positive energy in every zone of your home. Grow, jade plant, grow!

Feng shui for beginners

Stand inside your home with your back to the front door. Or inside your bedroom. (The following rules apply to both entire homes and individual rooms.) Look forward. According to the principles of feng shui, the space is divided into eight zones, each of which corresponds to a sector of your life. By placing certain items into certain zones, you activate that sector. Cool, right? Here, feng shui expert Catherine Brophy offers an introduction, with quick tips for stimulating each sector.

Your money

WHAT TO DO: Place fresh flowers or a jade plant here. This is also a good spot in which to keep cash or a valuable treasure (Grandma's wedding ring or your diamond graduation studs). Caveat: If you have a roommate, you probably want to place the money corner in your bedroom to avoid having to, say, store your gems on someone else's nightstand.

Your reputation

WHAT TO DO: In this area, display awards, accolades, your office softball MVP trophy (actually, you could probably put that in storage), and good-luck symbols.

Your relationships

WHAT TO DO: Bring in pairs of objects or motifs (especially anything involving lovebirds, butterflies, and cranes) or an image of two trees intertwined. If your living room is in this area, place a love seat, a pair of pillows, or two matching chairs here. Do not expect anything weird to happen between you and your roommate if you sit there together—it's not *that* powerful.

Your friends and travel

WHAT TO DO: Here, keep photo-booth strips, vacation postcards, and that portrait of you your graphic-artist friend doodled on a bar coaster.

Your family and health

WHAT TO DO: It's important to keep this area clean. (You know, if you don't have your health...) And it's the perfect spot for a family-photo wall.

Your knowledge

WHAT TO DO: Create a reading nook or an intimate spot for conversation. If you meditate, make this your regular "om base."

Your career

WHAT TO DO: This area should be as well lit as possible. If it falls around the entry, hang a bright pendant or chandelier. Put something here that relates to your passion or your job. A fashion designer might want a cool, vintage *Vogue* cover in a frame. If you play music, store your instrument here.

Your creativity

WHAT TO DO: Tack up a bulletin board, or make a craft or sewing zone. Make sure this spot is not boring. (Wacky wallpaper or bright art prints work wonders.)

WAIT—DON'T THROW THAT OUT, EITHER!

Even more smart and surprising repurposing ideas.

Pop a photo in an old **CD JEWEL CASE** for a desk display.

Before storing a breakable, zip it into a padded **LAPTOP SLEEVE** for cushy protection.

Prop up your laptop with a **RUBBER DOORSTOP.**

Use old **CROCS** as hanging planters (the holes are perfect for drainage). Line the toes with moss, plant pansies, and hang by the heel straps.

Stash plastic bags in an empty **TISSUE BOX** for easy access when the bathroom trash can needs a liner.

Use an orphaned **EARRING** in place of a pushpin—functional and pretty.

How to deal when your roommate has zero taste

In an ideal world, you would agree on everything, down to the wattage of the living-room bulbs. Decorators John Loecke and Jason Oliver Nixon share their tips for navigating roommate reality—even, or especially, when the truth is ugly.

If possible, have a conversation about the design aesthetic before you move in together.

If one person is crunchy granola and one is clean-lined, you're going to have a problem. But as with any relationship, you have to compromise, say Loecke and Nixon. Call in a third party to help you moderate the paring-down process for the common areas. This should be a neutral party you both trust. But, ultimately, whoever has the higher-quality and more comfortable stuff should win.

If you can't come to an agreement, then come up with a budget and go shopping together.

"Make the living room clean and spare with a few good pieces, rather than going to town to fill up every space," says Nixon. "That way, when it comes to that one big, sentimental eyesore your roommate won't get rid of, you're better able to fit it in."

Allow every room to have at least one ugly item.

Really, it won't kill you. "I think of Philippe Starck's hotel design," says Loecke. "He would always have one strange furniture item in there, and it was a conversation piece. Even if it was a wagon-wheel table or something—what the hell? It adds a bizarre element. Instead of hiding it, make it front and center."

CHAPTER 9

FAKING A CLEAN HOME

The lease is signed. You've put together all your furniture—and you have the 36 Allen wrenches to prove it. But what do you do when it's just, well, you, and that ancient, hulking radiator goes clunk in the night? Or you discover the "surprise" Mister Whiskers left on the flokati next to your bed?

In this chapter, we'll give you the dirt on keeping your place presentable and ready to host book club or a bachelorette party with minimal effort. (We know you've got better stuff than scrubbing planned for your weekend.)

The only cleaning kit you'll ever need

Want to make your place presentable with little fuss (and cost)? Stock up on these supplies and you're halfway home—even if you've never dusted a lampshade in your life.

Scrub brush

WHY YOU NEED IT: Because soap-scum rings don't respond to sweet talk. You'll also need this heavy-duty scrubber for floors, fireplaces, and other rough, textured surfaces.

WHAT TO LOOK FOR: Nylon bristles are the least likely to cause scratches, and a rubber handle is the most comfortable to grip.

Old toothbrush

WHY YOU NEED IT: Don't toss that relic of your last ill-fated relationship. Find a more fitting use: dislodging nasty gunk from the crevices larger tools can't reach (like the hinges of the toilet seat). It's therapy and thrift all in one!

WHAT TO LOOK FOR: Any soft-bristle model you're ready to retire.

All-purpose cleaner

WHY YOU NEED IT: It's the Ryan Gosling of cleaning products: hardworking, versatile, and welcome in almost any woman's home. You can use it to wipe down fixtures, clean the floor, and freshen the toilet—it will never complain.

WHAT TO LOOK FOR: The label should include the industry-regulated term "degreaser" or "cuts grease" and an Environmental Protection Agency (EPA) registration number indicating that the product is a proven disinfectant. Word to the wise: With a commercial-strength or concentrated solution, mix 1 part cleaner to 50 parts water, says Don Aslett, the author of *No Time to Clean!* This can be powerful stuff. More Clooney than Gosling—or more Fassbender than Clooney. Handle with care.

Mild abrasive cleanser

WHY YOU NEED IT: Containing mineral or metal granules, this product helps you scour scum on tubs and tile with a minimum of elbow grease.

WHAT TO LOOK FOR: Terms like "mild" and "gentle" are industry-regulated and tell you that the product is safe for most surfaces. Bonus points if the label says "chlorine-free" and "won't scratch," says Ellen Sandbeck, the author of *Organic Housekeeping*.

Microfiber cloths

WHY YOU NEED THEM: Their almost-magical nylon fibers lift and trap dirt like no other product. The cloths handle almost any chore with just water, and you can chuck them in the washing machine after each use.

WHAT TO LOOK FOR: Buy multipacks with various colors, then designate a different one for each task so you don't accidentally wipe the counter with the same cloth that cleaned the AC unit.

Microfiber duster

WHY YOU NEED IT: The dusting version of the microfiber cloths we're obsessed with, it acts like a magnet for debris and pet hair in even the most awkward and delicate areas (between window blinds, on the leaves of plants). Also, like the cloths, it requires no cleaning product, and the removable heads can be machine washed.

WHAT TO LOOK FOR: A comfy handle and a head with a thick or looped nap to grab the maximum amount of particles.

Mr. Clean Magic Eraser

WHY YOU NEED IT: This miracle product, which contains melamine foam, excels at tricky jobs,
like zapping scuff marks from walls and wiping out stovetop grease. What's more, if you cut one in half and toss it in the toilet tank, it will help keep the bowl clean.

WHAT TO LOOK FOR: Size matters. Choose one that's about three by six inches so that it fits in your hand but still covers a substantial area.

Disinfecting wipes

WHY YOU NEED THEM: Even your pig-pen room-mate can handle a countertop cleanup with premoistened wipes. They eradicate nearly 100 percent of bacteria just by showing up.

WHAT TO LOOK FOR: A label with a registration number from the EPA, which means the product has been proven to kill bacteria, fungi, and viruses. "Store the canister upside down so that the wipes don't dry out," says Donna Smallin, the author of *The One-Minute Cleaner Plain & Simple.*

Baking soda

WHY YOU NEED IT: To make brownies, obvs. And for neutralizing the leftover-chicken-vindaloo smell in the refrigerator. But perhaps its most impressive trick is performed during post-cooking cleanup. "If you have a pan with burned-on grease, put it on the stove with water and baking soda and boil the water," says Sandbeck. "The grease floats right off."

WHAT TO LOOK FOR: A label that says "pure baking soda" or "100 percent sodium bicarbonate."

White vinegar

WHY YOU NEED IT: Its high acidic level kills bacteria and removes mineral deposits from faucets and windows. Fresh out of it? Try another high-acidity kitchen staple with similar scouring power: lemons. They're not just a vodka-soda garnish!

WHAT TO LOOK FOR: Plain distilled white vinegar (not cider, balsamic, or white wine) with a solution of 5 percent acetic acid. Use it undiluted, or mix 1 cup with a gallon of water.

Spray bottle

WHY YOU NEED IT: The bottle makes cleaning large areas a snap: You just spritz and wipe. And it comes in handy for spraying homemade stain-removal solution on carpets and upholstery.

WHAT TO LOOK FOR: Buy professional-grade plastic spray bottles. (You can find them in most big-box stores.) Avoid metal ones, which may rust and compromise the contents.

Microfiber mop

WHY YOU NEED IT: Microfiber mops are the best at grabbing and holding dirt particles (at least until you throw the cloth heads into the washing machine). They don't need any special potions to get floors clean—plain water will do. And they don't weigh a ton, like those old-fashioned swab-the-deck string mops, which sit around sopping in their own drippings when you're done. (Note: They use these mops in many hospitals, and if your floor is dirtier than a hospital's, we need to have a serious talk.)

WHAT TO LOOK FOR: A telescoping handle and a swiveling head, which make it easier to maneuver the mop and allow you to finish more quickly, and removable, machine-washable cloths. Try to buy a brand that also sells heavy-duty scrubber pads that fit the base, for all those sticky spills you discover well after they've hardened into unidentifiable, shellaclike coatings.

Glass cleaner

WHY YOU NEED IT: Every single person who enters your home is going to look at your bathroom mirror (or rather his or her own reflection in it), and you don't want to subject them to the sight of makeup and toothpaste splatters or errant bits of your boyfriend's whisker trimmings.

WHAT TO LOOK FOR: One of the newfangled mix-with-water solutions that lets you reuse the same container over and over again. Or mix your own batch of all-natural stuff, combining ¼ cup white vinegar, 2 cups water, and a squirt of liquid Castile soap in a spray bottle. (Spray it on the glass, then wipe with newspaper—weird, but it works.)

Wood cleaner

WHY YOU NEED IT: Kitchen-cabinet fronts can get shockingly dirty (thanks, grubby fingerprints and airborne cooking grease). And side tables and bookcases collect dust like it's their calling in life.

WHAT TO LOOK FOR: For routine maintenance, a plant-based, food-safe spray is a good option. (It also allows you to exercise the five-second rule when you lose a nacho on the side table.)

Rubber gloves

WHY YOU NEED THEM: Part of being an adult is being ready to go into some gross nooks and crannies once in a while because no one else is going to do it for you. And whether you're more freaked out by the germs or by the heavy-duty cleaners you'll occasionally call upon to handle the worst of them, preserving your gel mani is—or should be—the least of your worries.

WHAT TO LOOK FOR: A good fit. "Big ones flop around; small ones are hard to remove," says Aslett. "You don't want to clean the toilet, then end up having to bite the glove ends to get them off." And a pair with a foam lining will absorb interior dampness better than those with cotton.

PLUS

▶ **DISH SOAP**

▶ **DRYER SHEETS**

▶ **SPONGES**

▶ **A TOILET-BOWL BRUSH**

▶ **A BROOM AND DUSTPAN**

▶ **A VACUUM CLEANER**

The quick and dirty guide to housecleaning

The difference between tidying and deep-cleaning is like the difference between doing leg lifts while watching Real Housewives *and enrolling in bikini boot camp. Whether your goal is to make your room spotless or just habitable by humans, here's a road map.*

Kitchen

THE HALF-ASSED APPROACH (*LOOKS* CLEAN): Have a dishwasher? It's a great place to hide dirty dishes—even items you'll hand wash later. Move small appliances (often a refuge for wayward crumbs) off the countertops, spritz the surface with all-purpose cleaner, and wipe down. (It's OK to brush the crumbs right onto the floor—we'll get to that in a sec.) Rinse the sink and dig out anything gross that has collected in the drain. Sweep the floor.

THE FULL MONTY (*IS* CLEAN): All of the above, plus: Actually clean the dishes, then spray all-purpose cleaner into the sink and let it soak. (That's how the bacteria die.) Scrub with a sponge, rinse well, and dry. Before disinfecting the countertops, wash the cabinet fronts with a soft sponge and a solution of warm water and dish soap, wiping from top to bottom. It's amazing how much grime accumulates up there. Then clean the counters (as previously described) and wipe dry with a microfiber cloth. Clean the refrigerator handle with disinfectant (on a wipe or a paper towel) and the outsides of appliances with wipes designed for the task. Finally, mop the floor: A few spritzes of an all-purpose cleaner and a damp microfiber mop will do the trick, and you won't have to wrestle with a messy, sloshing mop bucket that douses your Toms midtask.

BONUS POINTS: Deep-clean the larger appliances, starting with the refrigerator. Remove all the contents (and toss that half-used tub of ricotta from your Great Lasagna Experiment), then wash the interior with a stank-banishing solution of 3 tablespoons baking soda and 4 cups warm water. The oven is next. If yours doesn't have a self-cleaning function (Dear Appliance Manufacturers: Please design a self-cleaning function for all gadgets henceforth—especially the coffeemaker and the toaster), use a plastic scraper or an old credit card to dislodge the hardened bits of pizza cheese and bread crumbs on the racks and the drip pan that fill the kitchen with smoke every time you heat the damn thing up. Then wipe down the inside with an all-purpose cleanser. Last but not least, remove the forgotten crumbs from the darkest depths of the pantry cabinets with a vacuum hose attachment or a damp cloth.

Living room

THE HALF-ASSED APPROACH: Simply clearing away the clutter buys you a lot of leeway in the living room. First, tour the room with a laundry basket or a large tote bag and load up any out-of-place items—the Tracy Anderson DVDs, the wedding invitations, the catalogs—that have taken up residence on or near the sofa and side tables. (You can worry about truly putting them away later.) Then tend to any obvious surface dust, focusing on the areas that are at eye level when you're seated or standing: Grab a microfiber cloth in each hand for twice the efficiency. Scan the room for pet messes (cat-hair tumbleweeds, soggy dog bones) and other eyesores and whisk them away. Then fluff pillows and fold throws—the living-room equivalent of swiping on mascara and lipstick. Instant presentability!

THE FULL MONTY: Vacuum or dry-mop the floor. It's not just for looks—accumulated dirt can be abrasive enough to damage carpet fibers and wood floors over time. (Unlike your elbows, they do not benefit from exfoliation.) Prioritize the areas around doorways, which harbor the most tracked-in dirt. While you have the vacuum out, use the brush attachment to get dust off curtains (close them first), sofas, and chairs, cleaning under and behind cushions and flipping them to distribute wear evenly—and avoid perma-butt impressions. For blinds, wipe each slat with a damp microfiber cloth (a half-and-half solution of warm water and white vinegar works best). Dry with another cloth, then follow up with a dryer sheet (a used one is perfectly fine), which will leave behind a residue that helps repel dust and other nasty particles.

BONUS POINTS: Wash the windows, using glass cleaner and a lint-free material, such as an old T-shirt, to minimize streaking (while cutting down on that stockpile of college intramural tees). Pro tip: Cleaning with vertical strokes inside and horizontal ones outside—or vice versa—will let you see which side any remaining streaks are on. Spot-clean dirt, stains, and scuffs from the walls with a damp Magic Eraser, then use your microfiber duster to get behind, underneath, and on top of tall furniture. Finally, roll back rugs and clean the floor below. Yes, dirt can work its way through.

Bathroom

THE HALF-ASSED APPROACH: Start with the sink, since that's what everyone sees first (toothpaste globs and all). With a disinfecting wipe in hand, clean the basin and its fixtures, concentrating on the grime-magnet seams where the two meet. Grab another wipe or two to clean the edge of the bathtub, the toilet seat, and the tank's top and sides. Finish up by shining the mirror with glass cleaner and a microfiber cloth.

THE FULL MONTY: Deep-clean the toilet. Sprinkle baking soda around the inside edge and let it sit for a few minutes. While that's soaking, use a wipe or a fresh cloth and all-purpose cleaner to clean the seat around the base and the hinges. And don't forget to lift the seat. (Just because you never get that view doesn't mean that your male guests won't.) Return to the bowl and give stubborn rings a scrubbing with a sponge or a brush. Next, wash your hands, then spray the shower walls and the tub with all-purpose cleaner; scrub them from the top down so that the tub floor gets a good soaking to dissolve buildup. When the rest of the room is finished, use your microfiber mop to clean the floor, getting into all the awkward corners between the sink, the toilet, and the tub, where hair, dust, and styling products collect and may be secretly plotting a takeover.

BONUS POINTS: If your shower door has that distinctive frosted look—and it didn't come that way—wipe it down with lemon oil or a mild abrasive cleanser to remove the lime scale that's clouding it up. To dislodge mildew and mold, spray all-purpose cleaner on the offending areas. Let it soak in for 5 minutes, then scrub.

Bedroom

THE HALF-ASSED APPROACH: Shake out and straighten sheets and bedding. Next, damp-dust surfaces with a microfiber cloth, making your way around the room in a clockwise circle (to keep track of where you've been). Pay special attention to the knickknacky stuff that harbors dust in its crevices. Then do a quick floor fix. For a wood floor, run a damp (not wet) microfiber mop around the edges of the bed and other exposed areas. Remember—don't wet-mop hardwood floors; they could warp. Vacuum the same zones if you have carpeting. Make quick stowaway jobs easier by keeping one empty drawer or a storage trunk for temporary mess-masking. Short on space? Install a row of hooks on a wall for catching strewn clothing—they will be faster than hangers and neater than piles.

THE FULL MONTY: Get under the bed. And behind it, too. Vacuuming, or at least doing a pass with a duster, will help you purge the area behind the bed of sneeze-inducing dust particles and the disgusting microscopic mites that feed on them. While you're at it, tackle the closet floor, which can collect and then release its own stores of vile particles every time you go digging for that favorite pair of espadrilles. Dusting the shelves and wiping down the doors with a damp microfiber cloth will help keep the air clear, too.

BONUS POINTS: Address windows, walls, and lights. Use a microfiber cloth and a glass or all-purpose surface cleaner to clean panes, frames, and windowsills in one fell swoop, then wipe down light switches and fixtures and use a Magic Eraser to take any scuffs and stains off the walls.

HOW THE HECK DO I CLEAN…?
FOUL-AIR EDITION

A WOOLLY AIR CONDITIONER
During sweaty season, you'll want to clean the A/C monthly, lest its filter grow an internal pelt of lint and pet hair, then conk out on the day that you need it most. First turn off the power, then unplug the unit and pop off the front panel. Remove the spongy filter and soak it in the sink in equal parts warm water and white vinegar for about an hour. Use the vacuum's crevice attachment on the coils. After you've replaced the filter (wait until it's dry) and the front panel, dust the exterior and the control buttons with a disinfecting wipe. Have central air? Once a season, unscrew the vent covers and clean the slats on both sides with a damp cloth.

A CEILING FAN WITH A BEARD
For safety, first tape down the fan's switch. (Nobody needs to lose a finger!) Place a drop cloth or an old sheet on the floor, covering an area about twice the span of the blades. Fill a spray bottle with water and 2 tablespoons white vinegar; spritz generously into an old pillowcase. Climb up on a stepladder and slide the pillowcase over the blades one by one, rubbing gently to dust. The dirt will fall into the pouch, not on your head.

HOW THE HECK DO I CLEAN...?
MESSY KITCHEN EDITION

BLACKENED BAKING SHEETS
Place the crusty baking pan in the sink and top with a dryer sheet. Fill the pan with warm water and let soak overnight. (It's like a team of little elves came in while you were snoozing and chipped away at the burnt-on remnants, bless their tiny hearts!) Rub clean with a sponge, then rinse well.

RUST-STAINED KNIVES
Good ones (the kind you bother putting in the knife block) should never go in the dishwasher, because harsh detergents can pit the blades and high heat can damage the handles. Instead, hand wash with hot, soapy water and towel-dry. Never soak knives; this can cause handles to shrink and blades to rust. To remove stains on blades, try this all-natural (and oddly satisfying) idea: Stab a large onion a few times. The onion's acid will remove the rust. Wipe clean.

A STINKY GARBAGE DISPOSAL OR TRASH CAN
Just...when you open it...the smell...dear lord. To combat odors and keep disposal blades sharp, freeze ½ cup white vinegar mixed with water in an ice-cube tray, toss in a few cubes, and run the disposal. Take the trash can outside (or to your bathtub) and hose it down. Pat dry, then spray every inch of it inside and out with an enzyme cleaner (typically sold for pet messes, since it knocks out both bacteria and smells). Then pull on some rubber gloves and start scrubbing with your scrub brush. Rinse, pat dry, and then sprinkle some baking soda—just a tad, not enough to powder a doughnut—in the bottom of the can before you put it back in service.

Ewww, how do I get rid of this?

There are problems with obvious fixes, and then there are problems where you don't even know where to begin. Like a mystery smell that haunts your waking hours or an inexplicable stickiness on the kitchen wall. Here's how to deal.

THE PROBLEM: Your bad date must have bathed in Axe Body Spray. Now your sofa reeks.

THE SOLUTION: Like a wildebeest marking its territory, Mr. Saturday Night left you something to remember him by—every time you sit down on the couch with the remote. To banish the offending odor from your upholstery, sprinkle the surface with baking soda, then vacuum. Or fill a spray bottle with water, a tablespoon of baking soda, and 10 drops of essential oil for an all-natural deodorizer; spritz and let dry.

THE PROBLEM: Someone forgot to dump out the wet coffee grounds before you left on vacation, and now the coffee machine's filter basket looks like a poor man's terrarium.

THE SOLUTION: Scrape out the moldy muck right away and clean the filter basket and pot with warm water and a dish scrubber or an old toothbrush. Then fill the reservoir with water and 1 cup distilled white vinegar and run it through a brew cycle. Dump out the liquid and repeat; then run a cycle or two of only clean water, no vinegar.

THE PROBLEM: You saved a bundle on salon bills by DIY-ing your dye job. Unfortunately, now the bathroom counter is covered in Ruby Fusion, too.

THE SOLUTION: If you can, wipe up spills with a wet cloth before they dry. For the spots you discover a day later, spritz them with a mixture of water and white vinegar (¼ cup vinegar in a standard spray bottle full of water), then scrub. Nothing doing? Time to pull out your trusty Magic Eraser.

THE PROBLEM: Your hair and your boyfriend's hair have gradually built a putrid love nest deep within your shower drain.

THE SOLUTION: Don't immediately resort to a super-toxic, heavy-duty chemical drain cleaner. That stuff is rough on pipes and the environment both. Instead, hie ye to the hardware store and purchase a super-cheap flexible plastic drain-cleaning tool with little teeth on either side. (Picture a giant zip tie and you'll be on the right track.) Push the free end down into the drain as far as it will go, then gently tug until it pulls out one of the most revolting globs of organic matter you've ever seen. Then throw the whole thing away. (The tool is disposable.) Now that that's out of the way, pour ½ cup baking soda, then ½ cup vinegar, down the drain. Cover it with a wet cloth, wait 5 minutes, uncover, and flush with steaming-hot water.

THE PROBLEM: The refrigerator smells like death.

THE SOLUTION: There's still nothing better for absorbing fridge odors than baking soda. To get the job done, spread the stuff out on a cookie sheet (for maximum surface area) until the worst of the odor is gone. Then you can go back to leaving an open box on one of the shelves. (Of course, removing the source of the smell— whether it's a rotting grocery item, a container of leftovers, or merely an accumulation of odiferous spills—is the essential first step.) Vanilla extract is also an effective remedy: Soak a cotton ball in it, then leave the cotton ball exposed on a dish until dry.

THE PROBLEM: You had no idea how much your corgi was going to shed. (You were too distracted by those adorable stumpy legs!) There is literally nowhere in the house that is safe to sit, unless you purge your wardrobe of any garment that doesn't exactly match Stumpy's fur.

THE SOLUTION: Since you're not going to vacuum every time Stumpy moves his butt from the armchair to the dog bed, try this faster fix, which doesn't require buying whole cartons of lint rollers. Put on a damp rubber glove, then run your hand over the hair-covered upholstery. The hair will cling to the glove, not the sofa. Rinse off the rubber glove in the sink, with the drain catcher in place.

THE PROBLEM: A thin film of grease has built up on the kitchen wall and has started to trap minuscule debris, like some invisible spider web.

THE SOLUTION: What you need is a degreasing product. Look for the ingredient d-Limonene, which is made from lemon peels. (Note: This stuff can be toxic for cats, so use caution around your furry friends.) It will attach to the film and make a kind of gooey, gelatinous muck that is much easier to remove than the original film. Another good use for the stuff? Removing adhesive from the spots where you taped up all those quirky inspirational messages to yourself. They seemed like such a good idea at the time. (Thanks for nothing, Miranda July!)

THE PROBLEM: Last night's margarita rounds left water rings all over the coffee table.

THE SOLUTION: Those mysterious light-colored circles aren't an alien transmission—they're a sign that moisture has seeped into the wood's surface and become trapped. Let's assume your table is not an antique or an heirloom. (And if it is, buy some coasters, already! Then look for a furniture-restoration specialist.) The first step is to use a soft, damp cloth with one of these treatments: creamy white appliance polish; a paste made of baking soda and water; or a solution of nonsoapy ammonia. Lightly rub the affected finish in the direction of the grain, repeating the motion for 5 to 10 minutes, until you break through to the troublesome condensation. Next, dry and clean the area with a soft cloth, then seal the finish with furniture wax or paste wax. Or, lazybones, just squeeze a bit of non-gel toothpaste on a soft cloth and rub the affected area, then buff with a clean cloth. Still have a stubborn spot? Substitute full-fat mayonnaise for the toothpaste and leave it on for at least an hour before wiping clean and buffing with a clean cloth.

THE PROBLEM: **I have unwanted guests. With hairless tails. And whiskers.**

THE SOLUTION: Mickey and Minnie aren't so cute when they've taken up residence in your kitchen cabinets. Besides freaking out your friends, they can also transmit parasites and germs through their droppings, which can cause food poisoning. The U.S. Centers for Disease Control and Prevention (CDC) recommend a simple snap trap baited with some peanut butter. This may sound mean, but it's the most humane (read: quick) solution. Mice can squeeze through areas the size of a nickel (eek!), so you will need to plug any gaps in your walls, molding, and floorboards with steel wool.

THE PROBLEM: **You think mice are a problem? Try roaches.**

THE SOLUTION: Yes, these creepy crawlies can contaminate food and trigger asthma. They can also kill your social life if anyone sees them. To keep roaches at bay, prevention is key: Don't leave unwashed dishes in the sink, uncovered food on countertops, or pet food out overnight. And instead of using those little black disks that contain harsh chemicals, try disposable, nontoxic glue traps.

HOW THE HECK DO I CLEAN...?
GRODY GIZMOS EDITION

THIS FILTHY MOUSE
Unplug the mouse or remove its batteries. Spray compressed air on the underside to clear dust from the trackball and crevices. (If you don't have compressed air, run a Post-it between the buttons.) Clean the top, along with the mouse pad, using a disinfecting wipe. (Don't get the trackball wet.) Dry with a clean, soft, lint-free cloth.

CRUMB-CAKED REMOTE CONTROL AND VIDEO-GAME CONTROLLERS
Spray compressed air between the buttons if you see the remains of your last bag of Doritos. (See above if you don't have compressed air.) Then clean with disinfecting wipes, making sure they're not dripping wet.

STREAKY TV SCREENS
Make sure that the TV is off and cool; a warm screen is harder to clean. Everyday cleaning products can damage LCD and plasma screens, so a specialized kit with pretreated polishing cloths is best (and less work). Apply the cloth in a light, circular motion.

FINGER-SMUDGED TABLET OR SMARTPHONE
Wipe the screen with a slightly damp soft cloth. "But don't use glass cleaner on any touch screen," says digital-lifestyle expert Carley Knobloch. "It can destroy the protective coating."

DIRTY CONFESSIONS: A HOUSE CLEANER TELLS ALL

Candace Mills, a cofounder of New York City eco-friendly cleaning service Team Clean, spills on the most horrifying items she's unearthed within a piece of furniture.

I ALWAYS THINK IT'S STRANGE WHEN I find a whole piece of food. A crumb I can understand. But we've found whole pieces of pizza. It's also happened that a client has somehow left a dildo (!) in the couch. I would think that's the kind of thing you put away—how do you forget that? But we're not out to embarrass people, so when we run across something of that nature, we just clean the room top to bottom, spick-and-span, and then maybe just place it somewhere where it will be found, either on the sofa cushion or even back where it originally was.

Two of the most common mistakes cleaning newbies make are letting messes sit around instead of dealing with them right away and using toxic commercial products for every single little job. (Unsurprisingly, one often leads to another.) If something spills, just deal with it. If you let it sit, it's going to dry and harden—and it's going to become more of a problem in your head, too. When you handle spills immediately, there's no need to use the industrial-grade chemicals. You can use vinegar throughout almost your entire home. It's even effective on bathroom mold. Sure, there's some patience required with green products. You just have to go do something else while the baking soda or vinegar or whatever you're using is doing its thing. Is that really so bad?

There are a few spots that are pretty consistently the filthiest in every home we see: under the bed, above the fridge and the kitchen cupboards, the fridge handles, the space between the oven and the cabinets, and the area underneath the cabinets along the baseboard. Those all get pretty bad. Laundry rooms are often neglected, too—especially the space behind the machines. People don't think about it, so you'll find more critters and bugs back there. And last but not least, there's the commode. People get everything else around it, but not the space behind it or the exterior of the bowl. I'm fascinated. I want to plant a camera and see how the heck that gets so dirty. On second thought, maybe not.

I'll never forget my first...

...apartment, rodents and all.
By **J. Courtney Sullivan**

THE FIRST PLACE I EVER LIVED ALONE was a 300-square-foot jewel box on Cranberry Street, in Brooklyn. It had a fireplace, crown moldings, and a hardwood floor that had seen better days. I loved it.

There, I did things no one else would ever want to do with me. I watched Doris Day marathons. I read W. H. Auden aloud. Of course, there were downsides. Rodents, for example. One mouse darted in and out of an oven vent so often that I decided to make peace with him and named him Stuey.

One tragic night, I returned from a weekend away to find poor Stuey dead on the kitchen floor. I am a feminist, but if I could have thought of a man to call to come remove him, I would have done so. Instead, I called my father at home in Boston and made him stay on the phone with me as I picked Stuey up and brought him outside. I used about 14 garbage bags to do this. For some reason, I wore sunglasses. When it was over, I shouted, exultant, "I did it! And I didn't need a man to help me."

"Except for me," said my dad, who was still on the line.

While on Cranberry Street, I found a copy of a book called *Live Alone and Like It*. Written by Marjorie Hillis in 1936, this slim guide became my bible. Living alone, Hillis said, was "as nice, perhaps, as any other way of living, and infinitely nicer than living with... the wrong single individual." Happily, I met the right single individual, my future hus-band. When we decided to live together, I tried to convince him to move into my apartment. He pointed out that the space was so small that it could barely contain my belongings, let alone his. He was right, but I wept when I closed the door for the last time.

We now live 15 minutes from Cranberry Street. Sometimes I stare up at the fourth floor, trying to discern something, *anything*. "Look, my old air conditioner!" I've said at least 10 times, and for some reason this gives me comfort.

I have the strongest urge to ring the bell, to see how the apartment's newest inhabitant is doing. I'm certain she is a young woman who lives alone. I imagine slipping a note into her mailbox, which used to be mine. I'd tell her to treasure this place, mice and all. Things have a way of rolling forward, and try as you might, you can't go back.

J. COURTNEY SULLIVAN IS THE AUTHOR OF THE NOVELS *THE ENGAGEMENTS*, *MAINE*, AND *COMMENCEMENT*.

Be your own super

Many supers are anything but. So you'll be in better shape if you don't depend on them for Every. Single. Thing. Take care of these tasks on your own.

▶ Make sure your fire extinguisher is properly pressurized. Check the gauge, usually located between the handle and the nozzle. The needle should be in the green section. If it's not, replace the extinguisher.

▶ When you turn your clocks ahead for daylight savings time, make your next task replacing the batteries in your smoke alarms and carbon monoxide detectors. (Do the same later in the year, when you turn the clocks back again.) You'll rest easier, even after losing that hour of sleep.

▶ If new episodes of *How I Met Your Mother* were airing the last time you checked your clothes-dryer vent, it's been too long—especially since dust bunnies can clog up the works, creating a serious fire hazard. First off, you should clean out the dryer's lint trap after every use. To go to the next level, unplug the dryer and scoot the machine out from the wall. Disconnect the exhaust pipe (it's probably attached with a simple clamp and some screws). Remove as much lint as you can from the pipe and the part of the dryer it connects to, using a vent brush or a vacuum hose. Reattach the pipe, then head outside to the place where the vent comes through the wall and make sure there's nothing weird, like a bird's nest, clogging it. Also make sure the flap (or damper) opens and closes securely. If you discover a serious problem (or just more dirt and debris than your vacuum can stomach), hire a pro to get the job done right. (Look for a certified dryer exhaust technician at dryersafety.org.)

▶ To keep your radiators running, try this: Fit a bleed key (just a couple of bucks at most hardware stores) into each radiator's valve and turn it counterclockwise. Use a bucket to catch any trapped water, then close the valve—and commence bragging about your impressive new skills.

▶ Test windows for drafts by running a lit candle along the perimeter of each frame. If the flame flickers, the window may need caulking or weather stripping. Once it's sealed, you'll save money on heating costs and delay having to swap out your fave summer pj's for fall flannels.

▶ Lubricate locks and hinges on windows and doors. In winter, the dry air may cause them to stick, which you don't want to discover by getting locked out on the first subzero day. A little WD-40 is just the thing.

Who does what?

You got a roommate to save on rent and to have fun— not to practice playing Mom. But it's hard when she doesn't do the dishes or the laundry. Hello, this is not a day care! Avoid chore wars with the help of Irene S. Levine, Ph.D., a professor of psychiatry at the New York University School of Medicine, in New York City.

Start off on the right foot.

Ideally, you'll choose a roommate whose ideas about cleanliness are at least in the same ballpark as yours. But since that's not always the case, it's wise to have a convo about cleaning before you've amassed a mountain of crusted pots and pans that no one wants to claim. And try to do it IRL. "It's always best to have conversations that are somewhat sensitive in person," says Levine. "It allows for facial and body expression to help get the message across." A tip: No scowling!

Determine your strengths and weaknesses, or who hates what most.

An early diplomatic move is to have each roommate list one chore that she really hates doing and one chore that she doesn't mind—or maybe even kind of likes. (Some people do find vacuuming soothing, we're told.) All the neutral tasks can then be divvied up according to how much time they take on a weekly or monthly basis. Also an option: switching things up every month or two, which you might need to try if everyone shares the same loathing for tub-scrubbing.

Establish some standards.

"Expectations are extremely important—defining exactly what needs to be done and figuring out a schedule that makes sense for both of you," says Levine. You might think the shower should get a weekly scrubbing, while she would be perfectly comfortable waiting until the mildew starts to take over. These discrepancies *will* raise their ugly heads over and over again until you spell things out.

Post a schedule in a visible spot.

"Otherwise it's easy on a day-to-day basis to forget," says Levine. Or, you know, to "forget."

Be flexible.

"Be cognizant of each other's lives and schedules. If you see that your roommate is in a crunch at work, fill in for her, and she might do the same for you later," says Levine.

Keep communicating.

If you suspect that your roommate didn't actually dust that still-linty ledge, it's OK to say something. Just mind how and when you do it. "Raise issues when they're little, before they become big ones that interfere with the relationship," says Levine. "And ask some questions first. There might be a reason the person didn't do it." Also helpful: framing the issue as a joint problem that you want to resolve together. ("I feel like we're swimming in pizza boxes lately. Is there something we can do to make it easier to keep up with the cardboard recycling?")

Pick your battles.

Differentiate between the shared areas of the house, which are mutual territory, and the private ones—and only worry about the first kind. "If your roommate doesn't want to make her bed, that's fine," says Levine.

When all else fails, hire someone to get the job done.

Especially for the bigger tasks that don't fit into the weekly rotation. If neither of you is ever going to volunteer to scrub out the oven or the refrigerator, agree to put a few dollars in a jar each week to save up for a seasonal visit from a professional to tackle those more vexing (and weekend-killing) tasks.

IF YOU DO ONLY ONE THING...

"Before you head to the grocery store, take a moment to wipe down refrigerator shelves with a damp cloth and throw away food past its prime. There's nothing better than unloading groceries into a sparkling-clean fridge."

CAMILLE STYLES is the creator of the blog CamilleStyles.com and a spokesperson for Electrolux (swanky appliances).

The no-spin guide to doing laundry

You probably experienced a few wardrobe malfunctions back in college. And things only get more complicated as your wardrobe shifts from boyfriend jeans to office-ready separates. This compendium will help you sort through the frustrations—and, of course, your darks and your whites.

Sorting

With the advance of color-safe detergents, you no longer have to sweat it if a stray red sock gets mixed up with your whites. Separating is still a good rule, but it's only necessary if it's indicated on the care label. Instead, sort by fabric weight. Give hardy items—towels, denim, twill—their own cycle. These are heavier, tougher fabrics, so when they're washed with finer cottons or synthetics, they beat the heck out of them. Group T-shirts, knits, leggings, and any delicate items together in a different load.

Water temperature

In most instances, you can't go wrong if you launder everything in cold. It helps preserve the color and condition of fabrics, saves energy, and is effective at removing dirt. If you're skittish about a particular item, check the tag.

Laundry detergent

Buy a color-safe all-purpose detergent to handle the majority of your laundry. A liquid formula dissolves well and can pretreat stains, so it's more versatile than a powder. It's also good to keep on hand an oxygen bleach to tackle tough stains and brighten whites and a mild detergent for gentle-cycle items and hand-washables. Fabric softener is handy to soften crunchy towels and zap static cling. The chemicals in softener can build up, so don't add it to every wash, and use half the recommended amount. Bonus: Think how much longer each bottle will last!

Hand washing

Fill the sink with lukewarm water and add a capful of mild detergent; swirl to disperse the soap. This is a job where you should keep lights separate from darks in case the dyes bleed. Use one hand to twirl the garment around in a circular motion for two to five minutes. Drain the water from the basin, then fold the fabric over and gently press it against the side of the sink to squeeze out excess water. (Wringing can be harsher on fabric than the average spin cycle.) Refill the basin to rinse out the soap, and repeat until the suds are gone. Lay the garment on a clean towel, roll up the towel, and press down on it to absorb the water. Hang or lay flat to dry.

Wash. Dry. Repeat.

That's 90 percent of what you need to know about laundry. The other 10 percent is right here. These handy tips can help you make your clothes last longer and look better.

1 | Unfasten all buttons on button-down shirts, including the small ones on the cuffs and the collars, before laundering. When buttons are fastened, the agitation in the machine and the weight of other garments can cause buttonholes to tear.

2 | Surprise! Many knit sweaters made of cotton, synthetics, or blends can be machine-washed in cold water on the gentle cycle with all-purpose or mild detergent, sometimes even if the tag says otherwise.

3 | To keep jeans from fading or getting roughed up, zip up all zippers and turn the pants inside out before washing in a small load (more water than clothes) in cold water using a color-safe detergent. Dry on low or medium heat, then pull the jeans out while slightly damp. They'll last longer that way.

4 | To prevent that stiff, almost crunchy feel that can develop as sweaters air-dry, give them a spin in the dryer on low heat for 10 minutes before laying them flat on a mesh sweater rack or a towel.

5 | To minimize jeans shrinkage, step on the hems while pulling on the waistband after laundering.

6 | Yoga-pants funk is real. Because the synthetic fibers in moisture-wicking material often trap smelly bacteria, these garments need TLC. After a sweat session, launder in the hottest water temperature your gear can handle, along with an enzyme-formulated detergent to break down protein-based stains, such as perspiration. If you spent a lot on your exercise clothes, skip the spandex-damaging dryer.

7 | Hand washing is generally the best way to care for bras and lingerie. And you can wash these items while you shower. Get them wet, lather a pea-size amount of mild shampoo, and gently squeeze the suds through the fabric. Rinse and roll in a towel to absorb excess moisture, then hang to dry.

8 | To keep shapewear in top form, wash in a mesh lingerie bag on the delicate cycle in cold water. Ditch the fabric softener and the dryer; lay flat to dry.

HOW OFTEN SHOULD I WASH THIS?*

Some of you may be doing this on the sly already. Well, time to come clean. Say it loud, say it proud: *It's totally OK not to wash every item of clothing every single time you wear it!* Still, that's not a license to go full frat boy. There *is* a science to what's recyclable and how many times you can do it. For optimal freshness, hang up clothes at the end of the day to let them air out before cramming them back into the closet.

ANYTHING WHITE OR SILK: AFTER EVERY WEAR

BRAS: AFTER 3 TO 4 WEARS

DRESS PANTS AND SKIRTS: AFTER 5 TO 7 WEARS

DOWN PARKAS AND VESTS: 2 TIMES A SEASON

FLEECE JACKETS AND SWEATSHIRTS: AFTER 6 TO 7 WEARS

HATS, GLOVES, AND SCARVES: 3 TO 5 TIMES A SEASON

HOSIERY: AFTER EVERY WEAR

JACKETS AND BLAZERS: AFTER 5 TO 6 WEARS

JEANS: AFTER 4 TO 5 WEARS

LEATHER AND SUEDE JACKETS: ONCE A SEASON

LEGGINGS AND YOGA PANTS: AFTER 1 TO 3 WEARS

PAJAMAS: AFTER 3 TO 4 WEARS

SHAPEWEAR: AFTER 1 TO 3 WEARS

SHORTS AND KHAKIS: AFTER 2 TO 3 WEARS

SWEATERS: COTTON, SILK, AND CASHMERE, AFTER 2 WEARS; WOOL AND SYNTHETIC BLENDS, AFTER 5 WEARS

SWIMSUITS: AFTER EVERY WEAR

T-SHIRTS, TANKS, AND CAMISOLES: AFTER EVERY WEAR

TOPS AND DRESSES: AFTER 1 TO 3 WEARS; FORMAL DRESSES SHOULD BE DRY-CLEANED AFTER EVERY WEAR

WOOL COATS: 1 TO 2 TIMES A SEASON

*Disclaimer: The information provided here should be used as general guidelines only. It does not take into account sweltering 90-degree days and accidental squirts of sriracha. Also, you may want to do a sniff check before the next round juuust to make sure.

LAUNDROMAT ETIQUETTE

You can avoid people who give you the heebie-jeebs on mass transit. But it's harder to make nice with oddballs when you're stuck in a small space waiting for your unmentionables to finish the rinse cycle. Here, how to mind your p's and q's at the Duds n Suds.

Q. HOW DO YOU AVOID AWKWARD SMALL TALK WITH STRANGERS?

A. Unwanted chitchat is the worst, especially when you can't make a quick escape. Look busy: If a stranger initiates unwanted conversation, look anxiously at your phone and start reading your e-mail. Then you can say, "Sorry, I'd love to chat, but I really need to get this done for work."

Q. WHAT DO YOU DO IF YOU NEED THE MACHINE (AND IT'S FINISHED RUNNING) BUT THE PERSON HASN'T COME BACK YET? HOW LONG IS IT POLITE TO WAIT BEFORE YOU CAN REMOVE HIS CLOTHES?

A. Allow for a grace period—say, 30 minutes. After that point, it's fine to move someone's clothes, but be courteous about it. Don't put his clothes in the dryer, as you may wind up shrinking an expensive sweater. Move the clothes to a clean and obvious spot. If the clothes are in the dryer and they're still wet, put a few more quarters in the machine and leave a note. Think of it as paying it forward.

Q. WHAT IF YOU ACCIDENTALLY TOOK SOMEONE'S ELSE T-SHIRT? OR IF SHE TOOK YOURS?

A. If you're the one who swiped the shirt, tack up a flyer that says, "I'm sorry—I took this by accident," in the laundry room, with a photo of the piece of clothing and your cell-phone number or e-mail address. If you suspect that someone may have unintentionally grabbed yours, leave a short note asking (nicely) for it back. What if no one replies? Don't put up an accusatory note. A few lost items are among the regular perils of communal laundry.

Q. HOW MANY MACHINES IS IT ACCEPTABLE TO USE AT ONCE? IS IT RUDE TO CLAIM ALL OF THEM?

A. If you're going to use an atypically large number of machines, then get your stuff out promptly. Don't disappear for the day. Using just two machines—one for darks and one for lights—is fine. But don't monopolize all the machines if you can possibly avoid it.

Out, out damn spot!

Eating 1.8 meals per day at your desk practically guarantees a lap full of lo mein eventually. Since everybody's gotta spill, drip, or trip sometime, here's your first-things-first strategy for addressing common stains on machine-washable clothes. (Take the fancy stuff straight to the cleaners. Turn the page for details.)

Berries or juice

Scrape up any solids, then apply a solution of warm water and dishwashing soap. Remove soap residue with a damp towel; blot. If the stain persists, blot on an ammonia solution with a warm, damp towel.

Blood

First flush the area with cold water, then daub it with a paste made from an enzyme detergent (such as All brand laundry detergent) and let sit in a warm place for 30 minutes. Place diluted ammonia in an eye dropper and treat the area. Rinse and finish with a regular wash cycle.

Chocolate

Apply a solution made of 1 tablespoon enzyme detergent and 2 cups water to the delicious offender, let sit for 20 minutes, then rinse thoroughly. Use a combination of water and a mild detergent to clean the residue.

Clear alcohol (vodka, gin)

Mix 1 tablespoon white vinegar and ⅔ cup rubbing alcohol. Using a dry cloth, dab onto the spill.

Coffee or tea

In a spray bottle, combine 1 cup white vinegar and 1 cup water. Spritz the stain, then blot with a damp cloth. Next, dab with diluted ammonia (1 tablespoon clear ammonia in 1 cup water)—a step probably best saved for once you're home from the office, to avoid drawing attention to the aroma. Blot with a clean, damp cloth, followed by a dry cloth.

OUTSOURCE!

Nothing is more depressing than dropping cash on dry-cleaning bills—except having to buy a pricey new item because you destroyed the old one in the wash. Be smart and have these items professionally cleaned rather than mangling them at home.

▶ Down comforters and parkas

▶ Lined suits, work dresses, and blazers (especially wool), since the inner and outer fabrics may react differently to water and shrink in weird ways

▶ Anything made of leather or suede

▶ Rayon, viscose, or acetate clothing

▶ Untreated-silk garments

▶ Any item with elaborate sequins, beading, or other delicate embellishments or with lots of special pleats or creases (Tip: If you've worn it on New Year's Eve, it's probably not a wash-at-home candidate.)

Dirt

Let dry, then brush off any loose particles. Next, apply a solution of a little dish soap and warm water. Remove the soap residue with a damp towel; blot. Repeat until the stain is gone.

Grease (pizza, salad dressing)

Sprinkle cornmeal or talcum powder on the spot until it is absorbed. Brush off with a dry cloth.

Ink

Dip a clean toothbrush in a capful of rubbing alcohol. Shake off the excess and brush gently over the spot. Vow not to let this deter you from using actual pens. You don't want to completely lose the ability to write the old-fashioned way!

Ketchup and tomato sauce

Apply a combination solvent (as are most standard store-bought stain-fighters). Use an eyedropper and diluted vinegar to remove any remaining color. Finish by thoroughly flushing the spot with cool water in a regular wash cycle.

Lipstick

Apply an oil solvent, available at drugstores, and let dry, then remove as much residue as possible. Treat with a liquid detergent (like Woolite) and very little water. Rub to form suds, then rinse. Use an eyedropper and diluted vinegar to remove any remaining color. Rinse with cool water.

Red wine

Blot—don't rub—with a clean, damp cloth, then use a fresh cloth to apply white wine. (Who knew?) Blot again. Still there? Sprinkle on baking soda, let sit for 20 minutes, and remove with yet another cloth.

Snow and salt

The calcium chloride in salty melted ice is alkaline and can leave behind a brownish stain. First neutralize with a vinegar solution (1 part white vinegar to 1 part water). Blot with a towel from the edge of the stain inward. Follow this with a solution of warm water and dish soap, then remove with a damp towel.

Sticky stuff (gum, wax)

If the worst a toppled candle did was splatter your tablecloth or duvet with wax, consider yourself lucky. Hold some ice to the gunk until it hardens, then gently scrape it off with a butter knife. Dab on some clear dish soap to dislodge any residue. Rinse with a clean, damp cloth.

Sweat marks

Treat perspiration marks (holy awkward job interview!) with a prewash stain remover, then launder the clothes in the hottest water recommended for the fabric, using an enzyme detergent and an oxygen bleach.

Vomit

Apply a solution of warm water and dish soap (blot; don't rub). Remove soap residue with a damp towel; blot. Repeat if necessary. If the stain persists, blot on an ammonia solution (1 tablespoon clear household formula plus 1 cup water) with a damp towel.

White wine

Dab with water and a little clear dish soap. Rinse with a clean, damp cloth. Easy peasy.

IF YOU DO ONLY ONE THING...

"Know that dust under the sofa becomes dust in the nose, the eye, or the soup."

CHERYL MENDELSON is the author of the all-things-domestic bible *Home Comforts: The Art & Science of Keeping House*.

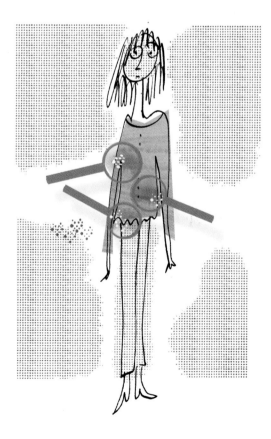

All you need in your...

Consider these three practical-life-supplies checklists the grown-up answer to the scouting-preparedness pledge. Stock your tool kit, desk drawer, and car trunk with these supplies and all manner of organizational crises will be averted.

TOOL KIT

☐ **MULTIHEAD SCREWDRIVER.** Phillips-head, flat-head, and Torx (six-point star shape).

☐ **12-VOLT CORDLESS DRILL.** For DIY work, like hanging curtains and mounting heavy artwork.

☐ **DUCT TAPE.** For quick fixes, like patching a torn bicycle seat.

☐ **NEEDLE-NOSE PLIERS.** For minor jewelry repairs and pulling out small nails.

☐ **METAL TAPE MEASURE.** Should be at least an inch wide so it won't flop when extended (so annoying!). For deciding where to best position that massive bookcase/room divider.

☐ **SLIP-JOINT PLIERS.** They adjust to grip items of various sizes.

☐ **ADJUSTABLE WRENCH.** Instead of a set with different sizes.

☐ **PUTTY KNIFE.** For removing old caulk, opening paint cans, or flipping burgers. (We kid—but it works.)

☐ **STANDARD FLAT-NOSE CLAW HAMMER.** One that weighs 12 to 16 ounces, with a steel head, for pounding in and pulling out nails.

☐ **ASSORTED FASTENERS.** Buy a kit with nuts, bolts, washers, anchors, and nails in various sizes.

☐ **WD-40.** For lubing bike chains and decreaking hinges.

DESK DRAWER

☐ **FOREVER STAMPS.** So you don't have to worry about the inevitable postal-rate changes that come right after you stock up.

☐ **BOX OF YOUR FAVORITE PENS.** Use (and lose) only one at a time instead of littering your desktop with dozens.

☐ **A DECENT STAPLER**

☐ **WEIGHTED TAPE DISPENSER.** One that holds a fat roll of tape.

☐ **BLACK PERMANENT MARKER.** For addressing packages and writing guests' names on plastic cups at parties.

☐ **ANGLE-TIP HIGHLIGHTER.** For color-coding credit-card bills and setting priorities on your overachiever-y lists.

☐ **SMALL AND LARGE POST-IT NOTES.** For reminders, shopping lists, epiphanies, and holding your place in a book.

☐ **AESTHETICALLY PLEASING PAPER CLIPS.** They cost about the same as standard ones and they're reusable, so why not?

☐ **CORRECTION TAPE.** To fix mistakes. (It's similar to the liquid stuff, but without the drying time—and the drying out.)

☐ **MECHANICAL PENCILS.** So you don't need a bulky sharpener.

☐ **TITANIUM SCISSORS.** Because they stay sharp for years.

CAR TRUNK

☐ **FLASHLIGHT AND EXTRA BATTERIES.** Plus a headlamp for hands-free illumination.

☐ **FIRST-AID KIT**

☐ **BASIC CAR-REPAIR KIT.** With wrenches, screwdrivers, pliers, hammer, socket set, a sharp blade, and a roll of duct tape.

☐ **JUMPER CABLES**

☐ **A GOOD TIRE IRON AND JACK.** The ones your car came with are probably crappy.

☐ **NONPERISHABLE SNACKS AND A FEW BOTTLES OF WATER**

☐ **REFLECTIVE OR BRIGHTLY COLORED OBJECT.** To signal distress. Consider safety flares, an LED strobe, safety triangles, or even an old orange or red rag to tie to the antenna.

☐ **HAND-CRANKED CELL-PHONE CHARGER.** Or a backup battery.

☐ **BLANKETS.** For keeping warm. A shiny Mylar space blanket traps heat like a boss.

☐ **EMERGENCY WHISTLE.** More noise, less effort.

☐ **SPARE TIRE, TIRE PATCH KIT, 12-VOLT AIR-COMPRESSOR CAN.** Good for refilling a tire with a slow leak. Or a can of Fix-a-Flat tire sealant. (Inform the auto-shop guys you used it before they remove a dud tire—it makes a real mess.)

☐ **MAPS.** Ones made of real paper—you can't count on always having cell service.

☐ **12-FOOT TOW ROPE.** In case you literally get stuck in a rut.

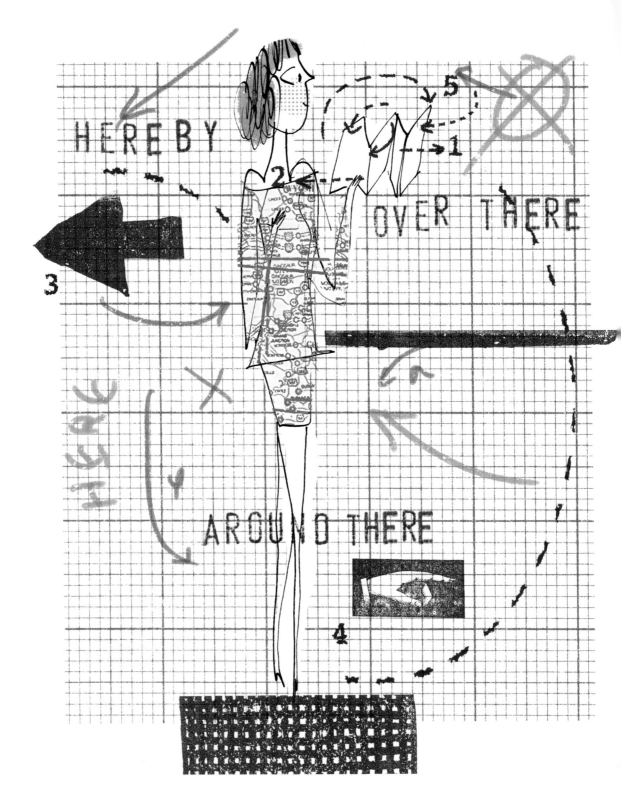

CHAPTER 10

DEALING

OK, we've told you how to get a mortgage, stock a pantry, and shop for clothes on a budget. But practical advice aside, life is squishy. And many of your toughest everyday challenges will center around not tangible, solvable problems (sorry) but dealing with people—all sorts of people, strangers and loved ones alike.

This final chapter helps you with the squishy: family feuds, friendship evolutions, social graces, etiquette breaches, breakups, makeups, breakups (again). Plus, it tells you how to write a killer thank-you note—very important, even nowadays. And we end with a little inspiration to send you on your way. Godspeed!

Etiquette rules for the real world

You weren't raised in a barn. You wouldn't do something flat-out rude, like belch in public. But everyday dilemmas are more vexing: Who gets custody of the airplane armrest—you or the other guy? How do you tell a hostess about your weird new diet? We'll tell you. (You're welcome.)

TABLE MANNERS

CAN I PUT MY ELBOWS ON THE TABLE? Yes, it's fine. Wrists, too. What you don't want to do is use your elbow as a fulcrum for bringing food to your mouth.

WHICH FORK AM I SUPPOSED TO USE? Work from the outside in, salad fork to dessert fork.

WHICH WATER GLASS IS MINE? Think *BMW*. Your *bread* plate is on your left; *meal* plate, in the middle; *water*, on the right.

CAN WE EAT YET? Wait until everyone has been served or the host gives you the green light. If there's a large number of people or a buffet, you can begin eating when you get your food. At weddings and in other situations where there's a preset menu, wait until the host gives the all-clear.

HOW SHOULD I PASS FOOD AROUND THE TABLE? Dishes should be passed counterclockwise, so that the right hand is free for serving. (You're out of luck, southpaws.) If you're asked to pass the salt or the pepper, pass both.

I CAN JUST...BARELY...REACH THE BUTTER. SHOULD I ASK FOR IT? If you can get the item you need without fully extending your arm, go for it. Otherwise ask for it to be passed.

I HAVE TO MAKE A PIT STOP. WHAT SHOULD I SAY? When you need to step away, say, "Excuse me. I'll be right back." No one needs to know the details.

Leave your napkin loosely on the table to the left of your plate, not on your seat.

PARTY MANNERS

WHAT'S THE DEAL WITH RSVP'ING? Always do it, and do it on time. Websites like Evite have features that allow the host to see who has read the invitation (and when). A snubbed or delayed RSVP comes off as ungrateful and careless.

CAN I BRING A "PLUS ONE"? Whoever is listed on the envelope is invited. If your boyfriend's name isn't included, he's not invited.

WILL MY LACTO-OVO MACROBIOTIC-PALEO DIET BE ACCOMMODATED? For large parties, you're on your own. Don't mention dietary needs to your host. For small dinner parties, let the host know as soon as possible. If you adhere to an especially tricky diet, ask if you can bring a dish.

WHEN SHOULD I SHOW UP? For a dinner party, show up 10 to 15 minutes after the scheduled time. Never show up early, because the host may not be ready. Any later than 15 minutes and you need to let the host know.

E-MAIL MANNERS

HOW FAST SHOULD I REPLY TO AN E-MAIL? Within 24 hours.

DO I HAVE TO INCLUDE A HELLO AND A SIGN-OFF (LIKE "SINCERELY, KATE") IN EVERY E-MAIL? It's OK to drop the "hello" and "many thanks" after some back-and-forth. Also, pay attention to a person's signature. Does she go by her full name or a nickname? Then echo her choice in future e-mails.

WHEN SHOULD I REPLY ALL? Click this only when you truly need to address the whole group. If what you have to say concerns only the sender, spare everyone else.

PUBLIC-TRANSPORTATION MANNERS

WHO GETS TO USE THE AIRPLANE ARMRESTS? The person in the middle seat gets both, because he doesn't have the aisle armrest or the window to lean on. If that's you, congrats.

ARE MY EARBUDS TOO LOUD? If your seatmates can discern that you have a soft spot for Iggy Azalea, then yes.

CAN I PUT MY FEET ON THE SEAT OR TAKE MY SHOES OFF? Keep them on the floor. For trips under three hours (this includes commuter trains), footwear stays on. If you do remove your shoes for longer flights, don't go bare. Bring along a pair of socks or slippers. Any issues with odor? Keep your feet contained.

SHOULD I GIVE THE PREGNANT LADY MY SEAT? Yes. And the same holds for children, the elderly, and anyone with a physical impediment.

NIGHTLIFE MANNERS

THE BARTENDER IS TOTALLY IGNORING ME. HOW DO I GET HIS ATTENTION? Make eye contact and smile. Tip well for the first round so that he'll check in with you later. What not to do: snap your fingers, flash a wad of cash, or use the hailing-a-taxi salute.

HOW DO I SQUEEZE PAST PEOPLE WITHOUT LOSING ALL MY DIGNITY? In a theater row, face the stage so that if you lose your balance, you can grab the back of the seat in front of you, not topple onto a stranger. When people scoot past you, stand up so that the seat folds up, then step back. However, if the show is under way, just move your legs to one side.

CAN I SNEAK A PEEK AT MY CELL? It should be off the table at a restaurant and turned off and put away at a theater. The glow of the screen distracts others in the audience.

WHO PAYS ON A DATE—ME OR THE GUY? The only rules you need to know are these: (1) Relationships should feel good, and (2) mutual graciousness is always in style. Old-fashioned chivalry may seem appealing, but rigid gender-based conventions—the kind that determine who makes decisions or acts in certain ways—are outdated. This is to say, it's up to you and your gentleman caller to decide who shells out when.

DO THIS, DON'T DO THAT

14 simple rules for keeping the manners police at bay

DO remove both earbuds when having a conversation.

DON'T clip your nails in public.

DO smile at coworkers as you pass in the hall.

DON'T block the climbing lane on the escalator.

DO cover your mouth when yawning.

DON'T wear so much perfume that people can smell it from more than an arm's length away.

DO be kind to restaurant and retail staff.

DON'T say that you'll be there in 10 minutes if it's going to be 20.

DO hold the door for the person behind you, and also grab the door when you're the one for whom it's being held.

DON'T blow your nose at the table.

DO put your shopping cart where it belongs instead of leaving it in a parking space to crash into a random car.

DON'T say "No problem" when you mean "You're welcome."

DO wipe down the exercise machine at the gym after you're finished.

DON'T get on an elevator or a train until the departing passengers have exited.

3 STEPS TO WRITING A BETTER THANK-YOU NOTE

Steve Fadie, the author of *Words to the Rescue,* helps demystify this essential missive.

WHAT TO SAY: Short really is sweet, says Fadie: "A lot of great notes are less than 30 words." Start the note with a spin on "thank you" ("You were so kind to…"). Avoid the semiapologetic phrase "I just wanted to say." Then get specific about how you'll enjoy the gift and what the gift giver means to you. Example: "Many thanks for the beautiful pen. It's a perfect graduation gift—and a great reminder of all the support you've shown me throughout my education." Boom. You're done.

HOW TO SEND IT: Handwritten is better. "We receive so few cards by mail these days, so it will stand out," says Fadie. Send thanks via e-mail or social networks only if you know there's no chance you'll send a card or if you're expressing gratitude for a smaller gesture and you've said "thank you" in person. But use a little thought here, too: Post an old, beloved photo of you and the gift giver on Facebook, for example, and craft a personalized message.

WHEN TO SEND IT: Ideally, you would get a note out the door within two weeks. If you get it together later, acknowledge the lapse, briefly, after you do the thanking. ("I apologize for the tardiness of this note. Please know I have been thinking of you with gratitude.") Better late…

How to make nice on the Internet

Did you get into a flame war on Twitter? Or accidentally swipe right on your ex on Tinder? Avoid future epic fails with this netiquette guide, courtesy of Catherine Newman, Real Simple's *manners columnist.*

The apps might be new, but many of your grandma's rules still apply: Be kind and respectful, responsible and trustworthy. Don't gossip; don't hurt anybody's feelings intentionally; don't embarrass people or make them feel excluded. Ask first. Show you care. Err on the side of caution. Follow the Golden Rule. (Would you be happy if someone posted a picture of you adjusting your bikini bottom?)

That said, the specifics of online life can pose fresh challenges, given that we're encouraged to share, to tag, to connect widely and instantly—and it can be hard to understand how our actions will affect other people. One good rule of thumb is to consider how they might. And another is to bear in mind that everything you do online is public and permanent. If you don't want Grams to see it, don't post it.

Perhaps even more important than how you use your technology is when you use it. Your boss isn't going to want to see a Facebook post timestamped from that afternoon meeting you were in. Your best friend might be over the moon about her wedding—but not about your live-tweeting it. And above all, remember to power off your gadgets and pay attention to the real people in your life—the ones who are right in front of you.

To avoid giving offense, follow these guidelines, tailored to each of the most popular social-media sites. (For expert tips on using the professional-networking site LinkedIn, go to page 41.)

FACEBOOK

The top pitfalls here include oversharing and underthinking. This is your public identity, so create it consciously.

DON'T POST ABOUT YOURSELF 24/7.
It's the nature of the medium, of course. And, sure, we all want affirmation. But try not to make every update about you and you alone. Try not to troll too frequently for compliments or sympathy. Actually, try not to post too frequently, period.

POST ONLY FLATTERING PICTURES OF OTHER PEOPLE.
Just because you're cool with being posted wolfing an entire deep-dish pizza doesn't mean your cousin, who was right there with you, will share your sentiments.

FRIEND WISELY.
Don't extend a request to your supervisor or a client. "You don't want them ga-ga-gooing at your baby niece or commenting on your Oktoberfest pics," says Newman. And if they friend you? Adjust your settings as needed, to keep at least a thin boundary between work and regular life.

SPARE US YOUR SYNCED GAMES.
No offense, but we don't even want to know that you're playing Diamond Dash, let alone receive tedious, spamlike invitations to join you.

ABSTAIN FROM VAGUE-BOOKING.
If you want to share something, please do. But, advises Newman, skip the ambiguous cries for attention: "It finally happened"; "ER visits suck"; or that frowny little emoji.

TWITTER

The 140-character limit of this social-networking service encourages brevity *and* frequency. You'll need to figure out what to post—and why.

MIND YOUR MEH.
The oatmeal you ate for breakfast? How much you hate Mondays? Unless you're a comic genius, a Nobel prize–winning neuroscientist, or Kate Middleton, your every mundane thought is probably not worth posting.

APPLY THE BILLBOARD TEST.
Assume that everyone in the world can and will see everything you post (the drunken rant, the gross joke), says Newman.

BE RESPONSIVE.
This is the quid pro quo rule: If someone you know follows you, follow him back; if someone tweets something nice about you, favorite it.

DON'T REQUEST RETWEETS.
Make the most of your 140 characters and people will want to share your tweets all on their own, without your asking.

SNAPCHAT

Because this picture- and video-messaging app allows you to create disappearing posts, the illusion of impermanence can lull you into a sense of safety. Don't be lulled.

REMEMBER THAT THE PICS ARE NOT NECESSARILY FLEETING…
"People can take screenshots of your snaps before they disappear," says Newman. "And those screenshots will then *not* disappear. Enough said."

…SO BE WARY OF POTENTIAL EMBARRASSMENT.
That goes for other people—and yourself. Just because this point can never be stressed enough: A nude snap is not going to do you any favors.

DON'T TAKE SCREENSHOTS OF OTHER PEOPLE'S SNAPS.
Creating permanent evidence violates the spirit of the medium. Folks using the app mean for their snaps to be transitory, and you should respect that intention.

TINDER

For those of you who haven't tried it yet, this hot-or-not matchmaking app shows you pictures of potential matches; you swipe right to like or left to pass. As with all dating apps, you'll want to balance being kind with protecting yourself.

THINK TWICE; SWIPE ONCE.
The quick-swipe style of Tinder makes it easy to like or skip the wrong people—and hard to correct your mistakes. Pay attention to what you're doing.

AVOID SHOWING GROUP SHOTS.
Potential dates are swiping to see who's out there; they don't want to waste time guessing which one is you.

DON'T SWIPE RIGHT ON A FRIEND OR *(EWW)* YOUR COUSIN.
If you're entirely confident that you're on the same page, says Newman, you can do the friendly-wave "OMG, we're both on Tinder" right swipe. But if they mistake you for romantically interested, things could get awkward fast.

IF YOU DON'T HEAR BACK, LET IT GO.
You've been matched with someone who doesn't respond to your initial message? Oh well. There are many potential reasons for this—some of them good ones—but only one solution: Move on.

BE SMART WITH STRANGERS.
Remember, for one thing, that anything you say or post can be saved as a screenshot. And, for another, that you should arrange first meetings in a public place, ideally as part of a larger group. (To quote your dad: *You can't be too careful.*)

INSTAGRAM

When you use this online photo-sharing service, you're asking people to look—so you'll want to think carefully about what you're showing them.

EDIT YOUR PHOTOS.
You went to Arizona and saw dozens of saguaro cacti that were uncannily human-shaped! Unless you're a professional cactus photographer, nobody wants to see more than two (or one).

GIVE CREDIT WHERE IT'S DUE.
Don't post other people's photos or quotes without clear attribution. This means no screen captures, even if you have the best intentions. Use a repost app instead.

RESTRAIN YOUR USE OF HASHTAGS.
A hashtag can provide a funny or interesting interpretation for your photo viewers. But more is not merrier, and overuse of them is a common pet peeve.

THINK OF THE FUTURE YOU.
Your tastes will change, as will your sense of humor, your idea of TMI, and your interest in privacy—but your photos will live on forever. Once more, with feeling: Use caution when posting.

IF YOU DO ONLY ONE THING...

Step away from the phone. "Everything is on my phone—work e-mails, Twitter, family, friends—so I constantly check it. But twice a day, I get away from it. At around 3 P.M., I keep my phone at my desk and take a 10-minute walk. When I get back, I feel refreshed. I also don't sleep with my phone. If you wake up in the middle of the night and look at your phone, that's not healthy. I leave it in the kitchen when I go to bed."

DOREE SHAFRIR is the executive editor of *BuzzFeed*.

The rules of attraction

Across the crowded Starbucks, you notice someone peering adorably at you over his laptop. The mysterious stranger smiles. You smile. You both remove your earbuds. Before you know it, you've fallen. Over the next few weeks, this person explodes into your world. No longer do you seem to have other thoughts or interests. (What friends? What family?) Here's why.

Q. Why am I drawn to certain people?

A. In general, you gravitate toward people like you. Beautiful people tend to go for equally beautiful people, and those from a particular socioeconomic background favor their own. Experts believe this happens because perceived equality contributes to a stable union. But once you get past the bone structure and the bank accounts and into personality attributes, opposites often attract. "We're apt to fall in love with those who are mysterious and challenging to us," says Helen Fisher, a professor of anthropology at Rutgers University, in New Brunswick, New Jersey, and the author of *Why Him? Why Her? How to Find and Keep Lasting Love.* "This pull to another biological type could also be adaptive," says Fisher. "If two very different people pool their DNA, they'll create more genetic variety, and their young will come to the job of parenting with a wider array of skills."

Q. Is love blind?

A. Not exactly—but once you're hooked, your vision gets, um, cloudy. "When you're in a relationship, you're aware of the other person's flaws, but your brain is telling you it's OK to ignore them," says Lucy Brown, a professor of neuroscience at the Albert Einstein College of Medicine, in New York City, who specializes in the brain's response to love. Some studies have found that when romantic partners look at each other, the part of the brain associated with social assessment and negative emotion is relatively dormant and critical judgment is dulled.

Q. Can love be addictive?

A. Love plays havoc with your body chemistry, causing you to act like an addict bent on scoring her next fix. Case in point: Obsessive-compulsive disorder is correlated with low levels of the brain chemical serotonin. And studies have shown that serotonin levels also decrease in the newly smitten, which is why you can't seem to get the other person out of your head. Also, norepinephrine and adrenaline levels increase, which can lead to more restlessness and distraction. Sound familiar?

Research by a team that included Brown and Fisher found that people who had recently fallen in love showed strong activity in the area of the brain that produces and receives dopamine, a neurotransmitter associated with addictive behavior whose activity increases when you expect to receive a reward. Gamblers and drug addicts experience similar dopamine activity. "You're not supposed to be satisfied," says Fisher. "You're supposed to be driven, so that you can win the person and eventually stabilize your internal chemistry."

When a relationship ends, you experience symptoms that are similar to an addict's withdrawal. Your dopamine levels go down, so your mood suffers. Your serotonin levels remain low, so your OCD-ish symptoms may not go away. In response to these imbalances, some scientists believe, risk-taking tendencies go up. "When you can't have someone but you're not willing to accept that, you try harder and become more extreme about it," says Fisher. Interestingly, she says, this compulsive behavior may help you move on faster: "Either you win the person back or you drive him away."

Q. Why do people cheat?

A. Attraction, romantic love, and attachment involve three overlapping but separate brain systems. "It's not hard for somebody to sexually desire one person, be infatuated with another, and still want to spend the rest of his or her life with a third," says Fisher. Because each kind of love serves a unique need and exists in a different context, cheaters are able to divide their emotional resources. Fisher suspects that the urge to stray may be stronger in people who have novelty-seeking, dopamine-sensitive personalities. But factors unique to the relationship—a need for attention, a desire to get out of the situation—are just as likely to fuel infidelity.

Q. Can love affect your health?

A. Yes. People in healthy, stable relationships tend to have less stress, which may translate into better health and immune function. Want more evidence? Creepily, people who are in conflict-ridden relationships might see cuts and bruises heal more slowly—by as much as 40 percent, according to one experiment at the Ohio State University College of Medicine.

Q. So what keeps people together?

A. Hormones and hard work. Restlessness sets in one to two years into a relationship, according to some research. That's the period in which the chemical activity associated with new love (high dopamine, for example) dies down.

Fortunately, there are ways to keep things exciting. Sexual contact drives up dopamine levels. Novelty does, too, which is the reason you felt so good about your significant other after you backpacked through Europe together. Frequent physical contact is most likely to maintain elevated oxytocin levels, which is why holding hands, stroking your partner, or any other kind of touch can create feelings of attachment. Besides being, you know, fun.

COMING OUT: A CHEAT SHEET

Sage advice on announcing the big news—and receiving it.

IF YOU COME OUT...

• Consider carefully whom you want to tell first. "People think they have to come out to their parents or best friends first," says Ellen Kahn, the director of the Children, Youth & Families Program at the Human Rights Campaign, a civil-rights organization working on behalf of lesbian, gay, bisexual, and transgender Americans. "But the stakes are higher with them. And you get better at having this conversation each time you do it. Come out first to someone you know will be supportive."

• Make sure you have a private space to talk and that the timing is right.

• Start by saying, "I have something really important to tell you. I'd appreciate if you can just be in listening mode so I can say what I need to," suggests Kahn. That way, you can (hopefully) make your announcement without being interrupted.

• Be prepared for not-so-great responses. "One bisexual woman came out to her parents, and they said that wasn't a valid identity. It had never occurred to her they would react that way," says Kahn.

• Tell the person whether this news is confidential or not. Ask yourself: Are there risks if this information travels further than you're ready for?

• Practice what you want to say. You do not need to label yourself as lesbian, bisexual, transgender, or anything else unless you wish to. You can even just say that you have questions about your sexual orientation or gender identity.

• Don't assume the person's first reaction will stick. "A lot of parents and close family members who initially seem neutral or not totally supportive evolve over time," says Kahn.

IF SOMEONE COMES OUT TO YOU...

• Express your compassion and admiration for that person. Remember that for many, coming out is still an act of courage.

• Avoid asking if she's certain about her orientation or gender identity—or anything along the lines of "But wait, you dated a guy last year, so what's up with that?"

• Don't say, "Well, duh," even if it was obvious to you. "You don't want to invalidate what a big deal this is," says Kahn.

• Offer your support, now and in the future. She may be afraid your relationship will change; show her it won't.

Come on—fight fair!

Three reasons why you need to learn the rules of engagement: Because you're old enough to know. Because (oh right) you care about this person. And because the faster you get through the argument, the faster you get to make-up sex.

PICK YOUR BATTLES. You do not have to address every injustice or irritation that comes along with your significant other. But it is a mistake to stay silent when an issue matters and the cost of silence is feeling bitter, resentful, or disconnected.

UNDERSTAND THE STAKES. Even if you think that you know your partner's issues, it can't hurt to pose a direct question. Be sure to ask, "What's your real concern here?"

WAIT UNTIL YOU'RE CALM. When emotions run high, disagreements can turn personal. ("Are you seriously going to watch *Game of Thrones* all day?" "I don't know. Is the alternative listening to you gripe at me?") And that's rarely productive. Recognize when emotions are charged, and don't have the conversation until you have a cool head. (And until *Game of Thrones* is over.)

BE RESPECTFUL. If he thinks you're listening thoughtfully, he is more likely to respond in kind. Saying "I understand how you feel" can go a long way.

SPEAK FOR YOURSELF. Rather than criticizing the other person, stick to expressing your own feelings and actions. ("I felt hurt when..." or "I'm concerned because....") No one wants to feel attacked.

Speaking of which, **DON'T INTERROGATE.** Try not to turn all prosecutor, with a litany of yes-or-no questions. This tack is aggressive and puts the other person on the defensive.

DON'T TRY TO WIN. In many instances, the disagreement will end in détente. It's more important to focus on understanding why he thinks differently than you do.

CONSIDER COMPROMISE. And remember: A compromise doesn't have to be equal to be acceptable. However, it is important for you to understand what you're both giving up and to be comfortable with that equation. You don't have to feel happy about a compromise, but you have to be able to live with it.

Girl, you'll be a woman soon

When did I first feel like an adult? At the moment when my dad convinced me to trust myself. By **Julia Fierro**

WHEN TWO OF MY COLLEGE FRIENDS asked me to share an apartment, I felt as if I'd struck gold. I'd have the second bedroom, with its own bathroom, all to myself. I fantasized about reading the thick novels I was studying for my 19th-century-literature courses in my very own tub surrounded by fruity-scented shower gels and candles. I had waist-length wavy hair and spent an embarrassing amount of time in front of the mirror each morning coating it with curl gel and crisping it with a hair dryer and a diffuser. Living in a dorm, I hauled my overstuffed shower caddy back and forth from my room to the bathroom. But in this new apartment I could perform my lengthy hairstyling ritual in the privacy of my own bathroom.

This great fortune was due to the fact that both of my new roommates would be men. Jerry and Rob insisted they were fine with sharing a bedroom and bath—and with the three of us splitting the rent equally. The apartment was spacious, had a view of D.C.'s Washington National Cathedral, and was a 10-minute tree-lined walk to our classes at the university. My new living arrangements couldn't have been more perfect.

At 20, I believed that there wasn't much of a difference between girls and boys. (The notion of my peers and me as women and men seemed to exist in the distant future.) Sure, this belief was challenged every time I went to a party and was hit on—sometimes with suggestions that I accompany this boy back to his dorm room. But I had made myself believe that I could handle not only myself but also any guy. I knew to say no firmly and not to go to parties alone, and I learned that I had to speak more loudly and butt into a discussion if I wanted to be heard over male voices.

So I didn't think twice about living with two men. Or, rather, I didn't until people kept asking: *What does your dad think? Is your dad OK with your living arrangements?* Again and again—until I, too, began to doubt my choice. My friends shared lots of suggestions that involved lying to my father, like "Don't tell your dad they're dudes" and "Tell your dad Jerry and Rob are in a relationship." I'm ashamed to admit, I was tempted to try the last one.

> I didn't think twice about living with two men. Or, rather, I didn't until people kept asking: *What does your dad think? Is your dad OK with your living arrangements?*

Why so much concern? My father had always trusted my judgment in the past. However, he had also been born into poverty in southern Italy in 1935, and his experiences were vastly different from my own privileged American life. I worried he would disapprove—and be disappointed in me. In retrospect, I realize I was not only fearful of my father's response; the problem was, I didn't yet feel comfortable trusting my own instincts and my ability to make life decisions.

Before I committed to living with Jerry and Rob, I called my father. Although he had met both guys when he had visited the college (and given them giant helpings of his baked ziti), I was nervous. What if my father, a sometimes emotionally unpredictable man, reacted the way so many of my friends expected him to?

"What do you think?" I nervously asked my father.

"You are a very smart woman," he said. "I trust you."

A subtle but powerful shift had occurred. I felt changed. It was certainly not the first time I had been called a woman, but it was the first time I had been called one by my father. His trust in me allowed me to take a step closer to trusting myself. For that, and for his gift of confidence in me and in my choices, I was grateful.

JULIA FIERRO IS THE AUTHOR OF THE NOVEL *CUTTING TEETH*.

Help! My friendship needs a fix

Don't throw sand. Take turns on the swing. If you followed some fundamental rules on the playground, you were guaranteed a pal for life—or at least until second grade. Playing nice as an adult is a little more complicated. Consult these strategies for seeing your friendships through a host of grown-up challenges.

THE PROBLEM: Caitlin knows exactly what you should do in every situation. And tells you.

WHAT TO DO: Speak up—ideally just after she has ordered you to reassess your choice of graduate school/roommate/lunch entrée. Use *I* statements to make your message seem less confrontational, suggests Christa Schmidt, an assistant professor of counseling psychology at Towson University, in Maryland, and be specific about what's irking you.

WHAT TO SAY: "I appreciate where you're coming from on this, and I know you care about me. But it's not your role to tell me how to live my life. What I need from you is to listen to me and be my friend instead of critiquing my decisions."

THE PROBLEM: Suzanne's idiot boyfriend is all kinds of inappropriate.

WHAT TO DO: Definitely don't complain to her, says Schmidt: "That will put distance between you two, because she won't want to discuss the relationship, a major part of her life, with you." Instead, rely on creative scheduling. Plan one-on-one activities with her that you know he won't want to have any part of—or organize a regular night out.

WHAT TO SAY: "Suzanne, instead of us all going out to dinner Friday night, how about you and I treat ourselves to a pedicure tomorrow?" Exception: If this guy's bad behavior is serious and you fear for her safety, then be direct. Verbal abuse, physical abuse, and cheating are all grounds for intervention. "Voice your concern for her as just that—concern, rather than an attack on her significant other," says Schmidt. And communicate that you will be there if the relationship goes belly-up.

THE PROBLEM: Xander needs to borrow some money. Again.

WHAT TO DO: Nothing is guaranteed to end a friendship faster than lending money. It creates an imbalance of power, and you could find yourself scrutinizing your friend's every cold-pressed-juice purchase, dropping hints about repayment, or morphing into the Mommy Warbucks of the relationship. Explain your answer as a long-standing personal policy rather than a decision specific to her situation, says Leah Ingram, the author of *The Everything Etiquette Book: A Modern-Day Guide to Good Manners,* and offer to help her find other ways to get what she needs.

WHAT TO SAY: "I'd love to help you get your new Etsy shop off the ground, but I'm not very good at mixing money and friendships. Can I help you research small-business grants instead?"

THE PROBLEM: Rachel is about to ruin her life, and you don't know how to stop her.

WHAT TO DO: Start by not saying, "What are you thinking?" Then clarify whether your friend wants advice or just a sympathetic ear, says Ingram. Even if she asks for help, you still need to tread lightly, since she probably wants her own thoughts reaffirmed. Try asking her a few strategic questions to steer her toward your perspective, suggests Don Gabor, a communications trainer and the author of *How to Start a Conversation and Make Friends.* Be careful to avoid leading questions, though, and keep your tone as genuinely inquisitive as possible. Finally, make sure you really listen to her answers; that may be what she needs most.

WHAT TO SAY: Begin with "I don't want to butt in, but do you need me to help you figure this out, or do you just want me to listen? I'm happy to do either." Then follow up with questions like "How do

you feel about marrying someone you've known for only a week?" rather than saying, "What, are you actually *hoping* to get divorced by 25?"

THE PROBLEM: Debra makes $5,000 more than you and wanted you to know. She has a cuter pug. Oh, and her triathlon time was two minutes faster.

WHAT TO DO: Try not to fall into her me-against-you mind-set, advises Schmidt. When you do feel a comparison coming on—your New Hampshire vacay may have been invigorating, but her solo trek to the top of Mount Kilimanjaro was life-altering—beat Debra to the punch with a preemptive, tongue-in-cheek strike about how much greater her story must be, says Millie Downing, a business-etiquette consultant. Say it with a smile and she might just get the message.

WHAT TO SAY: "Oh, I'm sure you got a much better deal than I did, but I'm happy with my choice." Or try a neutralizing statement like "I think we both killed that 5K."

THE PROBLEM: Mitchell is talking about his love issues. For the 20-zillionth time.

WHAT TO DO: Part of being a friend to someone is listening to his problems. But if you're starting to feel like a part-time therapist, you have to take action. It may help to set an unspoken time limit, like the few minutes it takes to steep a cup of chai, for letting Mitchell vent about how his boyfriend never remembers to text when he's going to be late. Then step in with a direct question about why he is unwilling or unable to address the issue. Afterward, steer the conversation to a more positive place. Ask him about something you know is going well (his internship, his band), so you get on a new topic without seeming as if you don't care about what's happening in his life.

WHAT TO SAY: Jokingly ask, "Didn't we play this out last month?" Or shoot straight: "What are your choices here? What is holding you back from making a change?"

3 ways to be a better friend

Bert and Ernie. Leslie Knope and Ann Perkins. Thelma and Louise. These duos knew what it took to create a meaningful bond. Here, expert suggestions for creating your own enduring relationships (none of which involve driving off a cliff).

1 | Be (genuinely) happy for your friend's success.

Friends want you to celebrate with them when good things happen. Sometimes that's harder than it sounds, especially if you're a little jealous. Swallow that emotion, because she doesn't only need a shoulder to cry on in a crisis. She's also looking for someone to cheer her triumphs. Joy shared is joy doubled.

JENNIFER LITCHMAN is one of the 10 lifelong friends who were the subject of the book The Girls From Ames, *by Jeffrey Zaslow.*

2 | Show a different side of yourself.

One great way to do that is to mix friends from different areas of your life—say, throw a get-together with your college buddies and your pals from work. You'll find yourself opening up more, and your friends will learn new things about you. Friendships benefit from a breath of fresh air.

SALLY HORCHOW is a coauthor of The Art of Friendship: 70 Simple Rules for Making Meaningful Connections.

3 | Make small gestures.

You don't have to go to great lengths, like throwing a surprise party or giving an expensive gift, to show your friends that you love them. Case in point: When I had surgery, about 50 people posted short comments online wishing me well. I was touched. You can also reach out in other ways. Leave your friend a compassionate voice message. It will mean the world.

JASON FALLS is a social-media consultant based in Louisville, Kentucky.

How to break up (nicely) with friends and significant others

It's a good thing most relationships aren't built to last. If you really want to skeeve yourself out, imagine yourself still being with your seventh-grade crush today. But this doesn't minimize the fact that, in the moment, breakups suck. Here, some pro tips for getting to the other side with your sanity—and maybe even your dignity—intact.

DO tell yourself that it's over—no wishy-washiness allowed. The more resolute you are about your decision, the easier it will be to broach the subject with the other person—and to hold your ground if and when things get emotional. "If you're honest with yourself about what's happening from your perspective, you can find a way to stay with your truth while still being kind," says Lisa Steadman, a relationship coach and the author of *It's a Breakup, Not a Breakdown.*

DON'T beat yourself up. Ideally, love and friend-ship last forever—which is why we can feel so much denial, shame, and blame when, more often than not, one or more parties want out. "Breaking up is a rite of passage, but it's also a big deal," says Andrea Bonior, Ph.D., a clinical psychologist and the author of *The Friendship Fix: The Complete Guide to Choosing, Losing, and Keeping Up With Your Friends.* And these feelings of loss are just as real, if not more so, with the dissolution of long friendships as with the loss of a lover.

DO try the slow fade first. Most of us are guilty of perpetuating phone tag, ignoring the occasional e-mail, or ditching a happy hour for a "work thing." And that's OK. "Breaking away slowly and passively is a natural first step," says Bonior. "Maybe you take a little more time getting back to the person; maybe you're not the one to initiate plans." But before you feel too relieved, take heed: It works only if the fade is a two-way street. "All too often," she says, "the slow fade leaves the other person wondering, Why isn't she returning my calls? Is she mad at me?"

DON'T let it go on too long if the other person is not getting the hint. If the relationship is still working well for her, she may not recognize—or acknowledge—your pulling back. "It can be especially hard to break up with a frenemy," says Steadman. If you're having a hard time cutting yourself loose, odds are you have to confront the situation.

DO try to break up in person. If you've spent every weekend hanging out with this friend, from your freshman year in college to last Friday night, it's not fair to ignore his birthday-party Evite and never show your face again. Think: How would you feel if the tables were turned and he was breaking up with you? Don't lean too heavily on technology if you've had a long-term, face-to-face relationship. "Most people don't want to sit at brunch and have a breakup conversation with a friend," says Bonior, "but if you've been friends for any period of time, it's what you owe him."

DO use a lot of *I* statements. This couples'-counseling trick applies to any tense conversation—especially when one or both parties are bound to walk away feeling hurt. Lean on it as things escalate, says Bonior: "Try 'I feel like I'm moving in a different direction,' or 'I feel that I just don't have the time.'" Global, accusatory statements like "You were never there for me when I needed you," even if true, will only put the dumpee on the defensive.

DON'T unload the accusations. "If the situation is truly irrevocable, then there's no need to take out a laundry list of everything she's done that you've hated," says Bonior. "If you have to get it out, vent to someone later or write in a journal."

DO end the conversation. You will require two things post-breakup: a stiff drink and some serious boundaries. "That means you don't take his calls anymore. You don't text each other all the time," says Steadman. It will help to have made peace with your decision before starting a conversation—and when it's finished, to have a few close friends on speed dial.

DON'T answer your (newly) ex-pal or partner's Gchat. We know: Silence can be deafening—and when you're caught up in the moment, shooting an emoji off into the ether will seem innocent enough. But in many cases holding back is the only way that either of you can move on. "It can feel harsh or cold, especially if you haven't filled the emptiness with another relationship, but remember—you've already said your piece," says Steadman. Give yourself the time to grieve—and the space to get your groove back.

How to get closer to your mom or dad

Your father is your bestie, except when he's driving you up the wall. You always ask your mother's opinion—but if you don't follow her advice, look out! Happily, with a little listening and sympathizing, the ties that bind you don't have to wind up in knots.

YOUR PARENT-KID RELATIONSHIP: Pals

WHY IT'S GOOD: Because this is a friendship built to last. And it's fun to spend the holidays with people you actually like.

WHY IT'S CHALLENGING: Sometimes a daughter needs a parent, not a partner in crime. Studies have confirmed what a lot of women know: When daughters face a big life change, like leaving home or getting a first job, they rely on their moms in particular to be experienced advisers, not buddies.

IMPROVING RELATIONS: Both parties need to be aware of their true roles. And that means you can't be super-close in all ways at all times. For example, you can tell your mom about your annoying girlfriend, but she shouldn't return the favor and disclose personal information about your father. Let your mom or dad know when you need each one to be a wise advisor, not just a friend.

YOUR PARENT-KID RELATIONSHIP: More like siblings

WHY IT'S GOOD: Because the bickering doesn't keep you from loving each other.

WHY IT'S CHALLENGING: Did you see where we mentioned bickering? Plus, if you have this kind of relationship, you might be more likely to have a bona fide rivalry. So you may compare yourself with your parent: *Oh, my dad is so much more successful than I'll ever be.* Or your Dad might be threatened by your burgeoning career success, especially if his work has hit the skids.

IMPROVING RELATIONS: To mitigate overly competitive feelings, try to understand the ways your parent might feel jealous or competitive, and be especially supportive in those areas. Talk about the way he seems to view your successes, and ask him to support your endeavors.

YOUR PARENT-KID RELATIONSHIP:
Sparring partners

WHY IT'S GOOD: Wait—we're thinking.

WHY IT'S CHALLENGING: It's confusing for a grown woman to fight with her mother or father about boyfriends or hair length or whether Tofurky is an acceptable Thanksgiving entrée. Parents typically feel ignored and react by badgering. Daughters feel, well, badgered and get defensive.

IMPROVING RELATIONS: Remind your parents that their opinions do indeed matter to you. Repeating comments in the context of "So you're saying..." lets Dad know that you're listening, even if his advice isn't always heeded.

YOUR PARENT-KID RELATIONSHIP:
Doppelgängers

WHY IT'S GOOD: Because you finish each other's sentences and make the same jokes.

WHY IT'S CHALLENGING: With the pressure to be the same, it's harder to create boundaries. When opinions differ, the stress of trying to gain the other's approval can be overwhelming. A daughter has to understand that Mom isn't responsible for her anymore. A mother needs to realize that all her kid's wins aren't her own wins; ditto for losses.

IMPROVING RELATIONS: These relationships are so intense because they're often driven by a fear of abandonment. Daughters should emphasize how deeply they value, say, their mothers' opinions, then make it clear that certain forthcoming decisions will be solo ones. So many women try to make their mothers agree with them. Don't try so hard; she'll love you anyway.

7 QUESTIONS TO ASK YOUR PARENTS

For years they took care of you: spoon-feeding pea puree, singing you to sleep, scouring the house till they found Binky. Now it's time for you to help them. Asking these tough-but-crucial Q.'s means you're ready for anything down the line.

▶ Are you on track to save for retirement?

▶ Have you consulted a reliable financial planner who can help anticipate your needs as you age?

▶ Have you written a will? Does someone you trust know where it is?

▶ Will you give me or another trusted person power of attorney over your financial affairs in case there's a time you can't handle them yourself?

▶ Have you thought about what kind of medical treatment you want in the future—and who would make those decisions if you can't make or communicate them on your own? Have you put these desires in writing?

▶ How do you feel about being kept alive with ventilators, feeding tubes, or other interventions? And under what circumstances would you want that?

▶ If you have advanced-care–planning documents, where do you keep them? Have you shared them with any family members, doctors, or clergy?

Why can't we just get along?:
A sibling problem-solver

No one knows you better: the good (your graduation party), the bad (your Bat Mitzvah party), and the ugly (two words: self-tanner fail). So it's no surprise that interactions with your sister or brother can get a little heated.

Why you fight

"There are running themes in sibling relationships," says Pauline Wallin, Ph.D., a clinical psychologist and the author of *Taming Your Inner Brat*. "Envy, bullying, control. From childhood to adulthood, your grumbling is still directed at the same person. The focus just changes from who controls the TV channel to who makes the decisions about your parents' estate." Jealousy often fuels adult conflict, as siblings get jobs, get promotions, and get significant others. "Now you're envious of the job, not the toy truck," says Avidan Milevsky, Ph.D., the author of *Sibling Relationships in Childhood and Adolescence*. Perceived parental favoritism at any age can continue to be a sore spot as well. (Does Mom visit him more often than me?)

What it looks like

You no longer wrestle with one another or grab toys (let's hope). As adults, it's all about words, from passive-aggressive e-mails to full-blown screaming matches, says Scott Myers, Ph.D., a professor of communication studies at West Virginia University, in Morgantown, and an expert on adult-sibling communication. Through his research, Myers has found that adults tend to be more verbally aggressive with siblings (saying things purposely to hurt them) than with anyone else. Think about it: If you spoke to a supervisor the way you speak to your sister, you would get demoted or worse. Other siblings who butt heads may cut off communication and become estranged.

The silver lining

Heated exchanges between siblings don't necessarily get in the way of friendship. (You can't push someone's buttons unless you're attuned to what makes him tick.) As siblings age, they mellow, and minor differences begin to pale in comparison with the powerful ties that they share. The Study of Adult Development at Harvard University Health Services, which followed adult subjects for decades, found a substantial correlation between having a strong bond with siblings in one's early 20s and being emotionally well-adjusted in later adulthood. And, wow, the sibling bond proved more pivotal to adult contentment than did having a successful career or a happy marriage.

How to make peace

Unlike kids, who have no choice but to see one another every day, adults with old rivalries can stop talking and let residual jealousy or stubbornness create permanent rifts. Or they may use family gatherings, such as the holidays, to revisit old slights. (Oh, I see. I still get the dinner plate with the big chip.) The good news is that you can begin to bridge what may seem like a gaping chasm with small acts, says Jane Isay, the author of Mom Still Likes You Best: Overcoming the Past and Reconnecting With Your Siblings. Here's how to get the goodwill flowing.

IDENTIFY THE REAL PROBLEM. If you're seething over your sister's new job, it's probably a sign that you're feeling insecure about your own career, says Milevsky. Instead of resenting her (no matter how annoying it is when she mentions her huge salary), try to let this knowledge motivate you to make a change or, at the very least, help you to be gracious toward her.

WORK ON YOUR COMPLIMENTS. If you have a strained relationship with your sister, you probably keep a mental laundry list of her faults. So make a point to say something nice: "I've always loved your sense of humor" or "You've done a great job balancing your new job and the kids' schedules." Says Wallin, "This forces you to look for the positive in her." Your kindness will not only foster goodwill (who doesn't love a person who gives compliments?) but also soften your sibling's attitude. It's hard to follow up a compliment with a sarcastic or nasty retort, no matter how outspoken your sibling may be.

PREEMPT! If you have a bossy brother, get a jump on his inevitable unsolicited advice and ask his opinion on something mundane: "I need new tires. Do you have any suggestions?" or "I'm tired of my usual dinner routine. Any recipe ideas?" This allows him to feel important (probably his real motivation, anyway) while you stay in control.

SPEAK UP. Many of us carry around old wounds that our siblings inflicted on us in childhood. Maybe you still feel self-conscious about your ears because your brother called you Dumbo. Or perhaps your sister has always teased you for being disorganized, even though your home is now as neat as a pin. It's time to confront your sibling about that hurt and ask that it come to an end. "We feel our siblings should be able to read our minds because we grew up together," says Myers. "But that's not necessarily so. It's OK to say, 'I know I was a chubby kid, but that joke isn't funny now. It's a sensitive issue for me.'" While your 12-year-old sister might not have taken your request seriously, your adult sibling probably will.

SAY YOU'RE SORRY. Any chance you're the sister who bullies? Sincere apologies go a long way. "Those simple words can work wonders to break a long-standing cycle of perceived slights and defensiveness," says Wallin. If even that seems scary, start with a baby step. "Sometimes a small olive branch, like offering to get a cup of coffee together, can open up the lines of communication," says Milevsky. That cuppa Joe could be a few bucks well worth spending.

10 helpful pieces of life advice

Adulthood is confusing. We seek coping strategies where we can find them: the Tao Te Ching, Yoda, The Rules According to JWoww. (OK, maybe not that last one.) We've put together a few more smart ideas for making your way in the world, from 10 truly impressive women. Take a few for the road.

1 | Begin the day with a good book.

I used to get up in the morning and immediately plunge into work. But about six months ago I started doing something different. Now, the very first thing I do is make a cup of coffee, take it back upstairs, and sit up in bed with the book that I was reading the night before. Currently it's a novel. Before that it was Jon Meacham's biography of Thomas Jefferson. It's always something that puts me in a world other than my work world. For the first 15 minutes of the day, I sip coffee and read and take intense pleasure in it all. The minute the cup of coffee is done—or once it's cold—I put the book down. I really believe that happiness is a collection of small, pleasurable experiences, like buying flowers or eating a square of chocolate. I try to have a few of these moments every day.

ANNE-MARIE SLAUGHTER has written widely on work-life balance. She is the president and CEO of the New America Foundation, a nonprofit think tank and civic enterprise based in New York City and Washington, D.C.

2 | Savor your coffee.

How long did it take you to down your last cappuccino? The next time, take a cue from the Japanese, whose formal tea ceremony can last four hours. Before taking a drink, participants raise their bowls in tribute to all the factors that came together to create that moment—from their ancestors to the farmers who grew the tea to the elders who taught them how to prepare it. Try this amended routine: Focus on the drink in front of you. Notice the smell, and relish the flavor. You'll find it's a wonderful daily exercise in mindfulness.

JENNIFER ANDERSON, PH.D., an expert on Japanese tea rituals, is a lecturer in anthropology at San José State University, in California.

3 | Be impatient.

Early in my career, I went to numerous meetings where I was the only woman present. I would want to contribute to the conversation but would think, If I say that, everybody will think it's really stupid. And then a man would say exactly what I had in mind, and the other participants would find it brilliant. I learned that you shouldn't wait to speak. I started listening actively, knowing that I was going to comment on something and having it in my mind that I would interrupt at the right moment. It's both polite and useful to say, "Well, before we proceed to the next subject, I would like to add the following." If you wait to be called on, often the discussion will move on so far that whatever you're talking about will not be germane.

MADELEINE ALBRIGHT was the first female U.S. secretary of state. She is currently the chair of the Albright Stonebridge Group, a global consulting firm, in Washington, D.C.

4 | Admit how you feel.

When something disturbing happens, I tend to gloss over it at first. But 5 or 10 minutes later, I have to ask myself what I'm feeling and why I feel that way. And then—it sounds so corny, but it really does work—I acknowledge the feeling. I identify it and own it. Then, usually, I can move on. Not that it's erased from my consciousness, but it's put in a place where I can move around it and deal with it. For example, I was recently talking on the phone to a friend, and she said something complimentary about someone who had hurt me. After the call, I was overcome with irritation. I thought, Why am I so grumpy?

Finally I admitted that I felt irritated, and then the feeling didn't nag me as much anymore. When an emotion is undefinable, it has more power than when you can see it for what it is.

ANNA HOLMES is the creator of the popular women's site Jezebel.com and the editor of The Book of Jezebel.

5 | Fake joy.

We think that we act because of how we feel. But we also feel because of how we act. So use this knowledge to change your mood. Jump up and down; getting both feet off the ground makes you feel childlike and energetic. Or go for a walk. Just this morning I got an unnerving e-mail from someone and felt lousy about it. So I headed out for a walk in Central Park with a friend. So many things that tend to make a person happy are wrapped up in one little thing—a walk. It really works! When I got home, I wasn't irritated anymore. I realized, Yeah, I've got my perspective back.

GRETCHEN RUBIN is the author of The Happiness Project *and* Happier at Home.

6 | Praise yourself.

Every thought we have, including self-criticism, paves a neural pathway. These pathways make it easier for us to have the same response the next time. Eventually some circuits get so big that the thoughts go on autopilot. Instead of going to the default—say, criticizing yourself for working too much instead of spending time with your family—give yourself credit for how much time you are spending with your loved ones. Tell yourself that you're doing a good job balancing things. At first you won't believe it. But do it day after day and you'll eventually build new neural pathways. The positive thoughts will become automatic.

LORETTA GRAZIANO BREUNING, PH.D., is the author of Meet Your Happy Chemicals.

7 | Stop imagining the ideal.

I often grow impatient when I want to be in control of a situation. To avoid getting antsy when I am writing and can't find specific words for my thoughts, I try to practice self-compassion. I tell myself that I'm not going to quit even if I become frustrated. I'll say out loud, "You're not perfect, but that's OK. Writing can be a messy process, and it's not ideal, but you can handle it." Talking to yourself may feel awkward and goofy, but it quells that feeling of impatience. And it certainly beats foraging for carbs, which I'm also apt to do when I'm agitated and have writer's block.

BRENÉ BROWN, PH.D., is a research professor at the University of Houston Graduate College of Social Work and the author of the book Daring Greatly. *You may have seen her widely viewed talk on TED.com.*

8 | Pluck the weeds.

I was miserable on and off in my life till age 39, blaming outside things, like my job or my relationship. And then it hit me: I am the leader of my life, and I can choose to believe what I want. It's such a simple idea, but it was a pivotal breakthrough. Now, whenever I have an anxious or negative thought, I use a technique that I learned from my love of gardening—one that I also teach to the girls I mentor. I think, Is this thought a weed that is taking up space and needs to be plucked? Or is it a flower that I need to tend and love and let thrive? I focus all my attention on the thoughts that are beautiful blooms and yank out the negative ones.

ELIZABETH KUNZ is the CEO of Girls on the Run, a nonprofit youth-development program.

9 | Let your heart break.

The world is full of what seem like intractable problems. Often we let that paralyze us. Instead, let it spur you to action. There are some people in the world that we can't help, but there are so many more that we can. So when you see a mother and her children suffering in another part of the world, don't look away. Look right at them. Let them break your heart, then let your empathy

and your talents help you make a difference in the lives of others. Whether you volunteer every week or just a few times a year, your time and unique skills are invaluable.

MELINDA GATES is a cochair of the Bill & Melinda Gates Foundation.

10 | Know when to listen and when to zone out.

My inner critic is the thing that keeps me doing draft after draft until the work is good. So I trust it and don't want to silence it completely. But you still need to quiet your mind. I try to meditate twice a day, which helps me feel calm and peaceful. I also exercise—not a class where you're held hostage by a teacher's personality, but one where there is dancing and no one is talking to you. It's impossible for me to worry about a script or scenes or salaries when I'm like, Wait— where do I put my foot?

JENNI KONNER is an executive producer of the HBO series Girls.

Should I tip this guy?

Everyone knows to leave a gratuity for the waiter. But how much should you give to, say, someone delivering pad thai or a settee? Here's a handy cheat sheet to help you figure out when and how much to make it rain.

ALWAYS TIP, NO MATTER WHAT
(or you'll get the stink eye)

Airport-shuttle driver

HOW MUCH: $1 to $3.

GOOD TO KNOW: Compensate extra if the driver waits for you, loads your luggage, or jams to get you to the gate quickly.

Airport skycap or porter

HOW MUCH: $1 to $3 a bag.

GOOD TO KNOW: Large or bulky items, like skis, deserve an extra dollar or two. If he tapes up an overstuffed suitcase or skips over other customers so you don't miss your flight, tip $5 to $20.

Appliance or furniture delivery

HOW MUCH: $5 to $10 a person.

GOOD TO KNOW: If they assemble your bed or shimmy your sofa up a narrow stairwell, throw in an extra $5 to $10.

Bartender

HOW MUCH: $1 a drink.

Bellhop

HOW MUCH: $1 to $2 per bag delivered to your room (up to $10 total).

Car washer

HOW MUCH: $2 for a standard sedan, $3 to $5 for a large vehicle, and 15 percent for detailing.

Caterer for a big event

HOW MUCH: 5 to 10 percent.

GOOD TO KNOW: If the caterer is also the owner, you can skip a tip. But pay it forward in other

ways: Post a thank-you on Yelp or the company's Facebook page.

Christmas-tree carrier

HOW MUCH: $2 to $5.

Cleaning person

HOW MUCH: Around the holidays, give money or a gift that's equivalent to one week's pay.

Coat checker

HOW MUCH: $1 per item.

GOOD TO KNOW: Add another buck if you also dropped off an umbrella and shopping bags.

Dog groomer or sitter

HOW MUCH: 15 to 20 percent.

GOOD TO KNOW: If your pup is a handful, make up for it with an extra 5 percent.

Emergency roadside-service provider

HOW MUCH: $5 to $20, as long as the service owner isn't coming to tow you himself—and as long as he's not gouging you on, say, the cost of the tow.

Food delivery

HOW MUCH: $2 to $4.

GOOD TO KNOW: Did he ride his bike through a monsoon with your pizza teetering on the basket? Add extra.

Groupon deal

HOW MUCH: Leave as much as you normally would on the full retail value of the service. Just because you got your manicure for half price doesn't mean you should half-ass the gratuity.

Hair shampooer

HOW MUCH: $3 to $5 (though at some places, you can forgo it entirely).

GOOD TO KNOW: Ask the front desk at the salon what to tip the shampooer. If they stare blankly in reply, then you'll know not to tip.

Hairstylist or colorist

HOW MUCH: 15 percent.

GOOD TO KNOW: If she squeezes you in on a busy day, add $3 to $5 more. In big cities, it is customary to tip a salon owner who styles your hair, too. If you're not sure whether the owner/stylist would expect a tip, check with the front desk.

Hotel concierge

HOW MUCH: $5 to $50.

GOOD TO KNOW: For standard reservations and recommendations, go low. If he finagles orchestra seats for the Lorde concert, up the ante.

Hotel housekeeping

HOW MUCH: $2 a night at a budget hotel; $3 to $5 a night at a high-end hotel.

GOOD TO KNOW: Leave this tip daily, since more than one housekeeper may clean your room.

Hotel-room delivery

HOW MUCH: $1 to $2 per item.

GOOD TO KNOW: Tip only for items or requests not included with the room. (Think toothpaste or laundry service.)

Hotel room service

HOW MUCH: $2 or 15 to 20 percent of the meal's cost.

GOOD TO KNOW: If a *service* charge appears on your tab, you still need to leave a tip (sorry). If a *gratuity* charge appears on the bill, skip the tip.

Laundry delivery

HOW MUCH: $2 to $5.

GOOD TO KNOW: Tip the same amount as for dry-cleaning delivery.

Manicurist or pedicurist

HOW MUCH: 10 to 20 percent.

GOOD TO KNOW: Err on the high side if your feet are particularly gnarly.

Massage therapist

HOW MUCH: 20 percent.

Movers

HOW MUCH: $20 to $50 a person.

GOOD TO KNOW: The harder the move (were five flights of stairs involved?), the bigger the tip.

Server

HOW MUCH: 15 to 20 percent.

GOOD TO KNOW: Even when the waiter messes up your drink order and forgets the dressing on the side, don't stiff him; just lower the amount to 12 percent and inform the manager of your complaint. And if your Bang Bang Shrimp was super burned, don't take out the chef's misstep on the server.

Server at a BYOB restaurant

HOW MUCH: If the waiter opened your bottle and kept your glass topped off, tip as if the wine were included in the check.

Server at a diner counter

HOW MUCH: 10 to 20 percent.

GOOD TO KNOW: Lean toward the high end if you have a complicated order, turned the counter into a satellite office, or are a regular.

Stripper at a bachelorette party

HOW MUCH: $100 to $200 per entertainer.

GOOD TO KNOW: Frequent tipping keeps Magic Mike moving, so make sure that your girls have plenty of dollar bills in hand.

Tattoo artist or body piercer

HOW MUCH: 20 percent for a tattoo; $5 for a piercing.

Taxi or car-service driver

HOW MUCH: 10 to 15 percent.

GOOD TO KNOW: Add an extra dollar or two if he helps lug your luggage.

Valet parking

HOW MUCH: $2 to $5.

GOOD TO KNOW: Tip the guy who returns your car, not the one who takes it away.

Waxer or threader

HOW MUCH: 20 percent.

TIPS APPRECIATED, NOT EXPECTED
(that is, the person went the extra mile, you're a pain in the butt, or you've had a good year)

Barista or counter person

HOW MUCH: Your spare change or up to $2.

GOOD TO KNOW: Don't feel pressured by the tip jar unless the employee goes above and beyond her job description (say, the fro-yo lady is heavy-handed on the chocolate crunchies).

Bartender at an open-bar event

HOW MUCH: $1 per drink.

GOOD TO KNOW: Definitely tip if you order many labor-intensive cocktails. ("Another round of mojitos, good sir!")

Doorman or superintendent

HOW MUCH: Tip only around the holidays; $20 to $100 a person.

GOOD TO KNOW: Now's your chance to make up for all the times you locked your keys in your apartment and needed to be let in at 2 A.M. Gauge according to how much help you received throughout the year (or what your budget will allow).

Facialist

HOW MUCH: $3 (small town) to $20 (big city).

Flower delivery

HOW MUCH: $2 to $5 an arrangement.

Gift wrapper

HOW MUCH: $1 to $5 per item.

GOOD TO KNOW: For the average wrap job, give a dollar or two. But if the end product looks like Buddy the Elf himself sprinkled magical fairy dust over it, the wrapper has earned a fiver.

Grocery delivery

HOW MUCH: $2 to $5.

GOOD TO KNOW: Schlepping several gallons of Poland Spring deserves a few bucks.

Hotel doorman

HOW MUCH: Opening the door, $0. Hailing a taxi, $1 (in the rain, up to $5). Helping remove luggage from a van, up to $2.

GOOD TO KNOW: If he's helpful with restaurant recommendations, directions, or other info, offer $5 to $10. No cash on hand? Leave the tip and a brief note for the doorman with the concierge.

Maître d' or hostess

HOW MUCH: Anywhere from $10 and up, depending on how fancy or in-demand the place is (and what you can reasonably spare).

GOOD TO KNOW: Was he able to reserve you a not-even-near-the-bathroom table at the newest hot spot without the slightest hint of condescension? Slip him something.

Parking-garage attendant

HOW MUCH: $2 to $5 for onetime parking.

GOOD TO KNOW: If you pay for monthly parking, tip only at the holidays ($25 and up) and give it to the garage manager.

Restroom attendant

HOW MUCH: $1 to $5.

GOOD TO KNOW: No need to tip if she just passed you a paper towel. But do so if she passed you some pomade to help you tame a cowlick or if she provided you with the pain reliever that your poor, achy head needed.

Group tour guide

HOW MUCH: $1 to $10 a person per day.

NO NEED TO REACH FOR YOUR WALLET (huzzah!)

- Acupuncturist
- Bed-and-breakfast owner
- Bicycle repair
- Bouncer
- Cable installer
- Chiropractor or physical therapist
- Cobbler
- Dry cleaner
- Grocery bagger
- House sitter
- Laser-hair-removal specialist
- Makeup artist or cosmetologist at a store counter
- Personal trainer or yoga instructor
- Plumber
- Repair person
- Sports instructor (swimming, tennis, surfing, etc.)
- Store employee who takes a heavy item to your car
- Tailor
- Tech expert/Geek Squad
- UPS or FedEx delivery person

INDEX

REAL SIMPLE

EDITOR Kristin van Ogtrop

EXECUTIVE EDITOR
Sarah Humphreys Collins

MANAGING EDITOR
Jacklyn Monk

DESIGN DIRECTOR
Abbey Kuster-Prokell

EDITOR, REALSIMPLE.COM
Lori Leibovich

THE REAL SIMPLE GUIDE TO REAL LIFE

EDITOR Noelle Howey

DESIGNER William van Roden

WRITERS Kera Bolonik,
Joanne Chen, Elizabeth
Passarella, Valerie Rains,
Ashley Tate, Yolanda Wikiel

WRITER-REPORTERS Kiley
Bense, N. Jamiyla Chisholm,
Carlos Greer, Catherine
Newman, Kaitlyn Pirie, Sarah
Robbins, Stephanie Sisco

RESEARCH CHIEF
Westry Green

RESEARCHER Maya Kukes

COPY CHIEF
Nancy Negovetich

COPY EDITORS
Pamela Grossman, Janet Kim,
Terri Schlenger

PRODUCTION MANAGER
Albert Young

ILLUSTRATOR Serge Bloch

REAL SIMPLE

GROUP PUBLISHER
Charles R. Kammerer

ASSOCIATE PUBLISHER
Julie Degarmo

**EXECUTIVE DIRECTOR,
DIGITAL**
Meg Power

VICE PRESIDENT, MARKETING
Kim Tan

**VICE PRESIDENT, CONSUMER
MARKETING**
Michelle Korchinski-Ogden

OXMOOR HOUSE

EDITORIAL DIRECTOR
Leah McLaughlin

CREATIVE DIRECTOR
Felicity Keane

ART DIRECTOR
Christopher Rhoads

**EXECUTIVE PHOTOGRAPHY
DIRECTOR** Iain Bagwell

EXECUTIVE FOOD DIRECTOR
Grace Parisi

SENIOR EDITOR Betty Wong

MANAGING EDITOR
Elizabeth Tyler Austin

**ASSISTANT MANAGING
EDITOR**
Jeanne de Lathouder

TIME HOME
ENTERTAINMENT INC.

PUBLISHER Margot Schupf

VICE PRESIDENT, FINANCE
Vandana Patel

**EXECUTIVE DIRECTOR,
MARKETING SERVICES**
Carol Pittard

PUBLISHING DIRECTOR
Megan Pearlman

**ASSISTANT GENERAL
COUNSEL**
Simone Procas

THANKS TO THESE EXPERTS:
Lashaun Dale, vice president of
Group X Creative at 24 Hour Fitness USA, Inc.; Phil Reed, senior
consumer advice editor at
Edmunds.com; Joshua Zeichner,
M.D., director of cosmetic and
clinical research in the department of dermatology at Mount
Sinai Hospital, in New York
City; American Dental Association; Walter Kaye, M.D., research
adviser for the National Eating
Disorders Association and director
of the Eating Disorder Treatment
and Research Program at the University of California, San Diego,
School of Medicine; Tom Spald-
ing, director of marketing and
communications at the Chimney
Safety Institute of America;
Steven Weisbart, Ph.D., senior
vice president and chief econo-
mist at the Insurance Information
Institute; Jodi R.R. Smith, president of Mannersmith, an etiquette
consulting firm in Boston and
author of *From Clueless to Class
Act: Manners for the Modern
Man/Woman*; Patricia Rossi, business etiquette consultant and
author of *Everyday Etiquette*.

SPECIAL THANKS TO:
Kiley Bense, Andra Chantim, Allison
Chesky, Tanya Christian, Rachel
Christensen, Danielle Claro, Sarah
Copeland, Julia Edelstein, Didi
Gluck, Betsy Goldberg, Marla
Hassner, Lindsay Hunt, Jenny Jin,
Dave Kanter, Charlyne Mattox,
Chelsea Renaud, Liz Welch.